To TKH

THE
MODERN WORLD-SYSTEM

Capitalist Agriculture and the Origins of the European
World-Economy in the Sixteenth Century

TEXT EDITION

Immanuel Wallerstein

ACADEMIC PRESS   New York   San Francisco   London

A Subsidiary of Harcourt Brace Jovanovich, Publishers

This is a volume in the series entitled

STUDIES IN SOCIAL DISCONTINUITY

Under the Consulting Editorship of Charles Tilly, *University of Michigan* and Edward Shorter, *University of Toronto*

ACADEMIC PRESS, INC.
111 Fifth Avenue, New York, New York 10003

United Kingdom Edition published by
ACADEMIC PRESS, INC. (LONDON) LTD.
24/28 Oval Road, London NW1

ISBN 0-12-785922-5

PRINTED IN THE UNITED STATES OF AMERICA

THE MODERN WORLD-SYSTEM

TEXT EDITION

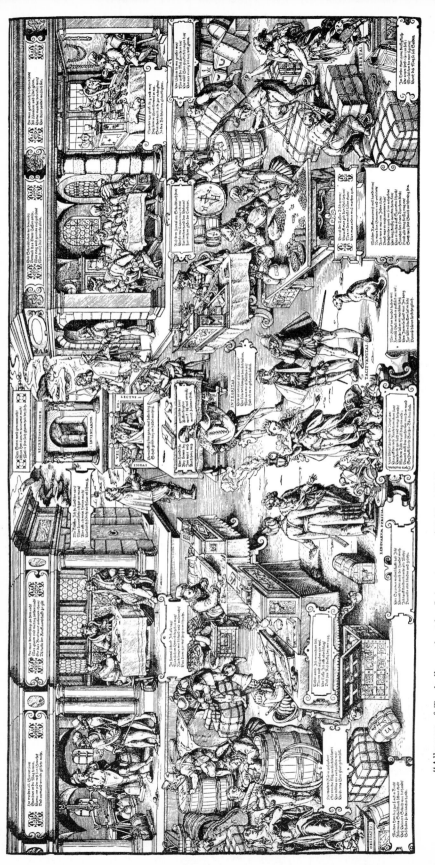

"Allegory of Trade," woodcut by Jobst Amman (1539–1591), who lived in Nuremberg. He was one of the "Little Masters." This bottom detail illustrated the house of a merchant of Nuremberg, still a flourishing center of trans-European trade.

CONTENTS

List of Illustrations   ix
Preface to the Text Edition   xi
Acknowledgments   xiii

INTRODUCTION: ON THE STUDY OF SOCIAL CHANGE   2

1. MEDIEVAL PRELUDE   14
2. THE NEW EUROPEAN DIVISION OF LABOR: c. 1450-1640   50
3. THE ABSOLUTE MONARCHY AND STATISM   92
4. FROM SEVILLE TO AMSTERDAM: THE FAILURE OF EMPIRE   114
5. THE STRONG CORE-STATES: CLASS-FORMATION AND INTERNATIONAL
   COMMERCE   146
6. THE EUROPEAN WORLD-ECONOMY: PERIPHERY VERSUS EXTERNAL ARENA   198
7. THEORETICAL REPRISE   228

Bibliographic Essay   240

LIST OF ILLUSTRATIONS

COVER: *Planisphere by Diogo Ribeiro (1529). Rome: Biblioteca Vaticana.*

FRONTISPIECE: *"Allegory of Trade," by Jobst Amman (1585-1586).*

INTRODUCTION: *"The Sack of Rome by Charles V." Illustration of book published ca. 1535. London: British Museum*

CHAPTER 1: *"The Foxhunt," by the Master of the Housebook (between 1475-1490). Wolfegg (Schloss), Germany.*

CHAPTER 2: *"The Negroes having exhausted the metallic veins had to be given work making sugar," by Theodore de Bry (1575). New York: The Rare Books Collection of the New York Public Library.*

CHAPTER 3: *"The Grand-Duke has the port of Livorno fortified," by Jacques Callot (between 1614-1620). Paris: Bibliothèque Nationale.*

CHAPTER 4: *"Massacre of the Innocents," by Pieter Breughel, the Elder (ca. 1565). Vienna: Kunsthistorisches Museum.*

CHAPTER 5: *"Two Beggars Fighting," by Jacques Bellange (between 1612-1617). Washington, D. C.: National Gallery of Art, Rosenwald Collection.*

CHAPTER 6: *"The (Dutch) fleet off Mozambique, and the capture of a (Portuguese) carrack near Goa." Illustration from a Journal (publ. 1651). Ithaca: Cornell University Library.*

CHAPTER 7:   *"Richmond Palace," an oil painting by David Vinckenboons (first quarter of the seventeenth century). Cambridge: Fitzwilliam Museum.*

The illustrations were selected and annotated with the assistance of Sally Spector.

PREFACE TO THE TEXT EDITION

The social sciences of the nineteenth and twentieth century have been the locus of a debate between the universalizers and the particularizers, between those who sought to discover the general rules of social behavior, and those who sought to delineate the particular and peculiar ways in which each unit developed. Most of the universalizers have called themselves economists or sociologists or political scientists. Most of the particularizers have called themselves historians or ethnographers.

Both groups however tended to share one premise in common: the unit of analysis was a politico-cultural structure, in existence or in potential existence. Whether the term they used for this unit was the state, or the people, or the nation, the concept always involved the assumption that there exist a multitude of such units whose position along a series of criteria could be compared, and that each such unit was proceeding down the road of history in its own separate way (for the universalizers, in parallel ways, albeit with time lags; for the particularizers, in idiosyncratic ways).

This book makes a radically different assumption. It assumes that the unit of analysis is an economic entity, the one that is measured by the existence of an effective division of labor, and that the relationship of such economic boundaries to political and cultural boundaries is variable, and therefore must be determined by empirical research for each historic case.

Once we assume that the unit of analysis is such a "world-system" and not the "state" or the "nation" or the "people", then much changes in the outcome of the analysis. Most specifically we shift from a concern with the attributive characteristics of states to concern with the relational characteristics of states. We shift from seeing classes (and status-groups) as groups within a state to seeing them as groups within a world-economy. And the debate of universalism vs. particularism as *alternative* modes of analysis becomes bypassed, since these terms reflect in fact a dialectical antinomy that pervades all social action.

Before we can begin to explore all the implications of an historical social science which refuses to choose between universalism and particularism and which insists that the only social system is that which is defined by an effective division of labor (and thus primarily world-systems), we must try to demonstrate that this picture has some relationship to empirical reality. This is the primary task of this work.

What kind of evidence would in fact be available for such an effort? It was unthinkable to start the search for data from scratch. I had to rely on the work of prior historians and other social scientists, fitting their work together in terms of my interpretative schema. I have tried to make my own work as explicit as possible in this regard. Thus, I used very extensive footnotes, partly as reference, partly as corroboration, and partly to pursue some by-paths of the central argument.

Extensive footnotes, I have discovered, are a controversial subject. There are those who appreciate the intellectual possibilities offered by them. And there are others who resent their intrusion, some even say their irrelevant intrusion. We have therefore decided on an experiment in this edition. We present the text without the footnotes (and the bibliography and the index). But we retain the numerical superscripts in the text. Hence those who find footnotes intrusive (or footnoted editions expensive) can have the text without them. And should they wonder about a few particular points, they can by means of the superscripts locate the footnotes in the complete edition. Instead of the bibliography which is extensive but undiscriminating, we offer a short bibliographical essay to outline major sources and suggest further reading.

Caveat emptor.

ACKNOWLEDGMENTS

It is always difficult to list the immediate sources of ideas and assis-tance—from authors, colleagues, and students—in the conception and writing of a book, and particularly so in a book that pretends to synthesize other people's empirical work. The great risk is neglect.

In the case of this volume the two authors whose voluminous writings most immediately inspired me on the path I finally decided to go were Fernand Braudel and Marian Malowist.

Once I had written a draft, Fernand Braudel read it carefully and gave me encouragement at a moment when I needed reassurance. Charles Tilly also read it carefully, and by raising pertinent questions forced me to clarify my argument. This was particularly so concerning the role of state-power and "absolutism" in general, and its counterpoint with the phenomenon of banditry in particular. Douglas Dowd put me onto Frederic Lane for which I thank him, since Frederic Lane is very worth being put onto.

As for Terence Hopkins, my debt is to our twenty years of intellectual discussion and collaboration. There is no sentence that can summarize this debt.

This book was written during a year's stay at the Center for Advanced Study in the Behavioral Sciences. Countless authors have sung its praises. Aside from splendid surroundings, unlimited library and secretarial assis-tance, and a ready supply of varied scholars to consult at a moment's notice, what the center offers is to leave the scholar to his own devices, for good or ill. Would that all men had such wisdom. The final version was consum-mated with the aid of a grant from the Social Sciences Grants Subcommit-tee of the Faculty of Graduate Studies and Research of McGill University.

C'est par une crise des revenus seigneuriaux que se termine le moyen-âge et s'ouvrent les temps modernes.

—MARC BLOCH

This collapse in real wage-rates [in Europe] formed the counterpart to the revolutionary rise of prices in the sixteenth century. The operation was fully paid for by the increased toil, hardships, impoverishments and dejection of the majority. Contemporaries were often aware that the deterioration was taking place.

—FERNAND BRAUDEL and FRANK SPOONER

The discovery of gold and silver in America, the extirpation, enslavement and entombment in mines of the aboriginal population, the beginning of the conquest and looting of the East Indies, the turning of Africa into a warren for the commercial hunting of black-skins, signalised the rosy dawn of the era of capitalist production. These idyllic proceedings are the chief momenta of primitive accumulation. On their heels treads the commercial war of the European nations, with the globe for a theatre.

—KARL MARX

INTRODUCTION:
ON THE STUDY OF
SOCIAL CHANGE

Figure 1: "The Sack of Rome by Charles V," a woodcut illustrating a book on "Imperial Practices and Prognostication . . ." published in Strassbourg circa 1535. This woodcut celebrates the event that brought the Holy Father to political dependence on the Holy Roman Emperor, and made Charles the uncontested power in Italy.

Change is eternal. Nothing ever changes. Both clichés are "true." Structures are those coral reefs of human relations which have a stable existence over relatively long periods of time. But structures too are born, develop, and die.

Unless we are to use the study of social change as a term synonymous to the totality of social science, its meaning should be restricted to the study of changes in those phenomena which are most durable—the definition of durability itself being of course subject to change over historical time and place.

One of the major assertions of world social science is that there are some great watersheds in the history of man. One such generally recognized watershed, though one however studied by only a minority of social scientists, is the so-called neolithic or agricultural revolution. The other great watershed is the creation of the modern world.

This latter event is at the center of most contemporary social science theory, and indeed, of the nineteenth century as well. To be sure, there is immense debate as to what are the defining characteristics of modern times (and hence what are its temporal boundaries). Furthermore, there is much disagreement about the motors of this process of change. But there seems to be widespread consensus that some great structural changes did occur in the world in the last several hundred years, changes that make the world of today qualitatively different from the world of yesterday. Even those who reject evolutionist assumptions of determinate progress nonetheless admit the difference in structures.

What are the appropriate units to study if one wishes to describe this "difference" and account for it? In a sense, many of the major theoretical debates of our time can be reduced to arguments about this. It is the great quest of contemporary social science. It is therefore appropriate to begin a work that purports to analyze the process of social change in the modern world with an intellectual itinerary of one's conceptual search.

I started with an interest in the social underpinnings of political conflict in my own society. I thought that by comprehending the modalities of such conflict, I might contribute as a rational man to the shaping of that society. This led me into two great debates. One was the degree to which "all history is the history of the class struggle." Phrased another way, are classes the only significant operating units in the social and political arenas? Or, as Weber argued, are they only one of a trinity of units—class, status-group, and party—which exist, the interactions among which explain the political process? Although I had my prejudices on the subject, I found, like others before me, that neither the definition of these terms nor the description of their relations was easy to elucidate. I felt increasingly that

3

this was far more a conceptual than an empirical problem, and that to resolve the debate, at least in my own mind, I would have to place the issues within a larger intellectual context.

The second great debate, which was linked to the first, was about the degree to which there could or did exist a consensus of values within a given society, and to the extent that such a consensus existed, the degree to which its presence or absence was in fact a major determinant of men's actions. This debate is linked to the first because it is only if one rejects the primordial character of social struggle in civil society that the question can even be raised.

Values are of course an elusive thing to observe and I became very uneasy with a great deal of the theorizing about values, which seemed often to combine the absence of a rigorous empirical base with an affront to common sense. Still it was clear that men and groups did justify their actions by reference to ideologies. Furthermore, it seemed clear also that groups became more coherent and hence more politically efficacious to the extent that they were self-conscious, which meant that they developed a common language and a *Weltanschauung*.

I shifted my area of empirical concern from my own society to Africa in the hope either that I would discover various theories confirmed by what I found there or that a look at distant climes would sharpen my perception by directing my attention to issues I would otherwise have missed. I expected the former to happen. But it was the latter that came to pass.

I went to Africa first during the colonial era, and I witnessed the process of "decolonization," and then of the independence of a cascade of sovereign states. White man that I was, I was bombarded by the onslaught of the colonial mentality of Europeans long resident in Africa. And sympathizer of nationalist movements that I was, I was privy to the angry analyses and optimistic passions of young militants of the African movements. It did not take long to realize that not only were these two groups at odds on political issues, but that they approached the situation with entirely different sets of conceptual frameworks.

In general, in a deep conflict, the eyes of the downtrodden are more acute about the reality of the present. For it is in their interest to perceive correctly in order to expose the hypocrisies of the rulers. They have less interest in ideological deflection. So it was in this case. The nationalists saw the reality in which they lived as a "colonial situation," that is, one in which both their social action and that of the Europeans living side by side with them as administrators, missionaries, teachers, and merchants were determined by the constraints of a single legal and social entity. They saw further that the political machinery was based on a caste system in which rank and hence reward was accorded on the basis of race.

② for Wallerstein society = politico-juridical system, &
colonality of society - natural colonial
hence → world-system.

African nationalists were determined to change the political structures within which they lived. I have told this story elsewhere and it is not relevant to refer to it here. What is relevant here is that I thereby became aware of the degree to which society as an abstraction was heavily limited to politico-juridical systems as an empirical reality. It was a false perspective to take a unit like a "tribe" and seek to analyze its operations without reference to the fact that, in a colonial situation, the governing institutions of a "tribe," far from being "sovereign," were closely circumscribed by the laws (and customs) of a larger entity of which they were an indissociable part, the colony. Indeed this led me to the larger generalization that the study of social organization was by and large defective because of the widespread lack of consideration of the legal and political framework within which both organizations and their members operated.

I sought to discover the general attributes of a colonial situation and to describe what I thought of as its "natural history." It quickly became clear to me that I had to hold at least some factors of the world-system constant. So I restricted myself to an analysis of how the colonial system operated for those countries which were colonies in the nineteenth and twentieth centuries of European powers and which were "overseas possessions" of these powers. Given this constant, I felt I could make generally applicable statements about the impact on social life of the imposition of colonial authority, the motives and modalities of resistance to this authority, the mechanisms by which colonial powers entrenched and sought to legitimate their power, the contradictory nature of the forces that were able to operate within this framework, the reasons why men were led to form organizations that challenged colonial rule, and the structural elements that made for the expansion and eventual political triumph of anticolonial movements. The unit of analysis in all of this was the colonial territory as legally defined by the administering power.

I was interested equally in what happened to these "new states" after independence. As the study of colonial territories seemed to focus on the causes of the breakdown of existing political order, the study of the postindependence period seemed to focus on the opposite issue: How legitimate authority is established and a sense of membership in the national entity spread among the citizenry.

This latter study ran into problems, however. In the first place, to study the postindependence politics of Afro-Asian states seemed to be a process of running after the headlines. There could perforce be relatively little historical depth. Furthermore, there was the tricky question of Latin America. There were many ways in which the situations there seemed parallel, and more and more people began to think of the three continents as a "Third World." But Latin American countries had been politically independent for 150 years. Their cultures were far more closely linked with the European tradition than anything in Africa or Asia. The whole enterprise seemed to be wavering on very shaky ground.

In search for an appropriate unit of analysis, I turned to "states in the period after formal independence but before they had achieved something that might be termed national integration." This definition could be taken to include most or all of Latin America for all or almost all of the time up to the present. But it obviously included other areas as well. It included for example the United States of America, at least in the period before say the Civil War. It surely included eastern Europe, at least up until the twentieth century and possibly up to the present. And it even included western and southern Europe, at least for earlier periods of time.

I was therefore forced by this logic to turn my attention to early modern Europe. This led me first into the question of what I would take as the starting point of this process, a process I provisionally formulated, for want of a better conceptual tool, as the process of modernization. Further-more, I had not only to consider the issue of starting points but of terminal points, unless I wished to include twentieth-century Britain or Germany as instances of this same social process. Since that seemed prima facie dubious, terminal points had to be thought about.

At this point, I was clearly involved in a developmental schema and some implicit notion of stages of development. This in turn posed two problems: criteria for determining stages, and comparability of units across historical time.

How many stages had there been? How many could there be? Is indus-trialization a turning point or the consequence of some political turning point? What in this context would the empirical meaning of a term like "revolution" mean, as in the French Revolution or the Russian Revolution? Were these stages unilinear, or could a unit go "backward"? This seemed to be a vast conceptual morass into which I had stepped.

Furthermore, getting out of the conceptual morass was very difficult because of the absence of reasonable measuring instruments. How could one say that seventeenth-century France was in some sense equivalent to twentieth-century India? Laymen might consider such a statement absurd. Were they so wrong? It was all very well to fall back on textbook formulae of the virtues of scientific abstraction, but the practical difficulties of comparison seemed immense.

One way to handle the "absurd" idea of comparing two such disparate units was to accept the legitimacy of the objection and add another vari-able—the world context of any given era, or what Wolfram Eberhard has called "world time." This meant that while seventeenth-century France might have shared some structural characteristics with twentieth-century India, they were to be seen as very different on the dimensions of world context. This was conceptually clarifying, but made measurement even more complicated.

Finally, there seemed to be another difficulty. If given societies went through "stages," that is, had a "natural history," what of the world-system itself? Did it not have "stages," or at least a "natural history"? If so, were we not studying evolutions within evolutions? And if that, was not the theory getting to be top-heavy in epicycles? Did it not call for some simplifying thrust?

It seemed to me it did. It was at this point that I abandoned the idea altogether of taking either the sovereign state or that vaguer concept, the national society, as the unit of analysis. I decided that neither one was a social system and that one could only speak of social change in social systems. The only social system in this scheme was the world-system.

This was of course enormously simplifying. I had one type of unit rather than units within units. I could explain changes in the sovereign states as consequent upon the evolution and interaction of the world-system. But it was also enormously complicating. I probably only had one instance of this unit in the modern era. Suppose indeed that I was right, that the correct unit of analysis was the world-system, and that sovereign states were to be seen as one kind of organizational structure among others within this single social system. Could I then do anything more than write its history?

I was not interested in writing its history, nor did I begin to have the empirical knowledge necessary for such a task. (And by its very nature, few individuals ever could.) But can there be laws about the unique? In a rigorous sense, there of course cannot be. A statement of causality or probability is made in terms of a series of like phenomena or like instances. Even if one were to include in such a series those that would probably or even possibly occur in the future, what could be proposed here was not to add a series of future possible instances to a network of present and past ones. It was to add a series of future possible instances to a single past-present one.

There had only been one "modern world." Maybe one day there would be discovered to be comparable phenomena on other planets, or additional modern world-systems on this one. But here and now, the reality was clear—only one. It was here that I was inspired by the analogy with astronomy which purports to explain the laws governing the universe, although (as far as we know) only one universe has ever existed.

What do astronomers do? As I understand it, the logic of their arguments involves two separate operations. They use the laws derived from the study of smaller physical entities, the laws of physics, and argue that (with perhaps certain specified exceptions) these laws hold by analogy for the system as a whole. Second, they argue a posteriori. If the whole system is to have a given state at time y, it most probably had a certain state at time x.

Both methods are tricky, and it is for this reason that in the field of cosmology, which is the study of the functioning of the system as a whole, there are wildly opposing hypotheses held by reputable astronomers. Just as there are in the explanations of the modern world-system, a state of affairs likely to remain so for some time. Actually, students of the operation of the world-system possibly have it easier than students of the operation of the universe in terms of the amount of empirical evidence at their disposal.

In any case, I was inspired by the epigram of T. J. G. Locher: "One should not confuse totality with completeness. The whole is more than the assembled parts, but it is surely also less."[1]

I was looking to describe the world-system at a certain level of abstraction, that of the evolution of structures of the whole system. I was interested in describing particular events only insofar as they threw light upon the system as typical instances of some mechanism, or as they were the crucial turning points in some major institutional change.

This kind of project is manageable to the extent that a good deal of empirical material exists, and that this material is at least partially in the form of contrapuntal controversial work. Fortunately this seems to be the case by now for a large number of the themes of modern history.

One of the major thrusts of modern social science has been the effort to achieve quantification of research findings. Utilizing the heavily narrative accounts of most historical research seems not to lend itself to such quantification. What then is the reliability of such data, and to what extent can one safely draw conclusions from the material about the operation of a system as such? It is a major tragedy of twentieth-century social science that so large a proportion of social scientists, facing this dilemma, have thrown in the sponge. Historical data seemed to them vague and crude, hence unreliable. They felt that there was little to be done about it, and that hence it was best to avoid using it. And the best way not to use it was to formulate problems in such a way that its use was not indicated.

Thus the quantifiability of data determined the choice of research problems which then determined the conceptual apparatuses with which one defined and handled the empirical data. It should be clear on a moment's reflection that this is an inversion of the scientific process. Conceptualization should determine research tools, at least most of the time, not vice versa. The degree of quantification should reflect merely the maximum of precision that is possible for given problems and given methods at given points of time. More rather than less quantification is always desirable, to the extent that it speaks to the questions which derive from the conceptual exercise. At this stage of analysis of the world-system, the degree of quantification achieved and immediately realizable is limited. We do the best we can and go forward from there.

Lastly, there is the question of objectivity and commitment. I do not believe there exists any social science that is not committed. That does not mean however that it is not possible to be objective. It is first of all a matter of defining clearly our terms. In the nineteenth century, in rebellion against the fairy-tale overtones of so much prior historical writing, we were given the ideal of telling history *wie es eigentlich gewesen ist.* But social reality is ephemeral. It exists in the present and disappears as it moves into the past. The past can only be told as it truly *is,* not was. For recounting the past is a social act of the present done by men of the present and affecting the social system of the present.

"Truth" changes because society changes. At any given time, nothing is successive; everything is contemporaneous, even that which is past. And in the present we are all irremediably the products of our background, our training, our personality and social role, and the structured pressures within which we operate. That is not to say there are no options. Quite the contrary. A social system and all its constituent institutions, including the sovereign states of the modern world, are the loci of a wide range of social groups—in contact, in collusion, and above all, in conflict with each other. Since we all belong to multiple groups, we often have to make decisions as to the priorities demanded by our loyalties. Scholars and scientists are not somehow exempt from this requirement. Nor is the requirement limited to their nonscholarly, directly political roles in the social system.

To be sure, to be a scholar or a scientist is to perform a particular role in the social system, one quite different from being an apologist for any particular group. I am not denigrating the role of advocate. It is essential and honorable, but not the same as that of scholar or scientist. The latter's role is to discern, within the framework of his commitments, the present reality of the phenomena he studies, to derive from this study general principles, from which ultimately particular applications may be made. In this sense, there is no area of study that is not "relevant." For the proper understanding of the social dynamics of the present requires a theoretical comprehension that can only be based on the study of the widest possible range of phenomena, including through all of historical time and space.

When I say the "present reality" of phenomena, I do not mean that in order to strengthen the political claims of a government, an archaeologist for example should assert that the artifacts he uncovers belong to one group when he in fact believes them to belong to another. I mean that the whole archaeological enterprise from its inception—the social investment in this branch of scientific activity, the research orientation, the conceptual tools, the modes of resuming and communicating the results—are functions of the social present. To think otherwise is self-deceptive at best. Objectivity is honesty within this framework.

Objectivity is a function of the whole social system. Insofar as the system is lopsided, concentrating certain kinds of research activity in the hands of particular groups, the results will be "biased" in favor of these groups.

Objectivity is the vector of a distribution of social investment in such activity such that it is performed by persons rooted in all the major groups of the world-system in a balanced fashion. Given this definition, we do not have an objective social science today. On the other hand, it is not an unfeasible objective within the foreseeable future.

We have already suggested that the study of world-systems is particularly tricky because of the impossibility of finding comparable instances. It is also particularly tricky because the social impact of statements about the world-system are clearly and immediately evident to all major actors in the political arena. Hence the social pressures on scholars and scientists, in the form of relatively tight social control on their activities, is particularly great in this field. This affords one further explanation to that of the methodological dilemmas for the reluctance of scholars to pursue activities in this domain.

But conversely this is the very reason why it is important to do so. Man's ability to participate intelligently in the evolution of his own system is dependent on his ability to perceive the whole. The more difficult we acknowledge the task to be, the more urgent it is that we start sooner rather than later. It is of course not in the interest of all groups that this be done. Here our commitment enters. It depends on our image of the good society. To the extent that we want a more egalitarian world and a more libertarian one, we must comprehend the conditions under which these states of being are realizable. To do that requires first of all a clear exposition of the nature and evolution of the modern world-system heretofore, and the range of possible developments in the present and the future. That kind of knowledge would be power. And within the framework of my commitments, it would be a power that would be most useful to those groups which represent the interests of the larger and more oppressed parts of the world's population.

It is therefore with these considerations in mind that I have embarked on this effort to analyze the determining elements of the modern world-system. It will take several volumes to accomplish this task, even in the preliminary format that this work must necessarily be.

I have divided the work, at least initially, into four principal parts, corresponding with what I think of as four major epochs, thus far, of the modern world-system. This first volume will deal with the origins and early conditions of the world-system, still only a European world-system. The approximate dates of this are 1450–1640. The second volume shall deal with the consolidation of this system, roughly between 1640 and 1815. The third shall deal with the conversion of the world-economy into a global enterprise, made possible by the technological transformation of modern industrialism. This expansion was so sudden and so great that the system in effect had to be recreated. The period here is roughly 1815–1917. The fourth volume will deal with the consolidation of this capitalist world-economy from 1917 to the present, and the particular "revolutionary" tensions this consolidation has provoked.

Much of contemporary social science has become the study of groups and organizations, when it has not been social psychology in disguise. This work, however, involves not the study of groups, but of social systems. When one studies a social system, the classical lines of division within social science are meaningless. Anthropology, economics, political science, sociology—and history—are divisions of the discipline anchored in a certain liberal conception of the state and its relation to functional and geographical sectors of the social order. They make a certain limited sense if the focus of one's study is organizations. They make none at all if the focus is the social system. I am not calling for a multidisciplinary approach to the study of social systems, but for a unidisciplinary approach. The substantive content of this book will, I hope, make it clear what I mean by this phrase, and how seriously I take it.

1

MEDIEVAL PRELUDE

Figure 2: "The Foxhunt," from *Das Mittelälterliche Hausbuch,* ink drawing by an anonymous German artist, active 1475–1490, known as the Master of the Housebook.

In the late fifteenth and early sixteenth century, there came into existence what we may call a European world-economy. It was not an empire yet it was as spacious as a grand empire and shared some features with it. But it was different, and new. It was a kind of social system the world has not really known before and which is the distinctive feature of the modern world-system. It is an economic but not a political entity, unlike empires, city-states and nation-states. In fact, it precisely encompasses within its bounds (it is hard to speak of boundaries) empires, city-states, and the emerging "nation-states." It is a "world" system, not because it encompasses the whole world, but because it is larger than any juridically-defined political unit. And it is a "world-*economy*" because the basic linkage between the parts of the system is economic, although this was reinforced to some extent by cultural links and eventually, as we shall see, by political arrangements and even confederal structures.

An empire, by contrast, is a political unit. For example, Shmuel Eisenstadt has defined it this way:

> The term "empire" has normally been used to designate a political system encompassing wide, relatively high centralized territories, in which the center, as embodied both in the person of the emperor and in the central political institutions, constituted an autonomous entity. Further, although empires have usually been based on traditional legitimation, they have often embraced some wider, potentially universal political and cultural orientation that went beyond that of any of their component parts.[1]

Empires in this sense were a constant feature of the world scene for 5,000 years. There were continuously several such empires in various parts of the world at any given point of time. The political centralization of an empire was at one and the same time its strength and its weakness. Its strength lay in the fact that it guaranteed economic flows from the periphery to the center by force (tribute and taxation) and by monopolistic advantages in trade. Its weakness lay in the fact that the bureaucracy made necessary by the political structure tended to absorb too much of the profit, especially as repression and exploitation bred revolt which increased military expenditures.[2] Political empires are a primitive means of economic domination. It is the social achievement of the modern world, if you will, to have invented the technology that makes it possible to increase the flow of the surplus from the lower strata to the upper strata, from the periphery to the center, from the majority to the minority, by eliminating the "waste" of too cumbersome a political superstructure.

I have said that a world-economy is an invention of the modern world. Not quite. There were world-economies before. But they were always transformed into empires: China, Persia, Rome. The modern world-economy might have gone in that same direction—indeed it has sporadically seemed as though it would—except that the techniques of modern capitalism and the technology of modern science, the two being somewhat linked as we know, enabled this world-economy to thrive, produce, and expand without the emergence of a unified political structure.[3]

What capitalism does is offer an alternative and more lucrative source of surplus appropriation (at least more lucrative over a long run). An empire is a mechanism for collecting tribute, which in Frederic Lane's pregnant image, "means payments received for protection, but payments in excess of the cost of producing the protection."[4] In a capitalist world-economy, political energy is used to secure monopoly rights (or as near to it as can be achieved). The state becomes less the central economic enterprise than the means of assuring certain terms of trade in other economic transactions. In this way, the operation of the market (not the *free* operation but nonetheless its operation) creates incentives to increased productivity and all the consequent accompaniment of modern economic development. The world-economy is the arena within which these processes occur.

A world-economy seems to be limited in size. Ferdinand Fried observed that:

> If one takes account of all the factors, one reaches the conclusion that the space of the 'world' economy in Roman antiquity could be covered in about 40 to 60 days, utilizing the best means of transport. . . . Now, in our times [1939], it also takes 40 to 60 days to cover the space of the modern world economy, if one uses the normal channels of transportation for merchandise.[5]

And Fernand Braudel adds that this could be said to be the time span of the Mediterranean world in the sixteenth century.[6]

The origins and the functioning of such a 60–day European world-economy[7] in the sixteenth century is our concern here. It is vital to remember, however, that Europe was not the only world-economy at the time. There were others.[8] But Europe alone embarked on the path of capitalist development which enabled it to outstrip these others. How and why did this come about? Let us start by seeing what happened in the world in the three centuries prior to 1450. In the twelfth century, the Eastern Hemisphere contained a series of empires and small worlds, many of which were interlinked at their edges with each other. At that time, the Mediterranean was one focus of trade where Byzantium, Italian city-states, and to some extent parts of northern Africa met. The Indian Ocean–Red Sea complex formed another such focus. The Chinese region was a third. The Central Asian land mass from Mongolia to Russia was a fourth. The Baltic area was on the verge of becoming a fifth. Northwest

Europe was however a very marginal area in economic terms. The principal social mode or organization there was what has come to be called feudalism.

We must be very clear what feudalism was not. It was not a "natural economy," that is, an economy of self-subsistence. Western Europe feudalism grew out of the disintegration of an empire, a disintegration which was never total in reality or even *de jure.*[9] The myth of the Roman Empire still provided a certain cultural and even legal coherence to the area. Christianity served as a set of parameters within which social action took place. Feudal Europe was a "civilization," but not a world-system.

It would not make sense to conceive of the areas in which feudalism existed as having two economies, a market economy of the towns and a subsistence economy of the rural manors. In the twentieth century, with reference to the so-called underdeveloped world, this approach has gone under the label of the "dual economy" theory. Rather, as Daniel Thorner suggests:

> We are sure to deceive ourselves if we think of peasant economies as oriented exclusively towards their own subsistence and term "capitalist" any orientation towards the "market." It is more reasonable to start by assuming that, for many centuries, peasant economies have had both orientations.[10]

For many centuries? How many? B. H. Slicher van Bath, in his major work on European agrarian history, marks the turning point at about 1150 A.D.. Even before then, he does not think Western Europe was engaged in subsistence farming, but rather from 500 A.D. to c. 1150 A.D. in what he calls "direct agricultural consumption," that is, a system of partial self-sufficiency in which, while most people produce their own food, they also supply it to the nonagricultural population as barter. From 1150 A.D. on, he considers Western Europe to have reached that stage of "indirect agricultural consumption," a stage we are still in today.[11]

What we should envisage then, when we speak of western European feudalism, is a series of tiny economic nodules whose population and productivity were slowly increasing, and in which the legal mechanisms ensured that the bulk of the surplus went to the landlords who had noble status and control of the juridical machinery. Since much of this surplus was in kind, it was of little benefit unless it could be sold. Towns grew up, supporting artisans who bought the surplus and exchanged it for their products. A merchant class came from two sources: On the one hand, agents of the landlords who sometimes became independent, as well as intermediate size peasants who retained enough surplus after payments to the lord to sell it on the market[12]; on the other hand, resident agents of long-distance merchants (based often in northern Italian city-states and later in the Hanseatic cities) who capitalized on poor communications and hence high disparities of prices from one area to another, especially when certain areas suffered natural calamities.[13] As towns grew, of course, they offered a possible refuge and place of employment for peasants which began to change some of the terms of relationship on the manor.[14]

Feudalism as a system should not be thought of as something antithetical to trade. On the contrary, up to a certain point, feudalism and the expansion of trade go hand in hand. Claude Cahen suggests that if scholars have often observed this phemonemon in areas *other than* western Europe,[15] perhaps they have failed to notice the same phenomenon in Western feudalism because of ideological blinkers. "Having thus noted the possibility of convergence, *up to a certain stage of development only,* of the development of feudalism and of commerce, we ought to reconsider, from this point of view, the history of the West itself."[16]

Yet a feudal system could only support a limited amount of long-distance trade as opposed to local trade. This was because long-distance trade was a trade in luxuries, not in bulk goods. It was a trade which benefited from price disparities and depended on the political indulgence and economic possibilities of the truly wealthy. It is only with the expansion of production within the framework of a modern world-economy that long-distance trade could convert itself in part into bulk trade which would, in turn, feed the process of expanded production. Until then, as Owen Lattimore notes, it was not really what we mean today by trade:

> As late as the time of Marco Polo (at least) the trade of the merchant who ventured beyond his own district depended delicately on the whims of potentates. . . . The distant venture was concerned less with the disposal of goods in bulk and more with curiosities, rarities and luxuries. . . . The merchant sought out those who could extend favor and protection. . . . If he were unlucky he might be plundered or taxed to ruination; but if he were lucky he received for his goods not so much an economic price as a munificent largesse. . . . The structure of the silk trade and that of much other trade was more a tribute structure than a trade structure.[17]

Thus, the level of commercial activity was limited. The principal economic activity remained food and handicraft production traded within small economic regions. Nonetheless, the scale of this economic activity was slowly expanding. And the various economic nuclei expanded therewith. New frontier lands were cultivated. New towns were founded. Population grew. The Crusades provided some of the advantages of colonial plunder. And then sometime in the fourteenth century, this expansion ceased. The cultivated areas retracted. Population declined. And throughout feudal Europe and beyond it, there seemed to be a "crisis," marked by war, disease, and economic hardship. Whence came this "crisis" and what were its consequences?

First, in what sense was there a crisis? Here there is some disagreement, not so much as to the description of the process as to the emphasis in causal explanation. Edouard Perroy sees the issue primarily as one of an optimal point having been reached in an expansion process, of a saturation of population, "an enormous density, given the still primitive state of agrarian and artisanal technology."[18] And lacking better plows and fertilizer little could be done to ameliorate the situation. This led to food shortages which in turn led to epidemics. With a stable money supply, there was a moderate rise in prices, hurting the rentiers. The slow deterioration of the situation was then rendered acute by the beginnings of the Hundred Years War in 1335–1345, which turned western European state systems toward a war economy, with the particular result that there was an increased need for taxes. The taxes, coming on top of already heavy feudal dues, were too much for the producers, creating a liquidity crisis which in turn led to a return to indirect taxes and taxes in kind. Thus started a downward cycle: The fiscal burden led to a reduction in consumption which led to a reduction in production and money circulation which increased further the liquidity difficulties which led to royal borrowing and eventually the insolvency of the limited royal treasuries, which in turn created a credit crisis, leading to hoarding of bullion, which in turn upset the pattern of international trade. A rapid rise in prices occurred, further reducing the margin of subsistence, and this began to take its toll in population. The landowner lost customers and tenants. The artisan lost customers. There was turn from arable to pasture land because it required less manpower. But there was a problem of customers for the wool. Wages rose, which was a particular burden for small and medium-sized landowners who turned to the State for protection against wage rises. "The disaggregation to manorial production, which becomes ever more severe after 1350, is proof of a continuous slump . . . [of] mediocrity in stagnation."[19]

Stagnation is, on the face of it, a curious consequence. One might have expected the following scenario. Reduced population leads to higher wages which, with rents relatively inelastic, would mean a change in the composition of demand, shifting part of the surplus from lord to peasant, and hence ensuring that less of it would be hoarded. Furthermore, a reduction of population in an economy that was largely agricultural should have led to parallel reductions in demand and supply. But since typically a producer will normally reduce production by eliminating the less fertile plots, there should have been an increased rate of productivity, which should have reduced prices. Both of these developments should have encouraged, not discouraged, trade. Nonetheless trade "stagnated" in fact.

What went wrong in the calculation is the implicit assumption about elasticity of demand. North and Thomas remind us that, given the state of the technology and the range of the volume of international trade, transactions costs were very high, and any reduction in volume (due to a decline in population) would set in train a process of rising costs which would lead to a further reduction in trade. They trace the process like this:

[Previously] merchants found it profitable to reduce transactions costs by stationing factors in a distant city to acquire information about prices and possible trading opportunities; as the volume of trade shrank, this was no longer expedient. Information flows dried up and trade volume was further reduced. It is thus not surprising that economic historians have found depression (for them meaning a decreased total volume of economic activity) even in the midst of this world where higher *per capita* income would presumably have followed the relatively increased real wage that peasant and worker must have been experiencing.[20]

R. H. Hilton accepts Perroy's description of events.[21] But he takes exception to the form of analysis which makes the crisis comparable to one of the recurrent crises of a developed capitalist system, thus exaggerating the degree to which financial and monetary dilemmas affect a feudal system in which the cash-flow element is so much smaller a part of human interaction than in capitalist society.[22] Furthermore, he suggests that Perroy omits any discussion of another phenomenon which resulted from the events Perroy describes, and which to Hilton is central, that of the unusual degree of social conflict, the "climate of endemic discontent," the peasant insurrections which took the form of a "revolt against the social system as such."[23] For Hilton, this was not therefore merely a conjunctural crisis, one point in an up and down of cyclical trends. Rather it was the culmination of 1000 years of development, the decisive crisis of a system. "During the last centuries of the Roman Empire as during the Middle Ages, society was paralyzed by the growing expense of a social and political superstructure, an expense to which corresponded no compensating increase in the productive resources of society."[24] Hilton agrees with Perroy that the immediate cause of the dilemma was to be found in technological limitations, the lack of fertilizer and the inability to expand fertilizer supply by expanding the number of cattle, because the climate limited the quantity of winter forage for cattle. But "what we should underline is that there was no large reinvestment of profits in agriculture such that would *significantly* increase productivity."[25] This was because of the inherent limitations of the reward system of feudal social organization.

What Hilton's emphasis on the *general* crisis of feudalism offers us over Perroy's sense of the conjunctural is that it can account for the social transformation these developments involved. For if the optimal degree of productivity had been passed in a system *and* the economic squeeze was leading to a generalized seignior–peasant class war, as well as ruinous fights within the seigniorial classes, then the only solution that would extract western Europe from decimation and stagnation would be one that would expand the economic pie to be shared, a solution which required, given the technology of the time, an expansion of the land area and population base to exploit. This is what in fact took place in the fifteenth and sixteenth centuries.

That peasant revolts became widespread in western Europe from the thirteenth century to the fifteenth century seems to be in little doubt. Hilton finds the immediate explanation for England in the fact that "in the 13th century most of the great estate-owners, lay and ecclesiastical, expanded their demesne production in order to sell agricultural produce on the market. . . . [As a result], labor services were increased, even doubled."[26] Kosminsky similarly talks of this period as being that of "the most intense exploitation of the English peasantry. . . ."[27] On the continent, there were a series of peasant rebellions: in northern Italy and then in coastal Flanders at the turn of the 14th century; in Denmark in 1340; in Majorca in 1351; the Jacquerie in France in 1358; scattered rebellions in Germany long before the great peasant war of 1525. Peasant republics sprang up in Frisia in the twelfth and thirteenth centuries, and in Switzerland in the thirteenth century. For B. H. Slicher van Bath, "peasant rebellions went with economic recession."[28] Dobb suggests that when such recession occurred, it fell particularly hard not on the lowest stratum of workers who probably never were very well off but on "the upper stratum of well-to-do peasants, who were in position to extend cultivation onto new land and to improve it, and who accordingly tended to be the spearpoint of revolt."[29]

The sudden decline of prosperity involved more than peasant discontent. The depopulation which accompanied it—caused by wars, famines, and epidemics—led to the *Wüstungen*, the recession of settlements from marginal lands, the disappearance of whole villages sometimes. The desertion of villages should not be seen exclusively as a sign of recession. For there are at least two other major reasons for desertion. One, which was a continuing one, was the search for physical security whenever warfare overtook a region.[30] A second, less "accidental" and more structural, was a change in agrarian social structure, the "enclosure" or "engrossing" of land. It seems clear that this process too was going on in the late Middle Ages.[31] And it is somewhat difficult at this stage of our knowledge to disentangle the three.

Two things seem clear about the cessation of clearings and the recession of settlements. It was, as Karl Helleiner remarks, a "selective process with respect to size of holdings. The percentage of small holdings abandoned in the course of the late Middle Ages appears to have been higher than that of full-sized farms."[32] It was also selective by regions. The *Wüstungen* seemed to have been extensive not only in Germany and Central Europe,[33] but also in England.[34] It was on the other hand far more limited in France.[35] No doubt this is in part explained by the fact that France was more densely settled and earlier cleared than other areas of Europe for both historical and pedological reasons.

At this time of contracting demand for agricultural products, urban wages and hence industrial prices were rising, because of the shortage

of labor bred by population decline. This in turn raised the cost of
agricultural labor while reducing rents (insofar as they were fixed while
nominal prices were inflating). This led to what Marc Bloch has called
the "momentary impoverishment of the seigniorial class."[36] Not only
were profits diminished but the costs of management rose, as they
always do in difficult times,[37] leading owners to consider shedding direct
management. The economic squeeze led to increased exactions on the
peasantry which were then counterproductive, and resulted in peasant
flight.[38] One path to the restoration of income for the nobility, one often
efficacious for the wealthiest stratum, was to involve themselves in new
and remunerative careers with the princes.[39] It was not however sufficient to counteract the effects of recession and therefore to stem the
decline of the demesne.[40] And it may incidentally, by removing seigniors
from residence, have encouraged disinterest in management.

What then happened to the large estates? They were sold or rented
for money to the principal group ready and able to engage in such a
transaction, the better off peasants, who were in a position to obtain
favorable terms.[41]

We must however remember that the social organization of agricultural production was not identical everywhere. The demesnes were the
largest in western Europe, in part because denser population had
required the relative efficiency of larger units. In central Europe, the
effects of economic recession led to the same desertion of marginal
lands, but the analysis of these *Wüstungen* is complicated by the fact that
they represented in part enclosures as well as abandonment.[42] Further
to the east, in Brandenburg and Poland, as we shall discuss later, where
population density was even thinner, the lords who collectively previously owned less land than the peasants "saw their estates acquiring all
the lands left deserted by the sudden demographic collapse."[43] How
profitable this would be for them in the sixteenth century, how profoundly this would alter the social structure of eastern Europe, how
important this would be for the development of western Europe—all this
was doubtless outside the ken of the participants in the fourteenth and
fifteenth centuries. But in the *nonmarginal* arable land areas of *western*
Europe, the *excessively large* demesne gives way to smaller landholdings.
Thus, simultaneously, there is the rise of a medium-sized peasantry on
arable land in western Europe, the beginning of enclosures of less arable
lands in western Europe (which would be the basis of expanded animal
husbandry), and the concentration of property into large estates in eastern
Europe (which would come to serve a new function as grain export areas).

Was this period of economic "collapse" or "stagnation" good or bad
for the development of a capitalist world-economy? It depends on the
length of one's perspective. Michael Postan sees the fifteenth century a'

a regression from the developments of the fourteenth,[44] a setback which to be sure was later overcome. Eugen Kosminsky sees it as part of the liquidation of feudalism, hence a necessary step in the development of a capitalist economy.[45] The facts are the same. The theoretical perspective is different.

Thus far, in this discussion, we have scarcely mentioned the developments in the political sphere, and in particular the slow rise of the centralized state bureaucracy. In the heyday of western feudalism, when the state was weakest, the landowner, the lord of the manor thrived. However much, in a later era, the state machinery might be utilized by the nobility to further their interests, they were doubtless better served still by the weakness of kings and emperors. Not only were they personally freer of control and taxation but they were also freer to control and tax the peasants. In such societies, where there is no effective link between the central authority with its legal order and the masses, the effect of violence was double, since as Bloch noted, "through the play of custom, an abuse might always by mutation become a precedent, a precedent a right."[46]

Lords of the manor then would never welcome the strengthening of the central machinery if they were not in a weakened condition in which they found it more difficult to resist the claims of central authority and more ready to welcome the benefits of imposed order. Such a situation was that posed by the economic difficulties of the fourteenth and fifteenth centuries, and the decline of seigniorial revenues.

Alongside the economic dilemmas occurred a technological shift in the art of war, from the long bow to the cannon and the handgun, from the cavalry war to the one in which infantry charged and hence in which more training and discipline was required. All this meant that the cost of war increased, the number of men required rose, and the desirability of a standing army over ad hoc formations became ever more clear. Given the new requirements, neither the feudal lords individually nor the city-states could really foot the bill or recruit the manpower, especially in an era of depopulation.[47] Indeed, even the territorial states were having a hard job of maintaining order, as the frequency of peasant revolts shows.[48]

The fifteenth century, however, saw the advent of the great restorers of internal order in western Europe: Louis XI in France, Henry VII in England, and Ferdinand of Aragon and Isabella of Castile in Spain. The major mechanisms at their disposition in this task, as for their less successful predecessors, were financial: by means of the arduous creation of a bureaucracy (civil and armed) strong enough to tax and thus to finance a still stronger bureaucratic structure. This process had started already in the twelfth and thirteenth centuries. With the cessation of the invasions, which had previously preoccupied and exhausted the princes, the growth of population, the revival of trade and hence the more abundant circulation of money, there was a basis for the taxation which could pay for salaried officials and troops.[49] This was true not only in France, England, and Spain but in the principalities of Germany as well.

Taxes are to be sure the key issue. And it is not easy to begin the upward cycle.[50] The obstacles to an effective taxation system in the late Middle Ages seem in retrospect overwhelming. Taxation can only in reality be on net production, and net production was low, as was the quantity of money, as well as its circulation. It was extremely difficult to verify taxes both because of a lack of personnel and because of the low level of quantified record keeping. It is no wonder that rulers constantly resorted to alternatives to taxation as sources of income: to confiscation, to borrowing, to selling state offices, to debasing the coinage. But each of these alternatives, while they may have solved financial dilemmas of the moment, had some negative long-term effects on the politico-economic strength of the king.[51] Still it would be false to emphasize the difficulties. It is the magnitude of the achievement that is impressive. The many compromises might be seen as essential steps on the road to success. Tax-farming[52] and the venality of office[53] can be seen precisely as two such useful compromises. Furthermore, the increased flow of funds to the king not only hurt the nobility by strengthening the state, but also by weakening the nobility's own sources of revenue, especially in the tighter economy of the fourteenth and fifteenth centuries, and especially for those not linked to the new bureaucracies. As Duby puts it: "A large part of the revenues extracted from the soil by the peasants still found its way into the lord's hands, but the endless progress of taxation had greatly enlarged the share taken by the agents of the State."[54]

And as the state grew stronger, monetary manipulation became more profitable. When in the fourteenth and fifteenth centuries, the financial crises of states beset by war were compounded by low profit margins in the countryside that could be taxed, the states had to find other sources of revenue, especially since depopulation meant that princes were offering exemptions from taxation to those who would recolonize devastated areas. Monetary manipulation thus had many advantages. Léopold Génicot points out that there are three possible explanations for the frequent debasements of the period: the reduction of state debts (although debasement also thereby reduces fixed revenues, which constituted the bulk of income from royal domains); scarcity of means of payment, at a time when trade was growing more than the stocks of silver and when public disorder encouraged hoarding of bullion; or a deliberate economic policy of lowering the exchange rate to arrest deflation, combat hoarders, facilitate exports and thus revive commerce. Whichever the explanation of the debasements, they were "very largely inflationary" and "reduced in this way the real value of fixed revenues."[55] The principal recipients of fixed revenues were the seigniorial classes, and hence they were weakened vis-à-vis the state.

The state? What was the state? At this time, it was the prince, the prince whose reputation was lauded, whose majesty was preserved, who little by little was removed from his subjects.[56] And it was the bureaucracy which emerged now as a distinctive social grouping with special characteristics and interests, the principal ally of the prince,[57] and yet one which, as we shall see, was to remain an ambivalent one. And it was the various parliamentary bodies the sovereigns created as mechanisms to assist them in the legislating of taxes, bodies composed largely of nobles, which the kings tried to use against the nobility and the nobility against the king.[58]

This state was a creation which dates not from the sixteenth century but from the thirteenth century in western Europe. Yves Renouard has traced how the boundary lines that determine to this day the frontiers of France, England, and Spain were more or less definitively settled in a series of battles which occurred between 1212 and 1214.[59] It was on the basis of these lines rather than some others (for example, a Mediterranean Occitanian state including Provence and Catalonia; or an Atlantic state including the western France of the Angevins as part of England) that later nationalist sentiments were constructed. First the boundaries, later the passions is as true of early modern Europe as, say, of twentieth-century Africa. It was at this period that not only were the boundary lines decided but, even more important, it was decided that there would be boundary lines. This is what Edouard Perroy calls the "fundamental change" in the political structure of western Europe.[60] In his view, it is between the middle of the twelfth century and the beginning of the fourteenth, in short at the height of commercial and agricultural prosperity of the Middle Ages, that we can date the transformation of Europe.

Why nation-states and not empires? Here we must be prudent about our terminology. Perhaps we should think of France of the thirteenth and fourteenth centuries as a nation-state, of France of the fifteenth and sixteenth centuries as an empire, of the seventeenth century as a nation-state again. This is what Fernand Braudel seems to think.[61] Why this pattern of alternation? Braudel suggests that "there was, with the economic expansion of the 15th and 16th centuries, a conjuncture stubbornly favorable to vast, even very vast States, to these 'thick States'. . . . In fact, history is, in turn, favorable and unfavorable to vast political structures."[62] Fritz Hartung and R. Mousnier suggest the need for a minimum size (but also a maximum?) for the establishment of an absolute monarchy, a form which did not succeed in little States. "Doubtless, the latter could not constitute military and economic units large enough to sustain an absolute monarchy."[63] These are but hints at answers to a problem worth considerable theoretical attention. V. G. Kiernan helps us perhaps the most with the following conceptual clarification:

> No dynasty set out to build a nation-state; each aimed at unlimited extension . . .
> and the more it prospered the more the outcome was a multifarious empire *man-
> qué*. It had to be large enough to survive and sharpen its claws on its neighbours,
> but small enough to be organized from one centre and to feel itself as an entity.
> On the closepacked western edge of Europe, any excessive ballooning of territory
> was checked by competition and geographical limits.[64]

Unless, of course, they extended their empires overseas.

What would happen to those empires *manqué* was that they would
develop different *raisons d'état* from empires, different ideologies. A
nation-state is a territorial unit whose rulers seek (sometimes seek, often
seek, surely not always seek) to make of it a national society—for reasons
we shall discuss later. The affair is even more confusing when we
remember that from the sixteenth century on, the nation-states of western Europe sought to create relatively homogeneous national societies at
the core of empires, using the imperial venture as an aid, perhaps an
indispensable one, to the creation of the national society.

We have discussed the crisis of western feudalism in the fourteenth
and fifteenth centuries as the background for, prelude to, the expansion
of Europe and its economic transformation since the sixteenth century.
Thus far the discussion and the explanations have been largely in terms
of the social structure (the organization of production, the state machinery, the relationship of various social groups). Yet many would feel that
the "crisis" of the fourteenth century and the "expansion" of the sixteenth could be accounted for, let us say in significant part, by factors
of the physical environment—climate, epidemiology, soil conditions.
These arguments cannot be lightly dismissed and the factors should be
assessed and given their due weight in accounting for the social change
that did occur.

The case for climate has been put most strongly by Gustaf Utterström.
The argument in summary goes like this:

> Thanks to industrialism, thanks not least to technical progress, man in our own
> day is less exposed to the whims of Nature than he was in previous centuries.
> But how often is it considered that another factor is that we are living in an age
> in which the climate, especially in northern Europe, is unusually mild? During
> the last 1000 years, . . . the periods of prosperity in human affairs have on the
> whole, though with important exceptions, occurred during the warm intervals
> between the great glaciations. It is in these same intervals that both economic life
> and the size of the populations have made the greatest advances.[65]

To strengthen his case, Utterström reminds us that climatic change
might have had special bearing on the earlier periods in the transformation of Europe. "The primitive agriculture of the Middle Ages must
have been much more dependent on favorable weather than is modern
agriculture with its high technical standards."[66]
Utterström points for example to the severe winters of the fourteenth

and early fifteenth centuries, the mild winters from 1460 to the mid-16th century, the severe winters of the second half of the seventeenth,[67] which corresponds *grosso modo* to economic recession, expansion, and recession.

> To regard population pressure as the decisive factor does not provide a satisfactory explanation of these economic developments. The fact that the population increased in the way it did raises a question which has not so far been asked: why did the population increase? . . . The great increase in population was . . . general throughout Europe. In northern and central Europe it got well under way during the period when the climate was unusually mild. This can scarcely be a chance coincidence: there must be a causal connection.[68]

In addition, Utterström makes epidemiological factors intervening variables. He explains the Black Plague by hot summers which led to the multiplication of the black rat, the host to the rat flea, one of the two carriers of the plague.[69]

Georges Duby acknowledges that this hypothesis must be taken seriously. Certainly some of the fourteenth century abandonments of cultivation (cereals in Iceland, the Scandinavian colonies in Greenland, the lowered forest limit in Sudetenland, the end of viticulture in England and its regression in Germany) are all plausibly explained by climatic change. But there are alternative plausible explanations. Most importantly, Duby reminds us that "agrarian recession, like the demographic collapse, started before the beginning of the fourteenth century,"[70] hence before the presumed climatic changes. Instead, Duby would see climatic factors and then epidemiology as being cumulative woes which, in the fourteenth century, "dealt a crushing blow to the already fragile demographic structure."[71] Similar skepticism about the temporal primacy of climatic change in explaining the ups and downs have been expressed by Helleiner,[72] Slicher van Bath,[73] and Emmanuel Le Roy Ladurie.[74]

Obviously, to the extent that there was climatic change, it would affect the operations of a social system. Yet equally obviously, it would affect different systems differently. Though opinions differ, it is probable that such glaciation as did occur was spread over the whole Northern Hemisphere, yet social developments in Asia and North America were clearly divergent from those in Europe. It would be useful therefore to return to the chronic factor of resource strain involved in the feudal system of social organization, or overconsumption by a minority given the overall low level of productivity. Norman Pounds reminds us of "how small the margin for security was for the medieval peasant even under conditions that might be termed normal or average. . . ."[75] Slicher van Bath tends to corroborate this hypotheses of prolonged undernourishment by observing that it was precisely in protein-producing regions that men were most resistant to the plague.[76]

If however there was first economic regression because of the chronic overexploitation and resulting rebellions discussed previously, and then climatic factors added on both food shortages and plagues, it is easy to see how the socio–physical conjuncture could achieve "crisis" proportions. The crisis would in turn be aggravated by the factor that the plague, once it spread, became endemic.[77] Furthermore, although fewer men should have meant more food since the landmass remained the same, it also meant a shift to pasturage and hence a reduction of caloric output. The demographic decline thus became endemic too.[78] Pierre Chaunu adds that "the collapse of rent, the diminution of profits and the aggravation of seigniorial burdens" may have worsened the situation further by turning capital investment away from the land.[79] And Dobb suggests that the resulting phenomenon of commutation may have further increased the burden of the peasant, rather than mitigating it as usually assumed, thereby adding to the dilemma.[80] Thus, intruding the variables of the physical environment does not undo our previous analysis. It enriches it by adding a further element to help explain a historical conjuncture so consequential in the future history of the world, a further instance in which long-term stabilities and slow secular changes can account for conjunctures which have the power to change social structures which are intermediate from the perspective of temporal duration.

The analysis thus far is as follows. In Europe in the late Middle Ages, there existed a Christian "civilization" but neither a world-empire nor a world-economy. Most of Europe was feudal, that is, consisted of relatively small, relatively self-sufficient economic nodules based on a form of exploitation which involved the relatively direct appropriation of the small agricultural surplus produced within a manorial economy by a small class of nobility. Within Europe, there were at least two smaller world-economies, a medium-sized one based on the city-states of northern Italy and a smaller one based on the city-states of Flanders and northern Germany. Most of Europe was not directly involved in these networks.

From about 1150 to 1300, there was an expansion in Europe within the framework of the feudal mode of production, an expansion at once geographic, commercial, and demographic. From about 1300 to 1450, what expanded contracted, again at the three levels of geography, commerce, and demography.

This contraction following the expansion caused a "crisis," one which was visible not only in the economic sphere but in the political sphere as well (internecine wars among the nobility and peasant revolts being the two main symptoms). It was also visible at the level of culture. The medieval Christian synthesis was coming under multitudinous attack in all the forms which later would be called the first stirrings of "modern" Western thought.

There are three main explanations of the crisis. One is that it was the product essentially of cyclical economic trends. The optimal point of expansion given the technology having been reached, there followed a contraction. The second is that it was the product essentially of a secular trend. After a thousand years of surplus appropriation under the feudal mode, a point of diminishing returns had been reached. While productivity remained stable (or even possibly declined as a result of soil exhaustion) because of the absence of structured motivation for technological advance, the burden to be borne by the producers of the surplus had been constantly expanding because of the growing size and level of expenditure of the ruling classes. There was no more to be squeezed out. The third explanation is climatological. The shift in European metereological conditions was such that it lowered soil productivity and increased epidemics simultaneously.

The first and the third explanation suffer from the fact that similar cyclical and climatological shifts occurred at other places and times without producing the consequence of creating a capitalist world-economy as a solution to the problems. The secular explanation of crisis may well be correct but it is inherently difficult to create the kind of serious statistical analysis that would demonstrate that it was a sufficient explanation of the social transformation. I believe it is most plausible to operate on the assumption that the "crisis of feudalism" represented a conjuncture of secular trends, an immediate cyclical crisis, and climatological decline.

It was precisely the immense pressures of this conjuncture that made possible the enormity of the social change. For what Europe was to develop and sustain now was a new form of surplus appropriation, a capitalist world-economy. It was to be based not on direct appropriation of agricultural surplus in the form either of tribute (as had been the case for world-empires) or of feudal rents (as had been the system of European feudalism). Instead what would develop now is the appropriation of a surplus which was based on more efficient and expanded productivity (first in agriculture and later in industry) by means of a world market mechanism with the "artificial" (that is, nonmarket) assist of state machineries, none of which controlled the world market in its entirety.

It will be the argument of this book that three things were essential to the establishment of such a capitalist world-economy: an expansion of the geographical size of the world in question, the development of variegated methods of labor control for different products and different zones of the world-economy, and the creation of relatively strong state machineries in what would become the core-states of this capitalist world-economy.

The second and third aspects were dependent in large part on the success of the first. The territorial expansion of Europe hence was theoretically a key prerequisite to a solution for the "crisis of feudalism." Without it, the European situation could well have collapsed into relative constant anarchy and further contraction. How was it then that Europe seized upon the alternative that was to save it? The answer is that it was not Europe that did so but Portugal, or at least it was Portugal that took the lead.

Let us look now at what it was in the social situation of Portugal that can account for the thrust toward overseas exploration which Portugal began right in the midst of the "crisis." To understand this phenomenon, we must start by remembering that Europe's geographical expansion started, as we have already suggested, earlier. Archibald Lewis argues that "from the eleventh to the mid-thirteenth century western Europe followed an almost classical frontier development."[81] He refers to the gradual reconquest of Spain from the Moors, the recuperation by Christian Europe of the Balaeric Islands, Sardinia, and Corsica, the Norman conquest of southern Italy and Sicily. He refers to the Crusades with its addition first of Cyprus, Palestine and Syria, then of Crete and the Aegean Islands. In Northwest Europe, there was English expansion into Wales, Scotland, and Ireland. And in eastern Europe, Germans and Scandinavians penetrated the lands of, conquered, and converted to Christianity Balts and Slavs. "The most important frontier [however] was an internal one of forest, swamp, marsh, moor, and fen. It was this wasteland which Europe's peasants settled and largely put into cultivation between the years 1000 and 1250."[82] Then, as we have seen, this expansion and this prosperity was brought to an end by a "crisis" which was also a contraction. In political terms, this involved the rally of the Moors in Granada, the expulsion of the Crusaders from the Levant, the reconquest of Constantinople by the Byzantines in 1261, the Mongol conquest of the Russian plain. Internally, in Europe, there were the *Wüstungen.*

The great explorations, the Atlantic expansion, was thus not the first but the second thrust of Europe, one that succeeded because the momentum was greater, the social and technological base more solid, the motivation more intense. Why however a thrust whose initial center was Portugal? In 1250 or even 1350, few would have thought Portugal a likely candidate for this role. And retrospectively from the twentieth century, it clashes with our sense of probability, our bias against the minor power Portugal has been in modern times and indeed throughout all of history.

We shall try to answer this question in terms of motivation and capabilities. The motivations were European in scope, though some of them may have been felt more acutely in Portugal. What were the explorers looking for? Precious metals and spices, the schoolboy textbooks tell us. And this was true, to be sure, up to a point.

In the Middle Ages, Christian Europe and the Arab world were in a symbiotic relationship in terms of gold and silver. In Andrew Watson's phrase, "in monetary matters, . . . the two regions should be treated as a whole."[83] The former minted silver, the latter gold. As a result of a long-term disequilibrium in prices, whose origins are complex and need not concern us here, the silver flowed eastward leading to an abundance in the Arab world. Silver exports could no longer lead to gold imports. In 1252, Florence and Genoa therefore struck new gold coins. The motive was there. One fact which made it possible was the expansion of the trans-Saharan gold trade in the thirteenth century.[84] Watson thinks it is implausible to talk of a gold shortage, therefore, in western Europe between 1250 and 1500, for it was a time of increasing supply. Still there remained a constant outflow of precious metals from Europe to India and China via Byzantium and the Arab world, although the disequilibrium was lessening. Watson talks, somewhat mysteriously, of the "strong power of India and China to attract precious metals from other parts of the world."[85] The demand for bullion thus remained high. Between 1350 and 1450, the silver mines in Serbia and Bosnia began to develop[86] and became an important source until the Turkish invasion of the fifteenth century cut them off from western Europe. Similarly, beginning in 1460, there was a sudden rise of silver mining in central Europe, made possible by technological improvements which permitted the exploitation of what had been theretofore marginal mines. Perroy estimates that between 1460 and 1530 silver production quintupled in central Europe.[87] Nonetheless, the supply was not keeping pace with the demand, and the search for gold by the maritime route (thus, for Sudanic gold, circumventing North African intermediaries) was unquestionably one consideration for the early Portuguese navigators.[88] When, therefore, the discovery of the Americas was to give Europe a richer source of gold than the Sudan and especially a far richer source of silver than central Europe, the economic consequences would be great.[89]

The bullion was sought to provide a monetary base for circulation within Europe but even more to export it to the Orient. For what? Again, every schoolboy knows: for spices and jewels. For whom? For the wealthy, who used them as the symbols of their conspicuous consumption. The spices were made into aphrodisiacs, as though the aristocracy could not make love otherwise. At this epoch, the relationship of Europe and Asia might be summed up as the exchange of preciosities. The bullion flowed east to decorate the temples, palaces, and clothing of Asian aristocratic classes and the jewels and spices flowed west. The accidents of cultural history (perhaps nothing more than physical scarcity) determined these complementary preferences. Henri Pirenne, and later Paul Sweezy, give this demand for luxuries a place of honor in the expansion of European commerce.[90] I am skeptical, however, that the exchange of preciosities, however large it loomed in the conscious thinking of the

European upper classes, could have sustained so colossal an enterprise as the expansion of the Atlantic world, much less accounted for the creation of a European world-economy.

In the long run, staples account for more of men's economic thrusts than luxuries. What western Europe needed in the fourteenth and fifteenth centuries was food (more calories and a better distribution of food values) and fuel. Expansion into Mediterranean and Atlantic islands, then to North and West Africa and across the Atlantic, as well as expansion into eastern Europe, the Russian steppes and eventually Central Asia provided food and fuel. It expanded the territorial base of European consumption by constructing a political economy in which this resource base was unequally consumed, disproportionately by western Europe. This was not the only way. There was also technological innovation which increased the yield of agriculture, innovation which began in Flanders as early as the thirteenth century and spread to England, but only in the sixteenth century.[91] But such technological innovation was most likely to occur precisely where there was dense population and industrial growth, as in medieval Flanders, which were the very places where it became more profitable to turn the land use to commercial crops, cattle-breeding and horticulture, which consequently "required the import of corn [wheat] in large quantities. Only then could the complicated interlocking system of agriculture and industry function to its fullest advantage."[92] Hence, the process of agricultural innovation fed rather than foreclosed the necessity of expansion.

Wheat was a central focus of new production and new commerce in the fifteenth and sixteenth centuries. At first, Europe found in northern forests and Mediterranean plains its "internal Americas," in the perceptive phrase of Fernand Braudel.[93] But internal Americas were not enough. There was expansion at the edges, first of all to the islands. Vitorino Magalhães-Godinho has put forward as a working hypothesis that agriculture was the major motivation of Portuguese colonization of the Atlantic islands, a hypothesis pursued by Joël Serrão, who noted that the development of these islands was speedy and in terms of "the tetralogy of cereals, sugar, dyes, and wine . . . . [There was] always a tendency towards monoculture, one or the other of the four products always being preferred."[94] The new wheat that was grown began to flow throughout the European continent, from the Baltic area to the Low Countries beginning in the fourteenth century[95] and as far as Portugal by the fifteenth,[96] from the Mediterranean to England and the Low Countries in the fourteenth and fifteenth centuries.[97]

Foods may be placed in a hierarchy in terms of their cost per 1000 calories. M. K. Bennett finds this hierarchy fairly stable over time and space. Milled-grain products and starchy roots and tubers are at the bottom of his eight tiers, that is, they are the cheapest, the most basic of the staples.[98] But on grains alone a good diet is not built. One of the most important complements in the European diet is sugar, useful both as a calorie source and as a substitute for fats. Furthermore, it can also be used for alcoholic drinks (particularly rum). And later on, it would be used for chocolate, a usage which the Spaniards learned from the Aztecs, and which would become a highly appreciated drink, at least in Spain, by the seventeenth century.[99]

Sugar too was a principal motivation for island expansion. And, because of its mode of production, with sugar went slavery. This started in the eastern Mediterranean in the twelfth century and then moved westward.[100] The Atlantic expansion was simply its logical continuation. Indeed, E. E. Rich traces African slavery in Portugal back to 1000 A.D., the slaves being acquired by trade with Mohammedan raiders.[101] Sugar was a very lucrative and demanding product, pushing out wheat[102] but then exhausting the soil, so that it required ever new lands (not to speak of the manpower exhausted by its cultivation).

Fish and meat are higher on Bennett's list of categories. But they were wanted as sources of protein. Godinho cites the expansion of fishing areas as one of the key dynamics of early Portuguese exploration.[103] Meat no doubt was less important than grain, and was considerably and steadily reduced in importance in the period from 1400 to 1750[104]—a proof of a point to which we shall return, that European workers paid part of the costs of European economic development.[105] Nonetheless the desire for meat was one of the motivations of the spice trade, not the Asian spices for the aphrodisiacs of the rich but the West African grains of paradise *(Amomum melegueta),* used as a pepper substitute as well as for the spiced wine known as hippocras.[106] These spices were "barely capable of making thin gruel acceptable."[107]

If food needs dictated the geographical expansion of Europe, the food benefits turned out to be even greater than could have been anticipated. World ecology was altered and in a way which, because of the social organization of the emergent European world-economy, would primarily benefit Europe.[108] In addition to food, the other great basic need was wood—wood for fuel, and wood for shipbuilding (and housebuilding). The economic development of the Middle Ages, and one must assume its crude forestry techniques, had led to a slow but steady deforestation of western Europe, Italy, and Spain, as well as Mediterranean islands. Oak became especially scarce.[109] By the sixteenth century, the Baltic area had begun to export wood in large quantities to Holland, England, and the Iberian peninsula.

One other need of provisioning should be mentioned, the need of clothing. There was of course the luxury trade, the demand for silks, whose ancient history was linked with the demand for jewels and spices. The growing textile industry, the first major industry in Europe's industrial development, was more than a luxury trade, however, and required materials for processing: dye-stuffs for cotton and wool textiles and gum used to stiffen the silks in the finishing process.[110]

Bullion was desired as a preciosity, for consumption in Europe and even more for trade with Asia, but it was also a necessity for the expansion of the European economy. We must ask ourselves why. After all, money as a means of payment can be made of anything, provided men will honor it. And indeed today we almost exclusively use nonbullion items as means of payment. Furthermore, Europe was beginning to do so in the late Middle Ages with the development of "money of account," sometimes deceivingly called "imaginary money."

It would however take centuries before metallic money approached the status of symbolic money.[111] It is not yet totally there even today. As a result Europe was beset by constant mutations of value through debasement, so constant that Marc Bloch calls it "the universal thread of monetary history."[112] Yet no one seriously suggested then dispensing with bullion.

There were various reasons why not. Those who advised the governments were self-interested in the system.[113] We must not forget that in the late Middle Ages, it was still the case that mints were commercial propositions serving private interests.[114] But more fundamental than self-interest was the collective psychology of fear, based on the structural reality of a weakly-articulated economic system. The money of account might always collapse. It surely was in no man's hands, however wealthy, to control it either singly or in collusion with others. Indeed, who knew, the whole monetary economy might once again collapse? It had before. Bullion was a hedge. The money of payment might always be used as a commodity, provided only the two uses of money, as measurement of value and means of payment, did not get too far apart.[115] For this, the use of bullion was essential. And hence without it, Europe would have lacked the collective confidence to develop a capitalist system, wherein profit is based on various deferrals of realized value. This is *a fortiori* true given the system of a nonimperial world-economy which, for other reasons, was essential. Given this phenomenon of collective psychology, an integral element of the social structure of the time, bullion must be seen as an essential crop for a prospering world-economy.

The motives for exploration were to be found not only in the products Europe wished to obtain but in the job requirements of various groups in Europe. As H. V. Livermore reminds us, it was the Iberian chroniclers of the time and shortly thereafter who first noted that "the idea of carrying on the *Reconquista* in North Africa was suggested by the need to find useful employment for those who had lived on frontier raids for almost a quarter of a century."[116]

We must recall the key problem of the decline in seigniorial income in the fourteenth and fifteenth centuries. M. M. Postan has called the consequent behavior of the English nobility "gangsterism," the use of illegal violence to recover a lost standard of income. Similar phenomena occurred in Sweden, Denmark, and Germany. One of the forms of this violence was surely expansion.[117] The general principle that might be invoked is that if feudal nobles obtain less revenue from their land, they will actively seek to have more land from which to draw revenue, thus restoring real income to the level of social expectations. If then we ask why did Portugal expand overseas and not other European countries, one simple answer is that nobles in other countries were luckier. They had easier expansions to undertake, closer at home, using horses rather than ships. Portugal, because of its geography, had no choice.

No doubt overseas expansion has been traditionally linked with the interests of merchants, who stood to profit by the expanded trade, and with the monarchs who sought to ensure both glory and revenue for the throne. But it may well have been that the *initial* motivation for Iberian explorations came primarily from the interests of the nobility, particularly from the notorious "younger sons" who lacked land, and that it was only once the trade network began functioning that the more prudent merchants (often less entrepreneurial than nobles threatened by being déclassé) became enthusiastic.[118]

Was the cause of expansion overpopulation? This is one of those questions which confuse the issue. Braudel tells us that there was of course overpopulation in the western Mediterranean, and as proof he cites the repeated expulsion of Jews and later the Moriscos from various countries.[119] But E. E. Rich assures us that, as a motivation for expansion in the fifteenth and sixteenth centuries, "overspill for redundant population was negligible. . . . The probability (for it can be no more) is that the increasing population went to the wars or to the cities."[120] Yes, perhaps, but how were those who went to the cities (or to the wars) fed—and clothed and housed, etc.? There was physical room for the population, even the growing population, in Europe. Indeed that was part of the very problem that led to expansion. The physical room was one element in the strength of the peasantry vis-à-vis the nobility, and hence one factor in the decline of seigniorial revenues, in the crisis of feudalism. European societies could have responded in various ways. One way was to define themselves (at least implicitly) as overpopulated and therefore in need of a larger land base.[121] Actually, what the nobility (and the bourgeoisie) needed, and what they would get, was a more tractable labor force. The size of the population was not the issue; it was the social relations that governed the interaction between upper and lower classes.

Finally, can overseas expansion be explained by the "crusading spirit," the need to evangelize? Again, the question obscures the problem. No doubt Christianity took on a particularly militant form in the Iberian peninsula where the national struggles had for so long been defined in religious terms. No doubt this was an era of Christian *defeat* by Moslem Turks in south-eastern Europe (to the very gates of Vienna). And Atlantic expansion may well have reflected a psychological reaction to these events, "a phenomenon of compensation, a sort of flight forward," as Chaunu suggests.[122] No doubt the passions of Christianity explain many of the particular decisions taken by the Portuguese and Spaniards, perhaps some of the intensity of commitment or overcommitment. But it seems more plausible to see this religious enthusiasm as rationalization, one no doubt internalized by many of the actors, hence reinforcing and sustaining—and economically distorting. But history has seen passion turn to cynicism too regularly for one not to be suspicious of invoking such belief systems as primary factors in explaining the genesis and long-term persistence of large-scale social action.

All that we have said of motivation does not conclusively answer: why the Portuguese? We have talked of *Europe's* material needs, a *general* crisis in seigniorial revenues. To be sure, we here adduced a particular interest of Portugal in solving this problem by Atlantic exploration; but it is not enough to be convincing. We must therefore turn from the issue of motivations to that of capabilities. Why was Portugal, of all the polities of Europe, most able to conduct the initial thrust? One obvious answer is found on any map. Portugal is located on the Atlantic, right next to Africa. In terms of the colonization of Atlantic islands and the exploration of the western coast of Africa, it was obviously closest. Furthermore, the oceanic currents are such that it was easiest, especially given the technology of the time, to set forth from Portuguese ports (as well as those of southwest Spain).[123]

In addition, Portugal already had much experience with long-distance trade. Here, if Portugal cannot match the Venetians or the Genoese, recent research has demonstrated that their background was significant and probably the match of the cities of northern Europe.[124]

A third factor was the availability of capital. The Genoese, the great rivals of the Venetians, decided early on to invest in Iberian commercial enterprise and to encourage their efforts at overseas expansion.[125] By the end of the fifteenth century, the Genoese would prefer the Spaniards to the Portuguese, but that is largely because the latter could by then afford to divest themselves of Genoese sponsorship, tutelage, and cut in the profit. Verlinden calls Italy "the only really colonizing nation during the middle ages."[126] In the twelfth century when Genoese and Pisans first appear in Catalonia,[127] in the thirteenth century when they first reach Portugal,[128] this is part of the efforts of the Italians to draw the Iberian peoples into the international trade of the time. But once there, the Italians would proceed to play an initiating role in Iberian colonization efforts because, by having come so early, "they were able to conquer the key positions of the Iberian peninsula itself."[129] As of 1317, according to Virginia Rau, "the city and the port of Lisbon would be the great centre of Genoese trade. . . ."[130] To be sure, in the late fourteenth and early fifteenth cen-

turies, Portuguese merchants began to complain about the "undue intervention [of the Italians] in the *retail* trade of the realm, which threatened
the dominant position of national merchants in that branch of trade."[131]
The solution was simple, and to some extent classic. The Italians were
absorbed by marriage and became landed aristocrats both in Portugal and
on Madeira.

There was one other aspect of the commercial economy that contributed
to Portugal's venturesomeness, compared to say France or England. It
was ironically that it was least absorbed in the zone that would become
the European world-economy, but rather tied in a significant degree to
the Islamic Mediterranean zone. As a consequence, her economy was relatively more monetized, her population relatively more urbanized.[132]

It was not geography nor mercantile strength alone, however, that accounted for Portugal's edge. It was also the strength of its state machinery.
Portugal was in this regard very different from other west European states,
different that is during the fifteenth century. She knew peace when they
knew internal warfare.[133] The stability of the state was important not only
because it created the climate in which entrepreneurs could flourish and
because it encouraged nobility to find outlets for their energies other than
internal or inter-European warfare. The stability of the state was crucial
also because it itself was in many ways the chief entrepreneur.[134] When
the state was stable, it could devote its energies to profitable commercial
ventures. For Portugal, as we have seen, the logic of its geohistory dictated
Atlantic expansion as the most sensible commercial venture for the state.

Why Portugal? Because she alone of the European states maximized
will and possibility. Europe needed a larger land base to support the expansion of its economy, one which could compensate for the critical decline
in seigniorial revenues and which could cut short the nascent and potentially
very violent class war which the crisis of feudalism implied. Europe needed
many things: bullion, staples, proteins, means of preserving protein, foods,
wood, materials to process textiles. And it needed a more tractable labor
force.

But "Europe" must not be reified. There was no central agency which
acted in terms of these long-range objectives. The real decisions were taken
by groups of men acting in terms of their immediate interests. In the
case of Portugal, there seemed to be advantage in the "discovery business"
for many groups—for the state, for the nobility, for the commercial bourgeoisie (indigenous and foreign), even for the semiproletariat of the towns.

For the state, a *small* state, the advantage was obvious. Expansion was
the most likely route to the expansion of revenue and the accumulation
of glory. And the Portuguese state, almost alone among the states of Europe
of the time, was not distracted by internal conflict. It had achieved moderate
political stability at least a century earlier than Spain, France, and England.

It was precisely this stability which created the impulse for the nobility.

Faced with the same financial squeeze as European nobles elsewhere, they were deprived of the soporific and financial potential (if they won) of internecine warfare. Nor could they hope to recoup their financial position by internal colonization. Portugal lacked the land. So they were sympathetic to the concept of oceanic expansion and they offered their "younger sons" to provide the necessary leadership for the expeditions.

The interests of the bourgeoisie for once did not conflict with those of the nobility. Prepared for modern capitalism by a long apprenticeship in long-distance trading and by the experience of living in one of the most highly monetized areas of Europe (because of the economic involvement with the Islamic Mediterranean world), the bourgeoisie too sought to escape the confines of the small Portuguese market. To the extent that they lacked the capital, they found it readily available from the Genoese who, for reasons of their own having to do with their rivalry with Venice, were ready to finance the Portuguese. And the potential conflict of the indigenous and foreign bourgeoisie was muted by the willingness of the Genoese to assimilate into Portuguese culture over time.

Finally, exploration and the consequent trade currents provided job outlets for the urban semiproletariat many of whom had fled to the towns because of the increased exploitation consequent upon the seigniorial crisis. Once again, a potential for internal disorder was minimized by the external expansion.

And if these conjunctures of will and possibility were not enough, Portugal was blessed by the best possible geographic location for the enterprise, best possible both because of its jutting out into the Atlantic and toward the south but also because of the convergence of favorable oceanic currents. It does not seem surprising thus, in retrospect, that Portugal made the plunge.

There is one last issue we must confront before we can proceed with the main part of the book. Thus far we have been concerned with explaining what it was that led Europe to the brink of creating a capitalist world-economy. Since our emphasis will be on how capitalism is only feasible within the framework of a world-economy and not within that of a world-empire, we must explore briefly why this should be so. The apt comparison is of Europe and China, which had approximately the same total population from the thirteenth to sixteenth centuries.[135] As Pierre Chaunu elegantly states:

> That Christopher Columbus and Vasco da Gama . . . weren't Chinese, . . . is something which is worth . . . some moments of reflection. After all, at the end of the 15th century, insofar as the historical literature permits us to understand it, the Far-East as an entity comparable to the Mediterranean . . . is in no way inferior, superficially at least, to the far-west of the Eurasian continent.[136]

In no way inferior? This requires the traditional comparison of technologies, and here the scholars are divided. For Lynn White, Jr., Europe expanded in the sixteenth century because Europe outstripped the rest of the world in the technology of agriculture as early as the ninth century A.D.:

> Between the first half of the 6th century and the end of the 9th century Northern Europe created or received a series of inventions which quickly coalesced into an entirely novel system of agriculture. In terms of a peasant's labor, this was by far the most productive the world has seen. [White is referring to the heavy plough, the three-field rotation system, open fields for cattle, the modern harness and horseshoe].... As the various elements in this new system were perfected and diffused, more food became available, and population rose. . . . And the new productivity of each northern peasant enabled more of them to leave the land for the cities, industry and commerce.[137]

White also argues that northern Europe pulled ahead in military technology in the eighth century and in industrial production in the eleventh. If one asks why this should be so, White attributes this to the profound upheaval of the barbarian invasions, to which the West presumably had a Toynbeean creative reaction.[138]

Other scholars however disagree on the factual assessment. Take military technology. Carlo Cipolla argues:

> It is likely that Chinese guns were at least as good as Western guns, if not better, up to the beginning of the 15th century. However, in the course of the 15th century, European technology made noticeable progress. . . . European artillery was incomparably more powerful than any kind of cannon ever made in Asia, and it is not difficult to find, in [16th century] texts echoes of the mixture of terror and surprise that arose at the appearance of European ordnance.[139]

Similarly, Joseph Needham, who is still in the midst of his monumental account of the history of Chinese science and technology, dates the moment of European technological and industrial advantage over China only at 1450 A.D.[140] What accounts for the European surge forward? Not one thing, says Needham, but "an organic whole, a packet of change."

> The fact is that in the spontaneous autochthonous development of Chinese society no drastic change parallel to the Renaissance and the "scientific revolution" of the West occurred at all. I often like to sketch the Chinese evolution as represented by a relatively slowly rising curve, noticeably running at a *much higher level than Europe* between, say, the 2nd and 15th centuries A.D. But then after the scientific renaissance had begun in the West with the Galilean revolution, with what one might call the discovery of the basic technique of scientific discovery itself, then the curve of science and technology in Europe begins to rise in a violent, almost exponential manner, overtaking the level of the Asian societies. . . . This violent disturbance is now beginning to right itself.[141]

Some scholars insist on the crucial role of the development of the rudder in Europe in the fifteenth century.[142] But Needham argues the exis-

tence of a rudder in China since ± first century A.D., an invention
probably diffused from China to Europe in the twelfth century A.D.[143]

If Needham's account of Chinese technological competence and superiority over the West until the latter's sudden surge forward is correct, then
it is even more striking that Chinese and Portuguese overseas exploration
began virtually simultaneously, but that after a mere 28 years the Chinese
pulled back into a continental shell and ceased all further attempts. Not
for lack of success, either. The seven voyages of the eunuch-admiral Cheng
Ho between 1405 and 1433 were a great success. He traveled the breadth
of the Indian Ocean from Java to Ceylon to East Africa in his seven voyages,
bringing back tribute and exotica to the Chinese court, which was highly
appreciative. The voyages ceased when Cheng Ho died in 1434. Furthermore, when, in 1479, Wang Chin, also a eunuch, interested in launching
a military expedition to Annam, applied to the archives to consult Cheng
Ho's papers on Annam, he was refused access. The papers were suppressed,
as if to blot out the very memory of Cheng Ho.[144]

The origins of the expeditions and the causes of their cession are equally
unclear. It seems to be the case that they were constantly opposed by
the official bureaucracy of Confucian mandarins.[145] The question is why.
They seem, on the contrary, to have been supported by the Emperor.
How else could they have been launched? Further evidence is found by
T'ien-Tsê Chang in the fact that, at the beginning of the fifteenth century,
the function of the Bureau of Trading Junks, a state institution since the
eighth century A.D., was shifted from that of collecting customs (which
now became a provincial function) to that of transmitting tribute, which
was to be sure of considerable importance in the era of Cheng Ho. Chang
asks of the decentralization of customs collections, which presumably permitted lowered barriers in some regions: "[Did not the Emperor] have
an eye to encouraging foreign trade the importance of which to China
was only too evident?"[146]

Only too evident, yet soon encouragement ceased. Why? For William
Willetts, this has something to do with the *Weltanschauung* of the Chinese.
They lacked, it is argued, a sort of colonizing mission precisely because,
in their arrogance, they were already the whole of the world.[147] In addition,
Willetts sees two more immediate explanations for the cessation of
exploration: the "pathological hatred felt by Confucian officialdom toward
the eunuchs"[148] and the "drain on Treasury funds occasioned by the fit-
ting-out of overseas missions."[149] The latter seems a strange reason, since
the drain would presumably have been compensated by the income colonial
enterprises might have generated. At least so it seemed to European
treasuries of the same epoch.

There are other explanations which argue in terms of alternative foci
of political attention diverting the initial interest in Indian Ocean
exploration. For example G. F. Hudson argues that the removal northward

of the capital, from Nanking to Peking in 1421, which was the consequence of the growing menace of the Mongol nomad barbarians, may have diverted imperial attention.[150] Boxer sees the distraction as having been the menace from the east in the *Wako* or Japanese piratical marauding bands that preyed on the coast of China.[151] M. A. P. Meilink-Roelofsz suggests that the pull of withdrawal may have been abetted by the push of expulsion by Moslem traders in the Indian Ocean.[152]

Even if all these things are true, it does not seem enough. Why was there not the internal motivation that would have treated these external difficulties as setbacks rather than as definitive obstacles? Was it, as some writers have suggested, that China simply did not want to expand?[153] Pierre Chaunu gives us a clue when he suggests that one of the things that was lacking to China was a lack of "groups with convergent wills" to expand.[154] This is more telling, since we remember that in Portugal what is striking is the parallel interests in overseas exploration and expansion shown by *varied* social groups. Let us review therefore the ways in which the European and Chinese world differed.

There is first a significant difference in agronomy. We discussed the emphasis on meat consumption in Europe, an emphasis which increased with the "crisis" of the fourteenth century. And while meat consumption for the mass of the population would later decline from the sixteenth to the nineteenth century, this did not necessarily mean a decline in the use of land for cattle rather than for grain. The absolute size of the upper classes going up from the sixteenth century on in Europe because of the dramatic rise in population, the same land area might have been used for meat. This would not be inconsistent with a relative decline in meat consumption by the lower classes, who would obtain their grains by import from peripheral areas as well as by more intensive cultivation in western Europe as the result of technological advance.

China by contrast was seeking a stronger agricultural base by developing rice production in the southeastern parts of the country. The emphasis on cattle in Europe led to the extensive use of animal muscular power as an engine of production. Rice is far more fruitful in calories per acre but far more demanding of manpower.

Thus, Chaunu notes, European use of animal power means that "European man possessed in the 15th century a motor, more or less five times as powerful as that possessed by Chinese man, the next most favored in the world at the time of the discoveries."[155]

But even more important than this technological advance for our problem is the implication of this different relationship of man to the land. As Chaunu puts it:

> The European wastes space. Even at the demographic lowpoint of the beginning of the 15th century, Europe lacked space. . . . But if Europe lacks space, China lacks men. . . .

The Western "take-off" occurs seemingly at the same date (11th–13th centuries) as the Chinese 'take-off' of rice-production, but it is infinitely more revolutionary, to the extent that it condemns the great Mediterranean area to the conquest of the Earth. . . .

In every way, the Chinese failure of the 15th century results less from a relative paucity of means than of motivations. The principal motivation remains the need, often subconscious, for space.[156]

Here at least we have a plausible explanation of why China might not want to expand overseas. China had in fact been expanding, but internally, extending its rice production within its frontiers. Europe's "internal Americas" in the fifteenth century were quickly exhausted, given an agronomy that depended on more space. Neither men nor societies engage in difficult tasks gratuitously. Exploration and colonization are difficult tasks.

One last consideration might be that, for some reason, the fifteenth century marked for China what Van der Sprenkel calls a "counter-colonization," a shift of population out of the rice-producing areas.[157] While this may have relieved the "over-population," a term always relative to social definition, it may have weakened China's industrializing potential without the compensating advantages of a colonial empire. The "take-off" may have thus collapsed.

There is a second great difference between Europe and China. China is a vast empire, as is the Turco-Moslem world at this time. Europe is not. It is a nascent world-economy, composed of small empires, nation-states, and city-states. There are many ways in which this difference was important.

Let us start with the arguments that Weber makes about the implications of the two forms of disintegration of an empire: feudalization, as in western Europe, and prebendalization, as in China.[158] He argues that a newly centralized state is more likely to emerge from a feudal than from a prebendal system. Weber's case is as follows:

> The occidental seigneurie, like the oriental Indian, developed through the disin-
> tegration of the central authority of the patrimonial state power—the disintegration
> of the Carolingian Empire in the Occident, the disintegration of the Caliphs and
> the Maharadja or Great Moguls in India. In the Carolingian Empire, however,
> the new stratum developed on the basis of a rural subsistence economy. [Hence,
> it was presumably at a *lower* level of economic development than its oriental counter-
> parts.] Through oath-bound vassalage, patterned after the war following, the
> stratum of lords was joined to the king and interposed itself between the freemen
> and the king. Feudal relations were also to be found in India, but they were not
> decisive for the formation either of a nobility or landlordism.
>
> In India, as in the Orient generally, a characteristic seigniory developed rather
> out of tax farming [presumably because the central power was still *strong* enough to
> insist on taxes and the economy *developed* enough and with enough money-circula-
> tion to furnish the basic surplus for taxation; as compared with the presumably
> less developed Occident of the early Middle Ages] and the military and tax

prebends of a far more bureaucratic state. The oriental seigniory therefore remained in essence, a "prebend" and did not become a 'fief'; not feudalization, but prebendalization of the patrimonial state occurred. The comparable, though undeveloped, occidental parallel is not the medieval fief but the purchase of offices and prebends during the papal seicento or during the days of the French Noblesse de Robe. . . . [Also] a purely military factor is important for the explanation of the different development of East and West. In Europe the horseman was technically a paramount force of feudalism. In India, in spite of their numbers, horsemen were relatively less important and efficient than the foot soldiers who held a primary role in the armies from Alexander to the Moguls.[159]

The logic of Weber's argument runs something like this: A technical factor (the importance of horsemen) leads to the strength of the intermediate warriors vis-à-vis the center during the process of disintegration of an empire. Hence the new social form that emerges is feudalism rather than a prebendal state, in which the center is relatively stronger than in a feudal system. Also, the economy of a feudal system is less developed than that of a prebendal system. (But is this cause or consequence? Weber is not clear.) In the short run, feudalization is obviously better from the standpoint of landlords, since it gives them more power (and more income?). In the long run, however, a prebendal land-controlling class can better resist the growth of a truly centralized monarchy than a feudal landowning class, because the feudal value system can be used by the king, insofar as he can make himself the apex of a single hierarchical system of feudal relations (it took the Capetians several centuries to accomplish this), to build a system of loyalty to himself which, once constructed, can simply shed the personal element and become loyalty to a nation of which the king is the incarnation. Prebendalism, being a far more truly contractual system than feudalism, cannot be conned by such mystical ties. (In which case, incidentally and in passing, we could see the growing prebendalism of eighteenth century France as regressive, and the French Revolution as an attempt to recoup the regression.)

Joseph Levenson, in a book devoted to the question, why not China?, comes up with an answer not too dissimilar from that of Weber:

Ideally and logically, feudalism as a sociological "ideal type" is blankly opposed to capitalism. But historically and chronologically it gave it stimulation. The very absence of feudal restraints in China put a greater obstacle in the way of the expansion of capitalism (and capitalistic world expansion) than their presence in Europe. For the non-feudal bureaucratic society of China, a self-charging, persisting society, just insofar as it was ideally more congenial than feudal society to elementary capitalist forms, accommodated and blanketed the embryonic capitalism, and ruined its revolutionary potential. Is it any wonder, then, that even in Portugal, one of the least of the capitalist powers in the end, a social process quite the reverse of China's should release the force of expansion instead of contracting it? It was a process in Portugal and Western Europe generally, of a protocapitalist extrication from feudalism and erosion of feudalism. And this was a process quite different from

the persistence in China of a non-feudal, bureaucratic society, a depressant of
feudalism—and of capitalism, too.[160]

Here we have an argument we shall encounter frequently: Initial receptivity
of a system to new forms does not lead to gradual continuous change
but rather to the stifling of the change, whereas initial resistance often
leads later on to a breakthrough.

Feudalization brought with it the dismantling of the imperial structure,
whereas prebendalization maintained it. Power and income was distributed
in the one case to ever more autonomous landlords, rooted in an area,
linked to a given peasantry, and in the other to an empire-wide stratum,
deliberately not linked to the local area, semi-universalistic in recruitment
but hence dependent upon the favor of the center. To strengthen the
center of an empire was a colossal job, one only begun in the twentieth
century under the Chinese Communist Party. To create centralized units
in smaller areas was impossible as long as the center maintained any
coherence, which it did under the Ming and then the successor Manchu
dynasty; whereas creating centralized units in a feudal system was, as we
know, feasible if difficult. Weber outlined the reasons quite clearly:

> A general result of oriental patrimonialism with its pecuniary prebends was that,
> typically, only military conquest or religious revolutions could shatter the firm struc-
> ture of prebendary interests, thus creating new power distributions and in turn
> new economic conditions. Any attempt at internal innovation, however, was wrecked
> by the aforementioned obstacles. Modern Europe, as noted, is a great historical
> exception to this because, above all, pacification of a unified empire was lacking.
> We may recall that, in the Warring States, the very stratum of state prebendiaries
> who blocked administrative rationalization in the world empire were once its most
> powerful promoters. Then, the stimulus was gone. *Just as competition for markets
> compelled the rationalization of private enterprise, so competition for political power compelled
> the rationalization of state economy and economic policy* both in the Occident and in
> the China of the Warring States. In the private economy, cartellization weakens
> rational calculation which is the soul of capitalism; among states, power monopoly
> prostrates rational management in administration, finance, and economic policy.
> . . . In addition to the aforementioned difference in the Occident, there were
> strong and independent forces. With these princely power could ally itself in order
> to shatter traditional fetters; or, under very special conditions, these forces could
> use their own military power to throw off the bonds of patrimonial power.[161]

There is another factor to consider in envisaging the relationship of
the regional center or the forward point of a system with the periphery
in a world-economy versus an empire. An empire is responsible for administering and defending a huge land and population mass. This drains
attention, energy, and profits which could be invested in capital development. Take for example the issue of the Japanese *Wako* and their presumed
impact on Chinese expansion. In principle, the *Wako* were less of a problem
to China than the Turks to Europe. But when the Turks advanced in
the east, there was no European emperor to recall the Portuguese expedi-

tions. Portugal was not diverted from its overseas adventures to defend Vienna, because Portugal had no political obligation to do so, and there was no machinery by which it could be induced to do so, nor any Europe-wide social group in whose interests such diversion would be.

Nor would expansion have seemed as immediately beneficial to a European emperor as it did to a Portuguese king. We discussed how the Chinese emperor may have seen, and the Chinese bureaucracy did see, Cheng Ho's expeditions as a drain on the treasury, whereas the need for increasing the finances of the state was one of the very motives of European expansion. An empire cannot be conceived of as an entrepreneur as can a state in a world-economy. For an empire pretends to be the whole. It cannot enrich its economy by draining from other economies, since it is the only economy. (This was surely the Chinese ideology and was probably their belief.) One can of course increase the share of the Emperor in the distribution of the economy. But this means the state seeks not entrepreneurial profits but increased tribute. And the very form of tribute may become economically self-defeating, as soon as political strength of the center wanes, because under such circumstances, the payment of "tribute" may be a disguised form of trade disadvantageous to the empire.[162]

There is a link too between military technology and the presence of an imperial framework. Carlo Cipolla raises the question as to why the Chinese did not adopt the military technological advantages they saw the Portuguese had. He suggests the following explanation: "Fearing internal bandits no less than foreign enemies and internal uprisings no less than foreign invasion, the Imperial Court did its best to limit both the spread of the knowledge of gunnery and the proliferation of artisans versed in the art."[163] In Europe with its multiplicity of sovereignties, there was no hope of limiting the spread of arms. In China, apparently, it was still possible, and hence the centralized system backed off a technological advance essential in the long run for the maintenance of its power. Once again, the imperial form may have served as a structural constraint, this time on technological development.

One last puzzle remains. There emerged in China at this time an ideology of individualism, that of the Wang Yang-ming school, which William T. Du Bary sees as comparable to humanist doctrines in the West, and which he calls a "near-revolution in thought," that however failed "to develop fully."[164] Did not individualism as an ideology signal the strength of an emergent bourgeoisie, and sustain it against traditionalist forces?

Quite the contrary, it seems, according to Roland Mousnier. His analysis of the social conflicts of Ming China argues that individualism was the weapon of the Confucian mandarins, the bureaucratic class which was so "modern" in outlook, against the eunuchs, who were "entrepreneurial" and "feudal" at the same time, and who represented the "nationalist" thrust of Ming China.[165] Mousnier argues as follows:

To advance their career [in Ming China], a large part of the educated classes of middle-class origin voluntarily became castrates. Because of their education, they were able to play a preponderant role and the Empire was in reality ruled by these eunuchs.

Once having obtained high posts, they aided their families, created for themselves a clientele by distributing offices and fiefs, became veritable powers within the Empire itself. The large role played by eunuchs seems to be therefore a function of the rise of the bourgeoisie. The princes of the blood and the men of importance [*les grands*] sought to defend themselves by creating a clientele also made up of educated men of middle-class origin whom they pushed forward in the civil service. . . . [This latter group] were sometimes disciples of Wang Yang-ming and invoked his precepts to oppose the eunuchs who were established in power. The eunuchs were for Chu Hi, defender of tradition and authority [to which the eunuchs had, at this point, primary access]. These struggles were all the more serious since princes of the blood, men of importance, and eunuchs all had a power base as land-controllers [*maîtres du sol*]. The Mings had sought to reinforce their position by creating a sort of feudalism of relatives and supporters. . . . The victim of this state of affairs was the peasant. The expenses of the State grew ceaselessly.[166]

So, of course, did they in Europe, but in Europe, these expenses supported a nascent bourgeoisie and an aristocracy that sought ultimately, as we shall see, to save itself by becoming bourgeois, as the bourgeois were becoming aristocratic. In Ming China, the ideology that served the western bourgeoisie to achieve its ultimate conquest of power was directed against this very bourgeoisie who (having achieved some power too early?) were cast in the role of defenders of tradition and authority. There is much that remains to be elucidated here, but it casts doubt on the too simple correlation of the ideology of individualism and the rise of capitalism. It surely casts doubt on any causal statement that would make the emergence of such an ideology primary.

The argument on China comes down to the following. It is doubtful that there was any significant difference between Europe and China in the fifteenth century on certain base points: population, area, state of technology (both in agriculture and in naval engineering). To the extent that there were differences it would be hard to use them to account for the magnitude of the difference of development in the coming centuries. Furthermore the difference in value systems seems both grossly exaggerated and, to the extent it existed, once again not to account for the different consequences. For, as we tried to illustrate, idea systems are capable of being used in the service of contrary interests, capable of being associated with quite different structural thrusts. The tenants of the primacy of values, in their eagerness to refute materialist arguments, seem guilty themselves of assuming a far more literal correspondence of ideology and social structure (though they invert the causal order) than classical Marxism ever was.

The essential difference between China and Europe reflects once again the conjuncture of a secular trend with a more immediate economic cycle.

The long-term secular trend goes back to the ancient empires of Rome and China, the ways in which and the degree to which they disintegrated. While the Roman framework remained a thin memory whose medieval reality was mediated largely by a common church, the Chinese managed to retain an imperial political structure, albeit a weakened one. This was the difference between a feudal system and a world-empire based on a prebendal bureaucracy. China could maintain a more advanced economy in many ways than Europe as a result of this. And quite possibly the degree of exploitation of the peasantry over a thousand years was less.

To this given, we must add the more recent agronomic thrusts of each, of Europe toward cattle and wheat, and of China toward rice. The latter requiring less space but more men, the secular pinch hit the two systems in different ways. Europe needed to expand geographically more than did China. And to the extent that some groups in China might have found expansion rewarding, they were restrained by the fact that crucial decisions were centralized in an imperial framework that had to concern itself first and foremost with short-run maintenance of the political equilibrium of its world-system.

So China, if anything seemingly better placed prima facie to move forward to capitalism in terms of already having an extensive state bureaucracy, being further advanced in terms of the monetization of the economy and possibly of technology as well, was nonetheless less well placed after all. It was burdened by an imperial political structure. It was burdened by the "rationality" of its value system which denied the state the leverage for change (had it wished to use it) that European monarchs found in the mysticality of European feudal loyalties.

We are now ready to proceed with our argument. As of 1450, the stage was set in Europe but not elsewhere for the creation of a capitalist world-economy. This system was based on two key institutions, a "world"-wide division of labor and bureaucratic state machineries in certain areas. We shall treat each successively and globally. Then we shall look at the three zones of the world-economy each in turn: what we shall call the semiperiphery, the core, and the periphery. We treat them in this order largely for reasons of historical sequence which will become clear in the exposition of the argument. It will then be possible to review the totality of the argument at a more abstract level. We choose to do this at the end rather than at the beginning not only in the belief that the case will be more convincing once the empirical material has been presented but also in the conviction that the final formulation of theory should result from the encounter with empirical reality, provided that the encounter has been informed by a basic perspective that makes it possible to perceive this reality.

 Igritarum ergo opera vfi funt Hifpani initiò in fcrutandis venis metallicis: verùm poft-
quam illæ fuerunt exhauftæ, horum minifterio vti cœperunt ad molas trufatiles quæ fac-
chariferas cannas comminuunt, ad faccharum coquendum & cogendum: in quo minifterio etiamnum hodie magna ex parte occupantur.   Nam cùm ea Infula humida fit &
calida, minimo negotio facchariferæ cannæ fiue arundines fuccrefcunt; ex quibus contufis, deinde
in lebetes coniectis, & decoctis, poftremum ritè repurgatis & in faccharum concretis,
magnum quæftum facere folent. Vtuntur præterea iftorum Nigritarum
opera in pafcendis armentis, & reliquis rebus adminiftrandis
quæ neceffariæ funt ad fuos vfus.

2

THE NEW EUROPEAN DIVISION OF LABOR C. 1450-1640

Figure 3: "The Negroes having exhausted the metallic veins had to be given work making sugar." This engraving of a sugar mill in Hispaniola was made in 1595 as part of a series begun by Theodore de Bry, a Flemish engraver, known as *Collectiones Peregrinationum*, celebrating the "discoveries" of West and East India. Reproduced by permission of the Rare Book Division, The New York Public Library, Astor, Lenox, and Tilden Foundations.

It was in the sixteenth century that there came to be a European world-economy based upon the capitalist mode of production. The most curious aspect of this early period is that capitalists did not flaunt their colors before the world. The reigning ideology was not that of free enterprise, or even individualism or science or naturalism or nationalism. These would all take until the eighteenth or nineteenth century to mature as world views. To the extent that an ideology seemed to prevail, it was that of statism, the *raison d'état*. Why should capitalism, a phenomenon that knew no frontiers, have been sustained by the development of strong states? This is a question which has no single answer. But it is *not* a paradox; quite the contrary. The distinctive feature of a capitalist world-economy is that economic decisions are oriented primarily to the arena of the world-economy, while political decisions are oriented primarily to the smaller structures that have legal control, the states (nation-states, city-states, empires) within the world-economy.

This double orientation, this "distinction" if you will, of the economic and political is the source of the confusion and mystification concerning the appropriate identification for groups to make, the reasonable and reasoned manifestations of group interest. Since, however, economic and political decisions cannot be meaningfully dissociated or discussed separately, this poses acute analytical problems. We shall handle them by attempting to treat them consecutively, alluding to the linkages, and pleading with the reader to suspend judgment until he can see the whole of the evidence in synthesis. No doubt we shall, wittingly and otherwise, violate our own rule of consecutiveness many times, but this at least is our organizing principle of presentation. If it seems that we deal with the larger system as an expression of capitalism and the smaller systems as expressions of statism (or, to use the current fashionable terminology, of national development), we never deny the unity of the concrete historical development. The states do not develop and cannot be understood except within the context of the development of the world-system.

The same is true of both social classes and ethnic (national, religious) groupings. They too came into social existence within the framework of states and of the world-system, simultaneously and sometimes in contradictory fashions. They are a function of the social organization of the time. The modern class system began to take its shape in the sixteenth century.

When, however, was the sixteenth century? Not so easy a question, if we remember that historical centuries are not necessarily chronological ones. Here I shall do no more than accept the judgment of Fernand Braudel, both because of the solidity of scholarship on which it is based, and because it seems to fit in so well with the data as I read them. Braudel says:

> I am skeptical . . . of a sixteenth century about which one doesn't specify if it
> is one or several, about which one gives to understand that it is a unity. I see

51

"our" century as divided in two, as did Lucien Febvre and my remarkable teacher
Henri Hauser, a first century beginning about 1450 and ending about 1550, a
second one starting up at that point and lasting until 1620 or 1640.[1]

The starting points and ending points vary according to the national perspective from which one views the century. However, for the European
world-economy as a whole, we consider 1450–1640 the meaningful time
unit, during which was created a capitalist world-economy, one to be sure
that was, in Braudel's phrase, "vast but weak."[2]

And where was this European world-economy? That too is difficult to
answer. For the historical continents are not necessarily geographical ones.
The European world-economy included by the end of the sixteenth century
not only northwest Europe and the Christian Mediterranean (including
Iberia) but also Central Europe and the Baltic region. It also included
certain regions of the Americas: New Spain, the Antilles, Terraferma,
Peru, Chile, Brazil—or rather those parts of these regions which were
under effective administrative control of the Spanish or Portuguese. Atlantic islands and perhaps a few enclaves on the African coast might also
be included in it, but not the Indian Ocean areas; not the Far East, except
perhaps, for a time, part of the Philippines; not the Ottoman Empire; and
not Russia, or at most Russia was marginally included briefly. There are no
clear and easy lines to draw, but I think it most fruitful to think of the
sixteenth century European world as being constructed out of the linkage
of two formerly more separate systems, the Christian Mediterranean system[3]
centering on the Northern Italian cities and the Flanders–Hanseatic trade
network of north and northwest Europe, and the attachment to this new
complex on the one hand of East Elbia, Poland, and some other areas
of eastern Europe, and on the other hand of the Atlantic islands and
parts of the New World.

In sheer space, this was quite an expansion. Just taking into account
formal overseas colonies of European powers, Chaunu notes that in the
five years between 1535 and 1540, Spain achieved control over more than
half the population of the Western Hemisphere, and that in the period
between then and 1670–1680, the area under European control went
from about three million square kilometers to about seven (to be stabilized
at that point until the end of the eighteenth century.[4] However, expanding
the space did not mean expanding the population. Chaunu speaks of a
"demographic scissors movement" wherein demographic growth in
Europe "is largely nullified at the planetary level by the decline in immense
extra-European sectors."[5] Hence, the land/labor ratio of the European
world-economy was immensely increased, one fundamental factor in
Europe's ability to sustain continued economic growth in this critical early
period of the modern era. But expansion involved more than an improved
land/labor ratio. It made possible the large-scale accumulation of basic

capital which was used to finance the rationalization of agricultural production. One of the most obvious characteristics of this sixteenth century European world-economy was a secular inflation, the so-called price revolution.
The connection between this particular inflation and the process of capital
accumulation has been a central theme of modern historiography. We
propose to try to sift through the complexities of this debate in order
that, in the light of the patterns we observe, we shall be able to explain
the particular division of labor that the European world-economy arrived
at by the end of this epoch.

The cyclical pattern of European prices has a voluminous history behind
it, and although scholars differ about dates and even more about causes,
the reality of the phenomenon is agreed. If we put together two recent
summaries[6] of the prices of grains, we get the following picture:

    1160–1260—rapid rise
    1260–1310 (1330,1380)—consistently high
    1310 (1330,1380)–1480—gradual fall
    1480–1620 (1650)—high
    1620 (1650)–1734 (1755)—recession
    1734 (1755)–1817—rise

If we take the more narrow segment with which we are presently concerned,
the sixteenth century, which appears on the above listing as "high," there
were of course economic fluctuations within that. Pierre Chaunu has un-
covered the following cycle, based on his monumental study of the records
of the *Casa de Contratación* in Seville, the key entrepôt of trans-Atlantic
trade. By using measures of volume (both overall and for specific merchan-
dises) and of value, Chaunu sees four periods:

    1504–1550—steady rise
    1550–1562/3—relatively minor recession
    1562/3–1610—expansion
    1610–1650—recession[7]

Volume and value measures are not to be sure identical. "The index of
flow is likened, in an exaggerated fashion, to the fluctuation of prices.
The peculiar price curve is flatter than that of trade-flow."[8] Chaunu considers his breaking point of 1610 to fit in with those of Elsas for Germany
(1627) and of Posthumus for the Low Countries (1637) for, as we shall
see, the decline set in at different times for different parts of Europe.[9]

These time discrepancies remind us that the world-economy was only
in the process of emergence. Chaunu points out that in the fifteenth century,
the three European trade areas (the Christian Mediterranean, the
northwest, and eastern Europe) were at three different price levels, ranging
respectively from expensive to inexpensive. The creation of a world-

economy can be precisely measured by the "fantastic spread of prices at the beginning [of the century], and in the long run the closing of the gap."[10] Though the long run is longer than the sixteenth century, progress in closing the gap can be seen. If in 1500, the price gap between the Christian Mediterranean and eastern Europe was on the order of 6 to 1, by 1600 it was only 4 to 1,[11] and by 1750 it was only 2 to 1. Henryk Samsonowicz says that from the early sixteenth century on, Prussian wages and prices came "closer and closer" to those in western Europe "despite the diametrically opposed directions of their social and economic development."[12] Despite? Should it not read "because of"?

One major explanation of the price rise of the sixteenth century has been that of Earl J. Hamilton. He first argued it in relation to sixteenth century Andalusian prices, later applying it more generally to western Europe:

> Throughout the period under investigation there was a close connection between the imports of American gold and silver and Andalusian prices. . . . Commencing with the period 1503–1505 there was an upward trend in the arrivals of treasure until 1595, while from 1503 to 1597 there was a continuous rise in Andalusian prices. The greatest rises in prices coincide with the greatest increase in the imports of gold and silver. The correlation between imports of treasure and prices persists after 1600, when both are on the decline.[13]

By 1960, Hamilton's theory had been subject to much attack, both empirical and theoretical. Nonetheless, he reasserted it even more vigorously:

> [The increase of bullion supply since 1500] was probably much greater percentage-wise than the price upheaval. So rather than seek ancillary causes of the Price Revolution, . . . one needs to explain the failure of prices to keep pace with the increase of stock of precious metals. Increased utilization of gold and silver for plate, ornamentation, jewelry and other non-monetary purposes as they became relatively cheaper through rising commodity prices neutralized some of the new bullion. . . . Liquidation of the unfavourable trade balance [with the Orient] absorbed large amounts of specie. . . . Conversion of produce rents into money payments, a shift from wages partially in kind to monetary renumeration and a decline in barter also tended to counteract the augmentation of gold and silver supply.[14]

As many of his critics have observed, Hamilton is working with Fisher's quantity theory of money which states that $PQ = MV$ and implicitly assuming that V and Q are remaining constant (P is equal to prices; Q is equal to the quantity of goods and services; M is equal to the quantity of money; and V is equal to the velocity of circulation). They have doubted the assumption and called for empirical enquiry.

In a major attack on Hamilton, Ingrid Hammarström argued that Hamilton had gotten his sequence wrong, that it was an increase in economic activity which led to an increase in prices which then accounts for the mining activities which produced the increased supply of bullion. To which Hamilton retorts:

> Obviously the "rise in prices" usually resulting from "economic activity which some-how comes about" . . . would curb, not increase, mining of the precious metal through rising costs of production in conjunction with *fixed mint prices* of precious metals. Furthermore, the rise in prices would decrease, not increase, the coinage of existing bullion by relatively cheapening it for nonmonetary use[15]

But why need the mint prices have been fixed? This was a policy decision and it would scarcely have benefited those who would profit by the flow of bullion in expanding times (which included the Spanish crown) to discourage its production when such a large quantity was suddenly available at such low real cost (given the form of labor). As Hammarström points out, the fundamental question is what explains the use to which the bullion was put:

> Why did Western Europe need the American bullion, not to be hoarded as treasure nor to be used as ornaments in the holy places (the use to which it was put in Asia and among the natives of America), but to form an important addition to its body of circulative coin—that is, as a medium of payment?[16]

Y.S. Brenner argues that a look at English data confirms Hammarström. He finds that the changes in the commodity-price level resulted "less from an increase, or lack of increase, in the European stock of metal, than from the manner in which this stock was employed."[17] He notes that the price rise antedates the arrival of American treasure.[18] Brenner argues that one should perceive that *all* the factors in Fisher's equation were variable at this time:

> In conclusion, the rise in prices during the first half of the 16th century was due to a combination of an increased velocity and volume of currency in circulation with a relatively decreased supply of, and intensified tightness of demand for, agricultural products. . . .
> The velocity (V) of the circulation was increased by the development of industry and the expansion of commerce; the sharp rise in the speculation in land and in the legalized market for funds; and by the transition of greater sections of society from rural self-sufficiency into urbanized communities dependent on markets (money-supply) for their food.[19]

Hence, Brenner is arguing, it was the general rise of capitalist activity that accounts for the *use* made of the bullion.

The bullion theory of economic expansion presumes, if not fixed velocities (V) and quantities of goods (Q), at least upper limits. Is there any evidence in support of this? On quantities of goods and services, it does not seem very plausible. For one thing, it implies, as Jorge Nadal reminds us, the hypothesis of full employment:

> Only then when the volume of goods produced cannot be increased, will any increase
> in expenditure (equivalent to the product of the quantity of money and velocity
> [*la masa monetaria en circulación*]) be translated into a proportionate increase in
> prices.[20]

Let us then not assume that an increase of bullion led to a price increase
directly but only via its ability to increase employment. Miskimin argues,
for example, that the "early mercantilist obsession with bullion flows" made
sense in that:

> Inflows of precious metals would presumably have set men and resources to work,
> and at the same time, tended to increase the funds available for government finance
> and thus lower the cost of fighting wars.

In which case, we can analyze which countries *utilized* the bullion most
effectively

> in terms of each country's ability, whether institutionally or physically determined,
> to extend the full employment constraint in order to convert the influx of bullion
> into real economic growth.[21]

What about limits on velocity? W.C. Robinson in his debate with Michael
Postan takes up the question of whether bullion flows are capable of explaining the fourteenth century downturn. He argues that in an economy with
primitive credit mechanisms, "the V was something close to the actual
physical turnover per coin per time period. . . ." Hence the thirteenth
century expansion which was stimulated by dehoarding and increases in
velocity was subject to inherent constraints:

> Eventually . . . the money supply reached its upper limit, save for modest annual
> increases, and velocity could increase no more. At this point trade was constricted
> and downward pressure on prices was felt. The buoyant optimism and high profits
> of the earlier period was replaced by pessimism and retrenchment. Hoarding of
> money began as a hedge against falling prices. In short, the downturn could become
> self-reinforcing.[22]

Postan, in his reply, argues that Robinson is factually wrong about a limit
having been reached since dehoarding was continuing, that credit
mechanisms were more flexible than Robinson suggests, and that the psychological attitudes of businessmen were a minor economic variable at
that time.[23] But basically he does not challenge the concept of a limit.
Miskimin does, and it seems to me effectively:

> It is also true, in all probability, that, given the level of development of credit
> institutions, there was a physical upper limit to the velocity of circulation of any given
> quantity of bullion, once it was struck into a finite number of coins. Debasement,
> however, by reducing the size of the units in which bullion circulated, would have the
> effect of raising the physical and institutional upper limits imposed on the velocity of

circulation of bullion. Under the combined pressures arising from internal migration, urbanization, and specialization, it would appear possible, indeed likely, that when debasement raised the technical limits on velocity, the new freedom was used, and that the many European debasements of the sixteenth century acted through the velocity term to increase prices *more* than proportionally, relative to the level of debasement itself.[24]

Hence we come back to the fact that it is the overall system with its structured pressures for certain kinds of political decisions (for example, debasement) which is crucial to explain the expansion. It was not bullion alone, but bullion in the context of a capitalist world-economy, that was crucial. For Charles Verlinden, it was specifically the monopolistic forms of capitalism in this early stage that accounted largely for the continued inflation of prices:

> In the explanation of cyclical crises, we must reserve a large place for speculation. "Monopoly" did not regulate price movements. It "deregulated" them in the short run, except for certain luxury products (wine). It is responsible for the catastrophic aspect of these movements. Indirectly it affected doubtless the peculiar movement. After each rise, partially artificial, prices did not come down to the pre-crisis level. Monopoly thus contributed, to a certain degree, to the intensification and acceleration of the long-term rise.[25]

Was the influx of bullion then good or bad? We are not posing a sort of abstract moral question. Rather were the consequences of the bullion inflow salutory for the creation of the new capitalist world-economy? Hamilton certainly seems to say yes. Joseph Schumpeter however thinks quite the opposite:

> Increase in the supply of monetary metals does not, any more than autonomous increase in the quantity of any other kind of money, produce any economically determined effects. It is obvious that these will be entirely contingent upon the use to which the new quantities are applied. . . . The first thing to be observed [about the sixteenth century] is that, as far as Spain herself is concerned the new wealth . . . served to finance the Hapsburg policy. . . . The influx provided . . . an alternative to the debasement of currency to which it otherwise would have been necessary to resort much earlier, and thus became the' instrument of war inflation and the vehicle of the familiar process of impoverishment and social organization incident thereto. The spectacular rise of prices which ensued was a no less familiar link in that chain of events. . . .
> In all these respects, the evolution of capitalism was indeed influenced, but in the end retarded rather than quickened, by that expansion of the circulating medium. The cases of France and England were different but only because effects were more diluted. . . . All the durable achievements of English industry and commerce can be accounted for without reference to the plethora of precious metals. . . .[26]

This argument is predicated on Schumpeter's firm conviction that "the inflationary influence—which the writer thinks, as a matter of both history and theory has been exaggerated, but which he does not deny—was almost wholly destructive."[27] Without accepting Schumpeter's bias for the rationally controlled as against the possibly impulsive and sometimes unpredictable consequences of inflation, his tirade does force upon us an awareness that the global effects of inflation were far less significant than the *differential* effects.[28]

Let us look first at food supply. Why, given a general economic expansion, was there a *decreased* supply of agricultural products? Well, first, there was not in an absolute sense.[29] It is only if one considers the figures for countries like England or Spain separately rather than the European world-economy as an entity that there is a decreased supply relative to increased population. In those countries where industry expanded, it was necessary to turn over a larger proportion of the land to the needs of horses.[30] But the men were still there; only now they were fed increasingly by Baltic grain.[31] It was, however, more expensive grain because of apparent shortage, transport, and the profits of middlemen.

Was then the increased supply of bullion irrelevant? Not at all. For it performed important functions for the expanding European world-economy. It sustained the thrust of the expansion, protecting this still weak system against the assaults of nature. Michel Morineau points out that in medieval Europe, wheat prices rose and fell in direct response to harvests. What happened in the sixteenth century was not so much that bullion raised prices but that it prevented their fall.[32] Indeed Carlo Cipolla is skeptical there was any *real* price rise at all.[33] Rather he believes that what is truly significant about the financial structure of the sixteenth century was not the rise of prices but the decline of the interest rate. He argues that in the late Middle Ages, the interest rate was about 4–5%, rising to a high point between 1520 and 1570 of 5.5%, and then dropping suddenly between 1570 and 1620 to an average of 2%. Bullion cheapened money.[34]

What this seems to indicate is that the critical factor was the emergence of a capitalist system which, as Marx said, could be said to date "from the creation in the sixteenth century of a world-embracing commerce and a world-embracing market."[35] The key variable was the emergence of capitalism as the dominant mode of social organization of the economy. Probably we could say the *only* mode in the sense that, once established, other "modes of production" survived in function of how they fitted into a politico–social framework deriving from capitalism. Still it is salutary to remember that, at least at this point, "there was not one capitalism, but several European capitalisms, each with its zone and its circuits."[36] Indeed, it is precisely this existence of several capitalisms which gave importance to the increased stock of bullion, for the velocity of its circulation was precisely less in the beginning in northwest Europe than in Mediterranean Europe. As Braudel and Spooner conclude, "the quantity theory of money has meaning when taken with the velocity of circulation and in the context of the disparities of the European economy."[37]

This brings us to the second half of the Hamilton argument. There was not only a price rise, but a wage lag. Here too the controversy about its existence and its causes is great.[38] Hamilton argued that as prices rose, wages (and rents) failed to keep abreast of prices because of institutional rigidities—in England and France, but not in Spain.[39] This created a gap, a sort of windfall profit, which was the major source of capital accumulation in the sixteenth century:

> In England and France the vast discrepancy between prices and wages, born of the price revolution, deprived labourers of a large part of the incomes they had hitherto enjoyed, and diverted this wealth to the recipients of other distributive shares. . . . Rents, as well as wages, lagged behind prices; so landlords gained nothing from labour's loss. . . .
> The windfalls thus received, along with gains from the East India trade, furnished the means to build up capital equipment, and the stupendous profits obtainable supplied an incentive for the feverish pursuit of capitalistic enterprise.[40]

The assertion that rents lagged behind prices has been subject to particularly heavy attack, notably by Eric Kerridge for sixteenth century England,[41] as well as by others for other places and times.[42] By 1960, Hamilton had retreated on rents but asserted this did not affect the thrust of the argument:

> [O]ne may assume that at the beginning of the Price Revolution wage payments represented three-fifths of production costs. . . . I guess that in 1500 the rent of land may have been one-fifth of national income in England and France and that, with the tendency for rising agricultural prices to raise rents and the infrequent removals of rent contracts to lower them offsetting each other, rents rose as fast as prices during the Price Revolution. The remaining fifth of national income went to profits, including interest. With three-fifths of the costs lagging far behind soaring prices, . . . profits must have reached high levels in England and France in the sixteenth century, continued on a high plateau for four or five decades, and remained high, into the great, though declining, gap between prices and wages, until the close of the seventeenth century.[43]

There have been other criticisms of Hamilton's wage lag hypothesis.[44] One important line of argument was contributed by John Nef, who suggested that recorded money wages were not equivalent to total wages, since there existed wages in kind which might have expanded to fill the gap, and also rises in wheat prices might not have been matched by rises in all basic commodity prices:

> In the first place, the index numbers hitherto compiled exaggerate the increase in the cost of subsistence during the price revolution. Secondly, the increase in the cost of the workingman's diet was borne to some extent not by them but by their employers. Thirdly, many workmen held small plots of land from which they obtained some of their necessary supplies. It follows that they were probably able to spend a more than negligible portion of the money wages on commodities other than food.[45]

Phelps-Brown and Hopkins agree that the deterioration in wages might have been less bad than it seemed, since grain prices did rise faster than manufactured products. Hence processed food products, increasingly important, rose less in price than basic grains, and improvements in manufacture further reduced the cost of such processed items.[46] Nonetheless more recent (1968) evidence, based on better data than Hamilton originally used, including evidence offered by Phelps-Brown and Hopkins, tends to confirm the general hypothesis that there was a decline in real wages in sixteenth century western Europe.[47]

The fall of real wages is strikingly exemplified in Table 1 compiled from Slicher van Bath.[48] It is the real wages of an English carpenter, paid by the day, expressed in kilograms of wheat.

TABLE 1 *Real Wages of English Carpenter*[a]

1251–1300	81.0
1300–1350	94.6
1351–1400	121.8
1401–1450	155.1
1451–1450	143.5
1501–1500	122.4
1551–1600	83.0
1601–1650	48.3
1651–1700	74.1
1701–1750	94.6
1751–1800	79.6
1801–1850	94.6

[a]1721–45 = 100.

Three facts are to be derived from this table. The real wages of an English carpenter are not strikingly different in 1850 from 1251. The high point of wages (155.1) was immediately preceding the "long" sixteenth century, and the low point (48.3) was at its end. The drop during the sixteenth century was immense. This drop is all the more telling if we realize that English wages in the period 1601–1650 were by no means at the low end of the European urban wage scale.

This dramatic drop in wages was itself the consequence of three structural factors which were the remains of features of a precapitalist economy not yet eliminated in the sixteenth century. Pierluigi Ciocca spells out in careful detail how these structures operated to reduce real wages in an era of sharp inflation and why each of these structural factors was largely eliminated in later centuries. The three factors are: money illusions, as well as the discontinuity of wage demands; wage fixing by custom, contract, or statute; and delay in payment. By money illusions Ciocca means the inability to perceive accurately gradual inflationary rises except at discontinuous points in time. Even, however, if they were perceived, wages could only be negotiated at intervals. Furthermore in the sixteenth century, the state often intervened, where custom or contract broke down, to forbid wage raises. Finally, at that time, many workers were only paid once a year, which in an inflationary era meant depreciated money. By the twentieth century, money illusions would be counteracted by the organization of trade unions, the spread of education, the existence of price indexes, and the accumulation of experience with inflation. Furthermore, the political organization of workers makes it more difficult for the state to restrain wages. And of course frequency of wage payment is a long-acquired right. But in this early capitalist era, workers did not have the same ability to maneuver.[49]

What strengthens the plausibility of this analysis, that there was a wage lag because of structural factors in the sixteenth century European world-economy based on early forms of world capitalism, is not only the empirical data which confirms it but the two known empirical exceptions: the cities of central and northern Italy, and of Flanders. Carlo Cipolla notes that in the late sixteenth and early seventeenth centuries, "labour costs seem to have been too high in Italy in relation to the wage levels in competing countries." The reason, according to Cipolla, was that "the workers' organizations succeeded in imposing wage levels which were disproportionate to the productivity of labour itself."[50] Similarly, Charles Verlinden finds that in the Belgian cities, wages followed the price of wheat products closely in the sixteenth century.[51] Why these two exceptions? Precisely because they were the "old" centers of trade,[52] and thus the workers were *relatively* strong as a politico–economic force. For this reason, these workers could better resist the galloping profiteering. In addition, the "advance" of capitalist mores had broken the old structures partially. It was, however, precisely as a result of the "strength" of the workers and the progress of capitalist mores that both northern Italian and Flemish cities would decline as industrial centers in the sixteenth century to make way for the newcomers who would win out: those of Holland, England and, to a lesser extent, France.

The thought that some workers (precisely those in the most "advanced" sectors) could resist the deterioration of wages better than others leads us to consider what were the *differentials in losses*[53] occasioned by the long-term inflation. Pierre Vilar suggests a simple core-periphery alternation.[54] This is however too simple a dichotomy. For it is not only the workers of the periphery, those who engage as we shall see in labor in Hispanic America and eastern Europe in the sixteenth century, who lost. Simultaneously the wage workers in most of western Europe lost as well, if not perhaps as much—do we know?—as the workers in eastern Europe (the "loss" being immeasureable for the workers of Hispanic America, since they had not previously been in the same economic system at all). And J.H. Elliott argues that the position of the Spanish worker in this decline more nearly approximates that of the east European worker rather than that of England.[55]

Thus if on some sort of continuum the Polish worker earned least and the Spanish next and let us say the Venetian most, where exactly was the English worker, representing the semiperipheral areas that were in the process of becoming core areas. Phelps-Brown and Hopkins suggest that one way to think of what was happening in these countries is to see that "the contraction of the [English] wage earner's basketful was mostly due to the changed terms of trade between workshop and farm."[56] On the one hand, the changed terms of trade falls most heavily on the wage earner (either landless or whose income from land is subsidiary). Phelps-Brown and Hopkins estimate the number of such wage earners as already one-third of the occupied population in England in the first half of the sixteenth century. As they say, "the other side of the medal [of the impoverishment of the wage earner] is the enrichment of those who sold farm produce *or leased farms at rents they could raise.*"[57] This throws some doubt on Hamilton's argument that the wage lag was a direct source of capital accumulation, or at least alerts us to the fact that the landowner in western Europe was a key intermediary in the accumulation of capital.

Still, Hamilton's fundamental point, endorsed by John Maynard Keynes, is well-taken. The inflation created a redistribution of incomes—a complicated one, because of the multiple layers of the European world-economy. It was nonetheless a method of taxing the politically weakest sectors to provide a capital accumulation fund which could then be invested by someone.[58] The landlords in particular kept finding new ways to extract payments from the peasants.[59] The argument, remember, is not only that there was a profit windfall, but that inflation encouraged investment.[60]

This brings us to one further objection to the wage-lag hypothesis, that of John Nef. He claims the argument falls because of the case of France, where, although it had the same wage lag as England, it did not make significant progress in industry at this time.[61] Furthermore, Nef points out that he is not dealing merely with a France–England comparison, for in terms of the industrial development, France's situation was, he asserts, comparable to that of southern Germany and the Spanish Netherlands, whereas England was comparable to Holland, Scotland, Sweden, and Liège. That is, the former all slowed down by comparison with the "age of the Renaissance" and the latter all speeded up. Yet wood and labor were *cheaper,* not dearer, in France than in England. Possibly the problem is that they were *too* cheap.[62]

But this comparison of Nef only undoes the Hamilton thesis if England and France are compared *in vacuo.* If, however, they are taken within the context of the European world-economy, this comparison merely places the French real wage level somewhere between that of Spain and England. What we could then argue is that within the world-economy as a whole there was an acute reduction of the distribution of produced income to the workers. The rates varied according to the country. The optimal situation for a local investing class would be to have access to profits from low wages in the periphery and further profits from medium (as opposed to high) wages in their own area. A medium wage level was optimum since whereas on the one hand a too high wage level (Venice) cut too far into the profit margin, on the other a too *low* wage level (France, a fortiori Spain) cut into the size of the local market for new industries. England and Holland came closest to this optimum situation in the Europe-wide system. The fact that it was a world-economy, however, was the sine qua non for the likelihood that inflationary profits could be profitably invested in new industries.

Inflation thus was important both because it was a mechanism of forced savings and hence of capital accumulation and because it served to distribute these profits unevenly through the system, disproportionately into what we have been calling the emerging core of the world-economy away from its periphery and its semiperiphery of "old" developed areas.

The other side of this picture, as the reader may already have gleaned from the discussion on the impact of inflation, is that there emerged within the world-economy a division of labor not only between agricultural and industrial tasks but among agricultural tasks as well. And along with this specialization went differing forms of labor control and differing patterns of stratification which in turn had different political consequences for the "states," that is, the arenas of *political* action.

Thus far we have tried to explain why it was that Europe expanded (rather than, say, China), why within Europe Portugal took the lead, and why this expansion should have been accompanied by inflation. We have not really faced up to the question of why this expansion should be so significant. That is to say, why was the creation of this world-economy the harbinger of modern industrial development, whereas previous imperial creations in the history of the world, apparently based on a relatively productive agricultural sector and a relatively strong bureaucratic political machinery, failed to go in this direction? To say it was technology is only to push us to ask what kind of system was it that encouraged so much technological advance. (Remember Needham's metaphor of the sudden spurt of Western technology.) E. L. Jones and S. J. Woolf see the distinctive features of the sixteenth century precisely as the fact that, for the first time in history, an expansion of agricultural productivity opened the way to the expansion of real income:

> One of the less palatable lessons of history is that technically advanced and physic-
> ally productive agricultures do not inevitably bring about a sustained growth of *per
> capita* real income, much less promote industrialization. The civilizations of Antiquity,
> with their elaborate agricultures. provide a starting-point. None of them, in the

> Middle East, Rome, China, Meso-America . . . led on to an industrial economy. Technically their farming organization was superb. . . . Equally, the physical volume of grain they produced was impressive. Yet their social histories are appalling tales of production cycles without a lasting rise in real incomes for the mass of people in either the upswings or the downswings. . . .
>
> The common fact, notably of the empires with irrigated agricultures, was the immense power of a state apparatus based on a bureaucracy concerned with defense against external threat and the internal maintenance of its own position. Taking a grand view of history, it would be fair to conclude that *these bureaucracies aimed at, and succeeded in maintaining, vast peasant societies through long ages and at all population densities in a state of virtual homeostasis.*[63]

The authors argue that in such a system, increase in gross production results simply in "static expansion,"[64] that is, an increase in the supportable population with a maintenance of the same absolute distribution of goods in the same relative proportions to different classes of society.

What was it about the social structure of the sixteenth century world-economy that accounts for social transformation of a different kind, one that could scarcely be called homeostasis? No doubt the bureaucracies of the sixteenth century did not have motivations very different from those Jones and Woolf ascribe to earlier ones. If the result was different, it must be that the world-economy was organized differently from earlier empires, and in such a way that there existed social pressures of a different kind. Specifically, we might look at the kinds of tensions such a system generated among the ruling classes and consequently the kinds of opportunities it provided for the mass of the population.

We have already outlined what we consider to be the pressures on Europe to expand. Expansion involves its own imperatives. The ability to expand successfully is a function both of the ability to maintain relative social solidarity at home (in turn a function of the mechanisms of the distribution of reward) and the arrangements that can be made to use *cheap labor far away* (it being all the more important that it be cheap the further it is away, because of transport costs).

Expansion also involves unequal development and therefore differential rewards, and unequal development in a multilayered format of layers within layers, each one polarized in terms of a bimodal distribution of rewards. Thus, concretely, in the sixteenth century, there was the differential of the core of the European world-economy versus its peripheral areas, within the European core between states, within states between regions and strata, within regions between city and country, and ultimately within more local units.[65]

The solidarity of the system was based ultimately on this phenomenon of unequal development, since the multilayered complexity provided the possibility of multilayered identification and the constant realignment of political forces, which provided at one and the same time the underlying turbulence that permitted technological development and political transformations, and also the ideological confusion that contained the rebellions, whether they were rebellions of slowdown, of force, or of flight. Such a system of multiple layers of social status and social reward is roughly correlated with a complex system of distribution of productive tasks: crudely, those who breed manpower sustain those who grow food who sustain those who grow other raw materials who sustain those involved in industrial production (and of course, as industrialism progresses, this hierarchy of productive services gets more complex as this last category is ever further refined).

The world-economy at this time had various kinds of workers: There were slaves who worked on sugar plantations and in easy kinds of mining operations which involved skimming off the surface. There were "serfs" who worked on large domains where grain was cultivated and wood harvested. There were "tenant" farmers on various kinds of cash-crop operations (including grain), and wage laborers in some agricultural production. This accounted for 90–95% of the population in the European world-economy. There was a new class of "yeoman" farmers. In addition, there was a small layer of intermediate personnel—supervisors of laborers, independent artisans, a few skilled workmen—and a thin layer of ruling classes, occupied in overseeing large land operations, operating major institutions of the social order, and to some extent pursuing their own leisure. This last group included both the existing nobility and the patrician bourgeoisie (as well as, of course, the Christian clergy and the state bureaucracy).

A moment's thought will reveal that these occupational categories were not randomly distributed either geographically or ethnically within the burgeoning world-economy. After some false starts, the picture rapidly evolved of a slave class of African origins located in the Western Hemisphere, a "serf" class divided into two segments: a major one in eastern Europe and a smaller one of American Indians in the Western Hemisphere. The peasants of western and southern Europe were for the most part "tenants." The wage-workers were almost all west Europeans. The yeoman farmers were drawn largely even more narrowly, principally from northwest Europe. The intermediate classes were pan-European in origin (plus mestizos and mulattoes) and distributed geographically throughout the arena. The ruling classes were also pan-European, but I believe one can demonstrate disproportionately from western Europe.

Why different modes of organizing labor—slavery, "feudalism," wage labor, self-employment—at the same point in time within the world-economy? Because each mode of labor control is best suited for particular types of production. And why were these modes concentrated in different zones of the world-economy—slavery and "feudalism" in the periphery, wage labor and self-employment in the core, and as we shall see sharecropping in the semiperiphery? Because the modes of labor control greatly affect the political system (in particular the strength of the state apparatus) and the possibilities for an indigenous bourgeoisie to thrive. The world-economy was based precisely on the assumption that there were in fact these three zones and that they did in fact have different modes of labor control. Were this not so, it would not have been possible to assure the kind of flow of the surplus which enabled the capitalist system to come into existence.

Let us review the modes of labor control and see their relation to product and productivity. We can then see how this affects the rise of the capitalist elements. We begin with slavery. Slavery was not unknown in Europe in the Middle Ages[66] but it was unimportant by comparison with its role in the European world-economy from the sixteenth to the eighteenth century. One reason was Europe's previous military weakness. As Marc Bloch has put it:

> Experience has proved it: of all forms of breeding, that of human cattle is one
> of the hardest. If slavery is to pay when applied to large-scale enterprises, there
> must be plenty of cheap human flesh on the market. You can only get it by war
> or slave-raiding. So a society can hardly base much of its economy on domesticated
> human beings unless it has at hand feebler societies to defeat or to raid.[67]

Such an inferior mode of production is only profitable if the market is large so that the small *per capita* profit is compensated by the large quantity of production. This is why slavery could flourish in the Roman Empire and why it is preeminently a capitalist institution, geared to the early preindustrial stages of a capitalist world-economy.[68]

Slaves, however, are not useful in large-scale enterprises whenever skill is required. Slaves cannot be expected to do more than what they are forced to do. Once skill is involved, it is more economic to find alternative methods of labor control, since the low cost is otherwise matched by very low productivity. Products that can be truly called labor-intensive are those which, because they require little skill to "harvest,"require little investment in supervision. It was principally sugar, and later cotton, that lent themselves to the assembling of unskilled laborers under brutal overseers.[69]

Sugar cultivation began on the Mediterranean islands, later moved to the Atlantic islands, then crossed the Atlantic to Brazil and the West Indies. Slavery followed the sugar.[70] As it moved, the ethnic composition of the slave class was transformed.[71] But why Africans as the new slaves? Because of exhaustion of the supply of laborers indigenous to the region of the plantations, because Europe needed a source of labor from a reasonably well-populated region that was accessible and relatively near the region of usage. But it had to be from a region that was outside its world-economy so that Europe could feel unconcerned about the economic consequences for the breeding region of wide-scale removal of manpower as slaves. Western Africa filled the bill best.[72]

The exhaustion of alternative supplies of labor is clear. The monocultures imposed on the Mediterranean and Atlantic islands ravaged them, pedologically and in terms of human population. Their soils were despoiled, their populations died out (for example, the Guanches of the Canary Islands), or emigrated, to escape the pressure.[73] Indian populations on Caribbean islands disappeared entirely. New Spain (Mexico) had a dramatic fall in population from approximately 11 million in 1519 to about 1.5 million in circa 1650.[74] Brazil and Peru seem to have had an equally dramatic decline.[75] The two immediate explanations of this demographic decline seem to be disease and damage to Indian cultivation caused by the domestic animals that the Europeans bred.[76] But sheer exhaustion of manpower, especially in the mines, must also have been significant. Consequently, at a relatively early point, the Spaniards and Portugese ceased trying to recruit Indians as slave labor in the Western Hemisphere and began to rely exclusively on imported Africans for plantation slaves. Presumably, the cost of transport still did not bring the cost to a higher point than the potential cost of preventing runaways by the remaining indigenous population. Besides the latter were rapidly dying off.

And yet slavery was not used everywhere. Not in eastern Europe which saw a "second serfdom." Not in western Europe which saw new forms of "rent" and the rise of wage labor. Not even in many sectors of the economy of Hispanic America where, instead of slave plantations, the Spaniards used a system known as *encomienda*. Why not slavery in all production in Hispanic America? Probably because the suppiy of African slaves, however large, was not unlimited. And because the economies of supervising an *indigenous* slave population (the amount of world-available nonindigenous slave labor making this the only reasonable other possibility), given the high likelihood of revolts, made it not worthwhile. This was especially the case since grain production, cattle-raising, and mining required a higher level of skill among the basic production workers than did sugar production. These workers therefore had to be compensated for by a slightly less onerous form of labor control.[77]

Since both the "second serfdom" in eastern Europe and the *encomienda* system in Hispanic America—synchronous be it noted—have been termed by many persons as "feudalism," much useless controversy has been generated as to whether and in what way these systems are or are not comparable to the "classic" feudalism of medieval Europe. The debate essentially revolves around whether the defining characteristic of feudalism is the hierarchical relationship of ownership (the awarding of a fief to a vassal, an exchange of protection for rents and services), the political jurisdiction of a seignior over his peasantry, or the existence of large domains of land upon which a peasant is somehow "constrained" to work at least part of his year in return for some kind of minimal payment (whether in the form of cash, kind, or the right to use the land for his own production for use or sale). Obviously, all sorts of combinations are possible.[78] Furthermore, not only the form of the subordinate's obligation to the superordinate may vary, but the degree of subordination may vary also, and as Dobb notes, "a change in the former is by no means always yoked with a change in the latter. . . ."[79]

From the point of view we are developing here, there is a fundamental difference between the feudalism of medieval Europe and the "feudalisms" of sixteenth century eastern Europe and Hispanic America. In the former, the landowner (seignior) was producing primarily for a local economy and derived his power from the weakness of the central authority. The economic limits of his exploitative pressure was determined by his need to furnish his household with the limited degree of luxury determined as socially optimal and by the costs of warfare (which varied over time). In the latter, the landowner (seignior) was producing for a capitalist world-economy. The economic limits of his exploitative pressure were determined by the demand–supply curve of a market. He was maintained in power by the strength rather than the weakness of the central authority, at least its strength vis-à-vis the farm laborer. To avoid any confusion, we shall call this form of "serfdom" by the name "coerced cash-crop labor," although the term is imperfect and awkward.

"Coerced cash-crop labor" is a system of agricultural labor control wherein the peasants are required by some legal process enforced by the state to labor at least part of the time on a large domain producing some product for sale on the world market. Normally, the domain was the "possession" of an individual, usually by designation of the state, but not necessarily a heritable property. The state could be itself the direct owner of such a domain, but in this case there was a tendency to transform the mechanism of labor control.[80] Using such a definition, this form of labor control became the dominant one in agricultural production in the peripheral areas of the sixteenth century European world-economy.

Henri H. Stahl makes very clear the way in which East Elbia's (and more generally eastern Europe's) "second serfdom" is "capitalist" in origin.[81] A number of other authors recognize that we are calling "coerced cash-crop labor" is a form of labor control in a capitalist and not a feudal economy. Sergio Bagú, speaking of Hispanic America, calls it "colonial capitalism."[82] Luigi Bulferetti, speaking of seventeenth century Lombardy, calls it "feudal capitalism."[83] Luis Vitale, speaking of the Spanish *latifundias,* insists they are "very capitalist enterprises."[84] Eric Wolf sees no inconsistency between a lord maintaining "patrimonial controls within the boundaries of his domain" and running his domain "as a capitalist enterprise."[85]

The pattern already began with the Venetians in Crete and elsewhere in the fourteenth century[86] and became widespread by the sixteenth century throughout the periphery and semiperiphery of the European world-economy. The crucial aspects from our perspective are twofold. One is to see that "coerced cash-crop labor" is *not,* as Pietro Vaccari puts it, "of a form that may be defined as a true reconstitution of the former feudal servitude;"[87] it is a *new* form of social organization. And second, it is *not* the case that two forms of social organization, capitalist and feudal, existed side by side, or could ever so exist. The world-economy has one form or the other. Once it is capitalist, relationships that bear certain formal resemblances to feudal relationships are necessarily redefined in terms of the governing principles of a capitalist system.[88] This was true both of the *encomienda* in Hispanic America and the so-called "second feudalism" in eastern Europe.

The *encomienda* in Hispanic America was a direct creation of the Crown. Its ideological justification was Christianization. Its chief function was to supply a labor force for the mines and cattle ranches, as well as to raise silk and to supply agricultural products for the *encomenderos* and the workers in towns and mines.[89] The *encomienda* was originally a feudal privilege, the right to obtain labor services from the Indians.[90]

When the exaggeration of early *encomenderos* threatened the supply of labor—for example, the Indians on the West Indian islands died off—a royal cedula of 1549 changed the obligations of *encomienda* from labor to tribute, thus shifting from a system akin to slavery to one we may call coerced cash-crop labor. As Silvio Zavala points out, the new version of *encomienda* was "free," but the threat of coercion lay in the background.[91] When "freedom" resulted in a significant drop in the labor supply, a further legal shift occurred, the institution of forced wage labor, called the *cuatequil* in New Spain and the *mita* in Peru.[92]

Consequently, although it is true that the *encomienda* in Hispanic America (as well as the *donatária* in Brazil) might have originated as feudal grants, they were soon transformed into capitalist enterprises by legal reforms.[93] This seems to be confirmed by the fact that it was precisely to avoid the centrifugal character of a feudal system that the *cuatequil* and *mita* were installed.[94]

Not only did the landowner have the Spanish Crown behind him in creating his capital, in coercing the peasant labor. He normally had an arrangement with the traditional chief of the Indian community in which the latter added his authority to that of the colonial rulers to the process of coercion.[95] The strength of chieftaincy was of course a function of pre-colonial patterns to a large extent.[96] The interest of the chief or *cacique* becomes quite clear when we realize how laborers were in fact paid. Alvaro Jara describes the system established in 1559 as it worked in Chile. There the Indians working on gold washing received a sixth of its value. This payment, called the *sesmo,* was however made not to individual Indians but to the collectivity of which they were members.[97] One can guess at the kinds of unequal division that were consequent upon this kind of global payment system.

The creation of coerced cash-crop labor in eastern Europe was more gradual than in Hispanic America, where it had been instituted as a result of conquest. In the twelfth and thirteenth centuries, much of eastern Europe (that is, East Elbia, Poland, Bohemia, Silesia, Hungary, Lithuania) went through the same process of growing concessions to the peasantry and growing transformation of feudal labor obligations into money obligations as did western Europe, and also Russia.[98] The process was gone through everywhere for the same reasons: the impact of prosperity and economic expansion on the bargaining relationship of serf and lord.[99] The recession of the fourteenth and fifteenth centuries however led to opposite consequences in western and eastern Europe. In the west, as we have seen, it led to a crisis of the feudal system. In the east, it led to a "manorial reaction"[100] which culminated in the sixteenth century with the "second serfdom" and a *new* landlord *class.*[101]

The reason why these opposite reactions to the same phenomenon (economic recession) occurred was because, for the reasons we previously explicated, the two areas became complementary parts of a more complex single system, the European world-economy, in which eastern Europe played the role of raw-materials producer for the industrializing west, thus coming to have, in Malowist's phrase, "an economy which, at bottom, [was] close to the classic colonial pattern."[102] A look at the nature of Baltic trade is sufficient to verify this. From the fifteenth century on, the products flowing from east to west were primarily bulk goods (cereals, timber, and later on, wool), although the older exports of fur and wax continued. And from west to east flowed textiles (both of luxury and of middling quality), salt, wines, silks. By the end of the fifteenth century, Holland was dependent on Baltic grain, Dutch and English shipping unthinkable without east European timber, hemp, pitch, and grease. Conversely, wheat had become the east's most important export, reaching even the Iberian peninsula and Italy.[103]

To be sure, this kind of colonial pattern of trade existed previously in terms of trade relations in Europe. There was the relationship of Venice and her colonies plus her sphere of influence.[104] There was Catalonia as a trade center in the late Middle Ages.[105] In the thirteenth and fourteenth centuries Portugal was a primary producer for Flanders,[106] as England was for the Hanse.[107] The production of primary products to exchange for the manufactured products of more advanced areas was always, as Braudel says of grain, a "marginal phenomenon subject to frequent [geographical] revisions." And, as he says, "each time, the bait [was] cash."[108] What was different in the sixteenth century was the existence of a market for primary products that encompassed a large world-economy. Slicher von Bath dates the creation of the international cereals market, centering in the Low Countries, only in 1544.[109]

If we take seriously Braudel's notion of "frequent revisions," then we must ask how an area gets defined as periphery rather than as core. In the Middle Ages, even the late Middle Ages, it was not at all clear that eastern Europe was destined to be the periphery of a European world-economy. A number of writers have emphasized the comparability of developments, east and west. Reginald R. Betts, for example, says of the fourteenth century: "Curiously [sic!], payments in specie were preferred not only by French and English large landowners . . . but by Czech, Polish and Hungarian landowners as well. . . ."[110] Similarly, Zs. S. Pach argues that as late as the fifteenth century, "the trend of rural development [in Hungary] was fundamentally concordant with that of the west European countries. . . ."[111]

Why then the divergence? One can answer in terms of the factors—geographical and social—which accounted for the spurt of western Europe. To some extent, we have already done this. One can also answer in part in terms of specific characteristics of eastern Europe. For one thing, the weakness of the towns was an important factor.[112] This was a small difference in the thirteenth century which became a big one in the sixteenth, since, as a result of the complementary divergence, western towns grew stronger and eastern ones relatively weaker. Or one can emphasize the fact that there already was a relatively more extensive cultivation of land in western Europe by the end of the thirteenth century, whereas there remained much more vacant space in eastern Europe.[113] A process of coerced cash-crop labor was relatively easier to institute on "new" lands.

But then we have to ask why even the slight differences between west and east? There is perhaps a single geopolitical explanation: the Turkish and Mongol–Tartar invasions of the late Middle Ages, which destroyed much, caused emigrations and various declines, and above all weakened the relative authority of the kings and great princes.[114]

What is at operation here is the general principle that in the course of social interaction small initial differences are reinforced, stabilized, and defined as "traditional." The "traditional" was then, and always is, an aspect of and creation of the present, never of the past. Speaking of the modern world, André Gunder Frank argues: "Economic development and under-development are the opposite face of the same coin. Both are the necessary result and contemporary manifestations of internal contradictions in the world capitalist system."[115] But the process is far more general than Frank indicates. As Owen Lattimore puts it, "Civilization gave birth to barbarism."[116] Speaking of the relationship between the sedentary and the nomadic at the frontiers of the world, Lattimore argues that the way to conceive of their origin and their relationship is to observe

> the formation of two diverging types out of what had originally been a unified society. These we may call, for convenience, "progressive" (agriculture becoming primary, hunting and gathering becoming secondary) and "backward" (hunting and gathering remaining primary, agriculture becoming secondary, in some cases not advancing beyond a desultory stage.[117]

Thus if, at a given moment in time, because of a series of factors at a previous time, one region has a *slight* edge over another in terms of one key factor, *and* there is a *conjuncture* of events which make this *slight* edge of central importance in terms of determining social action, then the slight edge is converted into a large disparity and the advantage holds even after the conjuncture has passed.[118] This was the case in the fifteenth and sixteenth centuries in Europe. Given the great expansion of the geographic and demographic scope of the world of commerce and industry, some areas of Europe could amass the profits of this expansion all the more if they could specialize in the activities essential to reaping this profit. They thus had to spend less of their time, manpower, land, and other natural resources on sustaining themselves in basic necessities. Either eastern Europe would become the "breadbasket" of western Europe or vice versa. Either solution would have served the "needs of the situation" in the conjuncture. The *slight* edge determined which of the two alternatives would prevail. At which point, the *slight* edge of the fifteenth century became the great disparity of the seventeenth and the monumental difference of the nineteenth.[119]

The crucial considerations in the form of labor control adopted in eastern Europe were the opportunity of large profit if production were increased (because of the existence of a world market) plus the combination of a relative shortage of labor and a large amount of unused land.[120] In the sixteenth century eastern Europe and in parts of the economy of Hispanic America, coerced cash-crop labor was thus desirable (profitable), necessary (in terms of the landowner's self-interest), and possible (in terms of the kind of work required). Slavery was impracticable because of the relative shortage of labor. *Indigenous* labor is *always* in short supply as slaves, as it is too difficult to control, and long-distance importation of slaves was not profitable for products that required as much supervision as wheat. After all, the cost of slaves was not negligible.

While presumably the peasant prefers a system of coerced cash-crop labor to slavery because of the minimal dignity and privileges involved in formal freedom, it is not necessarily the case that the material conditions of the coerced cash-crop laborer were better than those of the slave. Indeed Fernando Guillén Martinez argues that in Hispanic America, the Indian on the *encomienda* was more poorly treated than the slave, largely because of the insecure social situation of the *encomendero*.[121] Alvaro Jara argues similarly that the standard of living of the Indians on the *encomienda*, in this case in Chile, was "at a minimum level, using this concept in its strictest sense."[122]

Thus, in the geo–economically peripheral areas of the emerging world-economy, there were two primary activities: mines, principally for bullion; and agriculture, principally for certain foods. In the sixteenth century, Hispanic America provided primarily the former[123] while eastern Europe provided primarily the latter. In both cases, the technology was labor-intensive and the social system labor-exploitative. The surplus went overall disproportionately to supply the needs of the population of the core areas. The immediate profits of the enterprise were shared, as we shall see, between groups in the core areas, international trading groups, and local supervisory personnel (which include, for example, both aristocrats in Poland, and civil servants and *encomenderos* in Hispanic America). The mass of the population was engaged in coerced labor, a system defined, circumscribed, and enforced by the state and its judicial apparatus. Slaves were used to the extent that it was profitable to do so, and where such juridical extremism was too costly, the alternative of formally free but legally-coerced agricultural labor was employed on the cash-crop domains.[124]

In the core of the world-economy, in western Europe (including the Mediterranean Christian world), the situation was different in a number of respects. The population density was basically much higher (even in periods of demographic decline such as the fourteenth and fifteenth centuries).[125] The agriculture was hence more intensive.[126] In addition, part of the land was shifted from arable to pastoral use. The result was less coercion. In part, more skilled labor can insist on less juridical coercion. Or rather, the coercion has to be more indirect, via market mechanisms. In part, it was that in cattle breeding, it was always a temptation, especially in winter, to shift food from cattle to men. A manorial system was not able to deal with this problem effectively.[127] But the sixteenth century was a time of increased demand for meat, the demand for meat being elastic and expanding with a rising standard of living.[128] Also given the expansion of population, there was more demand for grain as well. The consequences were simple. Cattle-raising, which was profitable, required a different social organization of work. When it did not develop, for whatever reasons, pastoralism actually decreased.[129] Hence, Europe-wide, it became a matter of increased division of labor.

In the core area, towns flourished, industries were born, the merchants became a significant economic and political force. Agriculture to be sure remained throughout the sixteenth century the activity of the majority of the population. (Indeed this was true until the nineteenth century for northwest Europe and until the twentieth for southern Europe.) Nonetheless, the inclusion of eastern Europe and Hispanic America into a European world-economy in the sixteenth century not only provided capital (through booty and high-profit margins) but also liberated some labor in the core areas for specialization in other tasks. The occupational range of tasks in the core areas was a very complex one. It included a large remnant parallel to those in the periphery (for example, grain production). But the trend in the core was *toward* variety and specialization, while the trend in the periphery was toward monoculture.

The expansion of the sixteenth century was not only a geographical expansion. It was an economic expansion—a period of demographic growth, increased agricultural productivity, and the "first industrial revolution." It marked the establishment of *regular* trade between Europe and the rest of the inhabited world.[130] By the end of the century, the economy simply looked different and better.[131]

Thus far we have described the emergent forms of production and of labor control in the periphery and treated it in explicit and implicit contrast to the core areas. In fact, the core area structure is more complicated than we have indicated to this point. However before we treat this complexity we should look at the agricultural production of that third structural zone, the semiperiphery. We have not yet explicated the function of the semiperiphery for the workings of the world-system. Suffice it to say at this point that on a number of economic criteria (but not all), the semiperiphery represents a midway point on a continuum running from the core to the periphery. This is, in particular, true of the complexity of economic institutions, the degree of economic reward (both in terms of average level and range), and most of all in the form of labor control.

The periphery (eastern Europe and Hispanic America) used forced labor (slavery and coerced cash-crop labor). The core, as we shall see, increasingly used free labor. The semiperiphery (former core areas turning in the direction of peripheral structures) developed an inbetween form, share-cropping, as a widespread alternative. To be sure, sharecropping was known in other areas. But it took primacy of place at this time only in the semiperiphery. The *mezzadria* in Italy and the *fâcherie* in Provence were already known from the thirteenth century on; *métayage* elsewhere in southern France from the fourteenth. And as economic difficulties of lords of the manor increased in the fourteenth and fifteenth centuries the domains were increasingly leased in this form not as an entity but in smaller units, capable of sustaining a family rather than a whole village. Duby notes that by the mid-fifteenth century "the large-scale cereal-producing enterprises that were still able to exist in western Europe disappeared. . . ." He calls this "one of the fundamental transformations of country life. . . ."[132]

Why did the transformation, however, take this particular form? That is, why, if a transformation was threatened, did not the seignior turn to the state to force the peasants to stay on the land, as in eastern Europe? And, on the other hand, why, if there were concessions, did it take the form of sharecropping rather than the transfer of land to small farmers who either bought the land outright or paid a fixed rent, the principal (not, of course, the only) solution in northwest Europe?

Dobb, in comparing western and eastern Europe in terms of the seigniorial reaction to the phenomena of desertion and depopulation, and considering western Europe the arena of "concession" and eastern

Europe that of "renewed coercion," attributes the different reactions to the "strength of peasant resistance."[133] Ian Blanchard on the other hand agrees that the degree of peasant unrest is a factor but in a less direct way. The crucial factor was labor availability. He argues that up to the 1520s there was a labor shortage in England and that legislators did indeed seek to coerce laborers to remain on the land while landowners reluctantly enclosed *faute de mieux*.[134] Thus coercion, Blanchard argues, was used in England as well, as long as there was depopulation. It was only when population was growing that the peasants erupted, demanding in effect land.

Whatever the case, the amount of peasant resistance explains little since we would want to know why peasants resisted more in England than in Poland—does Dobb really believe this?[135]—why lords were stronger or weaker, why kings strengthened seigniorial authority or weakened it. We are most likely to discover the reasons in the fact of the complementary divergence within a single world-economy, for which we suggested two explanations: the comparative strength of the towns at the beginning point of the divergence, and the degree of vacancy of land.

"Vacancy" of land can be restated in terms of a land/labor ratio. If there is plenty of land, one can make do with relatively inefficient means of production. One can engage in extensive agriculture. One can use slaves or coerced cash-crop laborers. Intensive agriculture requires free laborers. But why then sharecropping? Obviously because the situation is somewhere inbetween.

Let us note that from the peasant's point of view, sharecropping is perhaps to be preferred to coerced cash-crop labor, but not by too much. The net return is low, although in times of prosperity it may rise. The coercion via debt mechanisms is often as real as legal coercion. For H.K. Takahashi, *métayers* are "semi-serfs," working for "usurious landowners."[136] Bloch sees developments in France as a process of slipping back from the gradual liberation of the peasant from the seignior which had been taking place in the late Middle Ages:

> If—absurd hypothesis—the [French] Revolution had broken out in about 1480, it would have turned over the land, via the suppression of seigniorial receipts (*charges seigneuriales*) almost exclusively to a mass of small farmers. But, from 1480 to 1789, three centuries passed in which large estates were reconstituted.[137]

Why sharecropping however and not tenantry on the one hand or coerced cash-crop labor on the other? Although sharecropping had the disadvantage, compared to coerced cash-cropping, of greater difficulty in supervision, it had the advantage of encouraging the peasant's efforts to increased productivity, provided of course the peasant would continue to work for the seignior without legal compulsion.[138] In short, when labor is plentiful, sharecropping is probably more profitable than coerced cash-cropping.[139]

As for tenantry, no doubt by this logic it is more profitable still than cash-cropping. However there is a proviso. Tenants have fixed contracts and gain at moments of inflation, at least to the extent that the contracts are relatively long-term. Of course, the reverse is true when the market declines. Sharecropping thus is a mode of risk-minimization.[140] It follows that sharecropping is most likely to be considered in areas of specialized agriculture where the risks of variance outweigh the transactions costs.

But this was precisely a moment of high risk. Continued price inflation is very unsettling. Sharecropping seemed the remedy.[141] In some areas, peasants were lucky enough to have legal defenses which make the enforcement of sharecropping too expensive for the landowner, who then found straight rental preferable. Such an instance was England. Cheung suggests that the key was freehold tenure, known in England but not for example in France.[142]

Legal factors are not alone determining. For we must still explain the discrepancy between northern France which moved extensively toward lease arrangements and southern France where sharecropping was the pervasive mode. The law in both areas was substantially the same. Duby locates the key differential in the relative affluence of the farmer in the north as contrasted to "the depressed economic conditions" of the southern peasant "working on land whose productivity had probably not been increased by improvement in techniques as in the north. . . ."[143]

If, however, it was just a question of technology, we are only pushed one step back, to ask why technological advances made in one area were adopted in another area not that distant either geographically or culturally. Braudel suggests that soil conditions in Mediterranean Europe and northwest Europe were fundamentally different, the former being poorer.[144] Porchnev suggests that a further consideration is degree of involvement in the world-economy, the existence of large estates (hence the absence of sharecropping) being correlated with high involvement.[145]

May we not then consider sharecropping as a sort of second best? Unable to move all the way to large estates based either on enclosure and tenancy as in England or coerced cash-crop labor as in eastern Europe, the landed classes of southern France and northern Italy chose the halfway house[146] of sharecropping, as a partial response to the creation of a capitalist world-economy, in the form of semicapitalist enterprises, appropriate indeed to semiperipheral areas.

If the semiperipheral areas remained semiperipheral and did not become the total satellites into which peripheral areas developed, it was not only because of the high land/labor ratio. It may also have been because the existence of a strong indigenous *bourgeoisie* has a particular impact on the development of *agricultural* production in times of distress. Duby points out that in areas where city merchants had been numerous and relatively powerful, many of the estates fell into the hands of these townsmen seeking protection against famine and the social status attached to land ownership, but not the trouble of actual farming. Giving out the land to sharecropping was a reasonable compromise.[147] How "reasonable" the compromise was from the point of view of the peasants is put into considerable doubt by G. E. de Falguerolles, since the orientation of these town bourgeois was toward short-run profit from their investment which had the effect of desolating the land over the following century.[148]

A second paradox, then, about the most "advanced" area. We already noted the strength of town workers keeping up the wage level, thus putting northern Italy at an industrial disadvantage vis-à-vis northwest Europe. Perhaps this same strength of workers accounted for maintaining disproportionate numbers of laborers in the rural areas by using guild restrictions to prevent their entry into urban employment, that is, in the sixteenth century period of demographic upsurge. This would have the result of weakening the bargaining position of the peasant. In any case, the "strength" of the town bourgeoisie seems to have led to a higher likelihood of sharecropping, and thus to the nonemergence of the yeoman farmer who would play such a large role in the economic advance of northwest Europe.

Let us now turn to those areas which would by 1640 be ensconced at the core of the European world-economy: England, the Netherlands, and to some extent northern France. These areas developed a combination of pasturage and arable production based on free or freer labor and units of relatively efficient size. As may be noted, Spain started down this path and then turned off it to become part of the semiperiphery. The reasons for this shift in economic role we shall expound at length in a later chapter.

In the crisis of the late Middle Ages, when a decline in population led to a lowered demand for agricultural products as well as higher wages for urban workers (and hence a better bargaining position for rural workers), the great demesnes declined in western Europe, as we have already seen. They could not become cash-crop estates as in sixteenth-century eastern Europe because there was no international market in a generally dismal economic scene. They had only two significant alternatives. On the one hand, they could convert feudal obligations into money rent,[149] which would reduce costs and increase income to the demesne owner, but involved a gradual transfer of control over the land. That is, it made possible the rise of the small-scale yeoman farmer, either as tenant on fixed rents or, if better off, as independent owner (who can be seen as someone who has, in the purchase of the land, paid a lump sum of rent for a number of years).[150] The alternative then open to the landlord was to convert his land to pasture: cattle or sheep. In the fifteenth century, both wool prices and meat prices had seemed to resist the effects of depression more, and in addition the costs in then scarce, hence expensive, labor were less.[151]

At this time, *both* England and Spain increased pasturage. With the expanding economy of the sixteenth century, wheat seemed to gain an advantage over wool,[152] but not over cattle which gave not only meat but tallow, leather, and dairy products, the consumption of all of which expanded with prosperity.[153] The most important thing to note about pasturage in the sixteenth century, especially livestock, was that it was becoming increasingly a regionally specialized activity. More cattle here, an advantage to large landowners, also meant less cattle elsewhere, which often meant a reduction in peasant consumption of meat and dairy products, a deterioration in his diet.[154] This overemphasis on livestock occurred in Spain, precisely. The two options—conversion of demesnes to leased land, and arable land to pasture—went hand in hand. For the latter made arable land all the scarcer, which made its rental value higher.[155] Furthermore, as arable land became scarcer, cultivation had to be more intensive, which meant that the quality of labor was very important, a further inducement to moving from labor services to money rent.[156]

The rise of sheep farming in the sixteenth century led to the great enclosures movement in England and Spain. But paradoxically it was not the large-scale proprietor who sought the enclosures but a new type, the small-scale independent proprietor.[157] It was of course the economic renewal of the sixteenth century that made possible the continued growth of these small-scale independent farmers.

For "sheep ate men," as the saying went, the rise of sheep farming thus creating the food shortages that had to be compensated both by more efficient arable production in England (the yeoman) and by Baltic grain (coerced cash-cropping).[158]

Furthermore, the increased enclosures made possible the growth in the rural areas of handicraft industries.[159] In Spain, however, the *Mesta* was too entrenched for the small-scale proprietor to make too much headway. And as we shall see later the imperial policies of Charles V gave some added strength to these large landowners. Instead of using its rural unemployed for industrial development, Spain would expel them and export them.

We must persist a little longer on this question of the development of western European agriculture and why it could not take the route of eastern Europe: large estates with coerced cash-crop labor. It was, in the end, because a capitalist world-economy was coming into existence. Paul Sweezy argues a sort of ecological continuum: "Near the centers of trade, the effect on feudal economy [of trade expansion] is strongly disintegrating; further away the effect tends to be just the opposite."[160] This is really too simple a formulation, as Postan argues and Dobb agrees.[161] The Sweezy case is based on the alternatives for the peasant, the ability to escape to the city, the "civilizing proximity of urban life."[162] He neglects the possibility that in many peripheral regions, for example eastern Europe, the peasant had the alternative of frontier areas, often quite as attractive as cities. Indeed, it was precisely because the peasant used this alternative that juridical means were introduced in the sixteenth century to bind him to the land.

The difference was less in the peasant's alternatives, though this played a role, than in the landowner's alternatives. Where was he to draw the largest and most immediate profit? On the one hand, he could turn his land over to other uses (pasture land at a higher rate of profit or lease for money to small farmers—both of which meant dispensing with the feudal labor-service requirements) and using the new profit for investment in trade and industry and/or in aristocratic luxury. On the other hand, he could seek to obtain larger profits by intensifying production of staple cash-crops (especially grain) and then investing the new profits in trade (but not industry and/or aristocratic luxury).[163] The former alternative was more plausible in northwest Europe, the latter in eastern Europe, largely because the *slight* differential already established in production specialties meant that profit maximization was achieved, or at least thought to be achieved, by doing more extensively and more efficiently what one already did best."[164] Hence, the state authorities encouraged enclosures for pasturing (and truck farming) in England, but the creation of large domains for wheat growing in eastern Europe.

As for why labor was contractual in northwest Europe and coerced in eastern Europe, it is insufficient to point to pasturage versus arable land use. For in that case, Hispanic America would have had contractual labor. Rather, demography plays the critical role, as we have already suggested. The western European alternative was one which assumed that there would be enough of a manpower pool at cheap enough rates to satisfy the landowner's needs without costing too much.[165] In eastern Europe and Hispanic America, there was a shortage of labor by comparison with the amount of land it was profitable to exploit, given the existence of world-economy. And in the presence of such a shortage "the expansion of markets and the growth of production is as likely to lead to the increase of labour services as to their decline."[166] Indeed, in Hispanic America, the decline in population was the very fact which explained the rise of cattle and sheep raising, both of which became widespread in the sixteenth century, and which took the form of large-scale enterprises with an important component of forced labor because of the labor shortage.[167]

Finally, let us look at what the rise of money tenancy meant. Remember that in western Europe the conversion of feudal dues to money rent became widespread in the *late Middle Ages,* as we discussed in the last chapter, because of population decline. One must not think of this as an either/or proposition. Feudal dues could be paid in labor services, in kind, or in money. It was often to the landowner's advantage to switch back and forth.[168] For this reason, the mere change in the *form* of feudal rent was not by itself critical. Indeed, Takahashi goes insofar as to argue that it is epiphenomenal,[169] but this seems to me to be quite overstating the issue.

Even if it might be true for the thirteenth and fourteenth centuries to some extent, the rise of payment of dues in money terms certainly *evolved into* a meaningful difference by the sixteenth century, precisely because the "extra-economic" coercive forces were pressuring not the rural laborers but instead the landowners to go further than they intended.[170] Or at least they were pushing some landowners. At a time of expansion, there was competition for labor. The richest landowners could afford to buy the labor away from others. The smallest often had little choice but to settle for obtaining tenants on his land. It was those of inbetween size who may have held on the longest to the old feudal relationships.[171]

England and France had followed the same path in the late Middle Ages. In both there was manumission of serfdom, the rise of money tenancy, and correlatively the rise of wage labor. Yet a curious thing happened in the sixteenth century. England continued on this path. Eastern Europe moved toward the "second serfdom." Southern France moved toward sharecropping. In northern France, transformation seemed to stop short. As Bloch notes, "villages which had not by [the sixteenth century] been able to obtain their liberty found it harder and harder to do so."[172]

One way to look at this is as a limitation on the ability of the serf to free himself. Bloch regards it rather as a limitation on the ability of the seignior to force the serf into a tenancy arrangement.[173] Bloch explains this crucial French–English differential in terms of prior differences. France was more economically developed than England, in the sense that the money economy had spread earlier and more extensively. England was more politically "developed" than France, in the sense that it had stronger central institutions, deriving ultimately from the fact that royal power originated in England in a conquest situation whereas French kings had to slowly piece together their authority amidst true feudal dispersion. Let us see the logic of each of these arguments.

First, France was more centrally located to the currents of European trade and technology than England, and therefore its landed classes developed earlier, the process of conversion of feudal dues to money rents also occurring earlier.[174] But since the counterpressures to the breaking up of manors occurred more or less simultaneously in England and France, it follows that English manors still remained relatively more intact than French at the onset of the "long" sixteenth century. Therefore, Bloch implies, English landlords were relatively more free to take advantage of new commercialization possibilities of large domains than French landlords. The English moved to a system of wage labor and continued manumission. The French had to make the best of a bad situation and landlords sought to increase their incomes by renewed old-style pressures.

The second argument deals with the relationship of the king and the nobility as early as the *twelfth* century. The English had established a strong central control on the judiciary. The other side of this achievement, however, was that *within* the manor the lord, although he lost power over criminal offenses, obtained full authority to do whatever he wished about tenure. In the fourteenth and fifteenth centuries, the manorial courts downplayed copyhold in their interpretation of customary law. When royal justice finally was able to intervene in such questions toward the end of the fifteenth century, they discovered that "customary law" permitted variable rents.

In France, however, there was no central criminal justice. On the other hand, the lord of the manor never had exclusive authority over land law. Hence patrimoniality could not be so easily undermined. Who the true "owner" was became an obscure legal question. By the sixteenth century, there were jurists who were willing to argue the tenant could not be dislodged. Unable, therefore, to change the rents, the seignior had to reacquire the land—by judicial manipulation of documents, and by expanding via "rediscovery" the obligations of feudal dues.[175] Over the long run, this difference would be crucial.[176]

Hence, what Bloch seems to be arguing is that because the English legal system allowed more flexibility to the landlord, money tenancy and wage labor continued to expand, allowing both great pastoral estates and the yeoman farmer becoming gentry to flourish. It also would force more rural labor into urban areas to form the proletariat with which to industrialize. In France, paradoxically the very strength of the monarchy forced the seigniorial class to maintain less economically functional, more "feudal," forms of land tenure, which would hold France back.

Resolving the tenure issue had in turn great consequences for the role a country would play in the world-system. A system of estate management as in eastern Europe requires large amounts of supervisory personnel. Had English landlords moved in this direction, there might not have been sufficient personnel to man the many new administrative posts required in the emerging world-economy—commercial managers, eventually overseas personnel, etc. It is not that landowners ceded their personnel for these other uses, but that as these other uses expanded, there were fewer persons left for supervisory positions on estates. Tenancy was a way out.

Note then the overall picture. Northwest Europe is in the process of dividing the use of her land for pastoral and arable products. This was only possible as the widening market created an ever larger market for the pastoral products,[177] and as the periphery of the world-economy provided cereal supplements for the core areas. The semiperiphery was turning away from industry (a task increasingly confided to the core) and *toward* relative self-sufficiency in agriculture. The agricultural specialization of the core encouraged the monetization of rural work relationships, as the work was more skilled and as landowners wished to rid themselves of the burden of surplus agricultural workers. Wage labor and money rents became the means of labor control. In this system, a stratum of independent small-scale farmers could emerge and indeed grow strong both on their agricultural products and on their links to the new handicraft industries. Given the increase in population and the decline in wages, it would then follow, as Marx said, that these yeomen farmers "grew rich at the expense both of their laborers and their land-lords."[178] They usurped (by enclosure) the lands of the former, arguing publicly the need to guarantee the country's food supply[179] and then hired them at low wages, while obtaining at fixed rentals more and more land from the owners of large demesnes. We do not wish to overstate the strength of this new yeoman class. It is enough to realize they became a significant economic, and hence political, force. Their economic strength lay in the fact that they had every incentive to be "en-trepreneurial." They were seeking wealth and upward mobility: the route to success lay through economic efficiency. But they were not yet burdened down either by traditional obligations of largesse or status obligations of luxury spending or town life.[180]

Obviously, such a redistribution of rural economic effort had a great impact on the character of the urban areas. What was going on in the towns? We know that the sixteenth century was a time of growing population in general and of growing town sizes, in absolute terms everywhere, but relatively in core areas. We know it follows, logically and from empirical evidence, as Helleiner says, that "one has to assume that, in the [16th century], the pressure of population on its land resources was mounting."[181] In eastern Europe, some people moved into frontier lands. From the Iberian peninsula, some went to the Americas, and some were expelled (Jews, later Moriscos) to other areas of the Mediterranean. In western Europe generally, there was emigration to the towns and a growing vagabondage that was "endemic."[182] There was not only the rural exodus, both the enclosed and ejected rural laborer, and the migratory laborer who came down from the mountains to the plains for a few weeks at harvest time, the "true rural proletarians" for Braudel.[183] There was also the vagabondage "caused by the decline of feudal bodies of retainers and the disbanding of the swollen armies which had flocked to serve the kings against their vassals. . . ."[184]

What did all these wanderers do? They of course provided the unskilled labor for the new industries. In Marx's view, "the rapid rise of manufac-tures, particularly in England, absorbed them gradually."[185] And as we have seen, their availability was one of the conditions of the willingness of landlords to commute feudal services to rents.[186]

This picture of an expanding labor force, not producing food, is hard to reconcile, however, with another fact. Jones and Woolf argue that a precondition to industrial development, and one that was historically met for the first time in sixteenth century northwest Europe, is that, along with an increase in productivity and a wider market, there was "a breathing space from intense population pressure during which income rather than men might be multiplied. . . ."[187]

But what about the surplus population then that swelled the towns of the core states, that wandered the countryside as vagabonds? Well, for one thing, they kept dying off in large quantity. Some were hanged for being vagabonds.[188] Famines were frequent, especially given "the slowness and prohibitive price of transport, [and] the irregularity of harvests. . . ."[189] As Braudel and Spooner put it, an analysis of this economy "must take into account the 'youth' of this [vagabond] population whose life-span was on the average short because of famines and epidemics. . . ."[190]

This would then account for an otherwise puzzling phenomenon noted by Braudel: "The proletariat of the towns could not have maintained its size, still less have grown, were it not for constant waves of immigration."[191] It also helps to explain the puzzling circumstance noted by Phelps-Brown and Hopkins, that, despite the significant fall in wages of the workers, there was so relatively little social upheaval. They say: "Part of the answer may be that it was a fall from a high level [of the 15th century], so that great though it was it still left the wage-earner with a subsistence . . ."[192]

But this subsistence survival of the northwest European worker's wage level was only made possible by having a periphery from which to import wheat, having bullion to make the flow possible, and allowing part of the population to die off; which part would be a fascinating subject to pursue. Is it not probable that, already in the sixteenth century, there were systematic ethnic distinctions of rank within the working class in the various cities of Europe? For example, Kazimierz Tyminiecki notes precisely this phenomenon in the towns of sixteenth century East Elbia, where German workers excluded Slavic migrants from higher occupations.[193] Not much research seems to have been done on the ethnic distribution of the urban working class of early modern Europe, but my guess would be that Tyminiecki's description might be shown to be typical of the whole of the world-economy. It is not only that, within this world-economy, towns were unevenly distributed, but that within the towns, ethnic groups were probably unevenly distributed. We must not forget here the concept of layers within layers.

If we must be careful to look at whom we mean by urban workers, we must be careful when we look at the upper classes. In medieval Europe, high status was held by warrior–landowners called nobles. For the most part, they were an occupationally homogeneous group, distinguished largely by rank which correlated roughly with size of domain and the number of vassals. To be sure, individuals and families moved up and down the rank scale. There were also a few towns in which emerged an urban patriciate. We have already discussed in the previous chapter some of the conceptual confusions of identity to which this gave rise.

But, in the sixteenth century, was the landowner–merchant aristocrat or bourgeois? It is clear that both generically and specifically this was unclear. The picture had become murky with the creation of a world-economy based on commerce and capitalist agriculture. Let us look successively at the international merchants and then the "industrialists," and see both their geographic distribution and their links to landowning classes.

In many ways the techniques of commercial gain used in the sixteenth century were merely an extension of the methods the towns learned to use vis-à-vis their immediate hinterland in the late Middle Ages. The problem of the towns collectively was to control their own market, that is, be able both to reduce the cost of items purchased from the countryside and to minimize the role of stranger merchants.[194] Two techniques were used. On the one hand, towns sought to obtain not only legal rights to tax market operations but also the right to regulate the trading operation (who should trade, when it should take place, what should be traded). Furthermore, they sought to restrict the possibilities of their countryside engaging in trade other than via their town. The result was what Dobb calls a sort of "urban colonialism."[195] Over time, these various mechanisms shifted their terms of trade in favor of the townsmen, in favor thus of the urban commercial classes against both the landowning and peasant classes.

But the profits in this, while important, were small by comparison with what might be earned by long-distance trade, especially colonial or semicolonial trade. Henri Sée estimates the profit margins of the early colonial commercial operations as being very high: "sometimes in excess of 200 or 300% from dealings that were little more than piracy."[196] There were really two separate aspects to this high profit ratio. One was the "monopsony" situation in the colonial area, that is, monopsony in the "purchase" of land and labor. This was arranged, as we have seen, by the use of legal force, whether in Hispanic America or in eastern Europe. The second was the effective lack of competition in the areas of sales of the primary products, western Europe. This lack of competition was the consequence, in part, of the lack of technological development, and in part of vertical linkage chains of merchandising.

To be sure, the technology of business transactions had seen some very important advances in the late thirteenth and early fourteenth centuries: deposit banking, the bill of exchange, brokers, branch offices of central commercial organizations. Chaunu estimates that these techniques enabled commercial capitalism to increase, "perhaps tenfold," its ability to skim surplus and thus have "the ships, the men, the means needed to feed the adventure of exploration and then of exploitation of new space, in close liaison with the state."[197] Nonetheless, the sum total of these commercial innovations was insufficient to make it possible for long-distance traders to enter the world market without substantial capital and usually some state assistance. Hence, not many could so enter, and those who were already in did not actively seek to alter this situation.[198]

Even more important were the vertical links. The sources of capital were limited. Let us remember, even the state apparatuses were large-scale borrowers. The profits of Portuguese sugar plantations based on slave labor, for example, went not merely to the Portuguese directly involved, but to persons in the more "advanced" European economies, who provided both initial capital and an industrial outlet.[199] It was not merely that northwest Europe could develop the factories, but that their vertical commercial links encouraged a financial dependence. Indeed it would not be extreme to talk of a system of international debt peonage, first perfected by Hanseatic merchants vis-à-vis Norwegian fishermen and furtrappers in the late Middle Ages[200] and later by the Germanic merchants of such towns as Riga, Reval, and Gdańsk vis-à-vis the east European hinterland. The technique was known elsewhere, being used by the merchants of Toulouse, the Genoese in the Iberian peninsula, and in parts of the wool trade of England and Spain. What was the method? Very simple: it involved the purchase of goods in advance of their production, that is, payments in advance for supplies to be delivered in the future. This prevented sale on an open market. It allowed the merchants rather than the producers to decide the optimum moment for world resale. And since the money lent tended to be expended by the time of delivery of the goods, if not overspent, the producer was always tempted to perpetuate the arrangement. In theory forbidden by law, this system could only be applied by merchants who had the means and influence to be able to sustain the practice, that is "foreign merchants, or rich merchants who had easy access to foreign markets."[201] These merchants could thereby take the profits of the price revolution and multiply them. The way in which this system involved a vertical network of exploitation and profit making is clearly described by Malowist as it operated in Poland:

> In the sixteenth and beginning of the seventeenth centuries, when the Gdańsk merchants were paying less attention to the sea trade, they began to exert an increasing influence on agriculture in all parts of Poland. Towards the end of the sixteenth century when conditions for the export of grain were particularly favorable, agents of the Gdańsk merchants were regularly to be seen at the markets in the towns and villages of Poland, where they bought up grain. . . . [In] the seventeenth century, the rich merchants of Gdańsk, like the merchants of Riga, made advance payments not only to the lesser gentry, but even to the wealthy nobles of Poland and Lithuania. . . . This great flourishing of Gdańsk trade in the extensive hinterlands can be explained by the immense increase in the wealth of the Gdańsk merchants during the time of the revolution in prices. . . . The Gdańsk merchants received advance payments from the Dutch, and . . . the latter sometimes collected for that purpose certain sums from merchants in Antwerp.[202]

This system of international debt peonage enabled a cadre of international merchants to bypass (and thus eventually destroy) the indigenous merchant classes of eastern Europe (and to some extent those of southern Europe) and enter into direct links with landlord–entrepreneurs (nobility included) who were essentially capitalist farmers, producing the goods and keeping control of them until they reached the first major port area, after which they were taken in hand by some merchants of west European (or north Italian) nationality[203] who in turn worked through and with a burgeoning financial class centered in a few cities.

If the international merchants in the European world-economy were largely of certain nationalities, was this also true of "industrialists," and what was the relation of these two groups? Industrial production existed already in the Middle Ages, but it was scattered, small-scale, and mostly geared to a luxury market. It was only with the rise of a capitalist system within the framework of a world-economy that there could emerge industrial entrepreneurs.[204]

It was precisely in the areas of greater agricultural specialization that there was a thrust to industrialize, not only in moments of expansion but in moments of contraction as well. Marian Malowist talks to the conjuncture in these areas of the growth of a cloth industry and agricultural crisis of the fourteenth and fifteenth centuries.[205] Joan Thirsk notes how the rural thrust, the need to find alternate employment possibilities for ejected rural labor, continued to operate in sixteenth century England.[206]

This rural pressure however did not operate in the most "advanced" areas because the fact that many of these industries were then located in rural areas was a function not only of the rural search for employment, but of the urban rejection. Many of the centers of the medieval textile industry in Flanders and northern Italy had their capital invested in luxury good production and were unable or unwilling to shift to the new market first made necessary by the monetary crisis of the fourteenth and fifteenth centuries and then made profitable by the creation of a world-economy in the sixteenth century. These entrepreneurs were not concerned in this case about frontiers.[207] One famous and key move of this kind was the flight of Flemish capitalists to England. What we must bear in mind is that at this stage the industries all had a shaky base. They rose and fell. They were like wanderers searching for a haven: "They resembled a thousand fires lighted at the same time, each fragile, in a vast field of dry grasses."[208] It is clear that the old advanced centers, the controllers of international trade, were not necessarily the centers of imagination and daring. It seems to bear out Henri Pirenne's belief in the noncontinuity of capitalist entrepreneurs.[209]

We are thus led to be prudent in the use of our terminology. Bourgeois and feudal classes, in an explanation which uses class categories to explain social change, should not be read, as it usually is, to mean "merchants" and "landowners." During the long period of the creation of the European

world-economy, in the core countries of this world-economy, there were
some merchants and some landowners who stood to gain from retaining
those forms of production associated with "feudalism," namely ones in
which peasant labor was in some way systematically and legally made to
turn over the largest part of its product to the landowner (e.g., corvée,
feudal rents, etc.). And there were some merchants and some landowners
who stood to gain from the rise of new forms of industrial production,
based on contractual labor. In the sixteenth century, this division often
corresponded, as a first approximation, to big and small. Big merchants
and big landowners profited more from the old feudal system; small
(medium-size? rising?) ones from the new capitalist forms. But the big–small
dichotomy should be used with caution and nuance and it only holds at
this point of historical time. Theoretically, of course, it makes a lot of
sense. New forms of social organization usually tend to have less appeal
to those doing well under an existing system than to those who are energetic
and ambitious, but not yet *arrivé*. Empirically, it is complicated by other
considerations.

Whatever their origins, this new class of "industrialists," some coming
out of the yeoman farmer ranks and some reconverted merchants, were
committed to what Vilar terms the essential characteristic of a modern
economy: "the achievement of medium-sized profits in much larger markets: selling more selling in quantity, while earning less on a per-unit
basis.[210] Part of the profit came from the wage-lag.[211] Part were windfall
profits. Part were low real interest rates. Part were profits borrowed
against the future in terms of noncalculated depreciation.[212] But profit
there was. And the amount of profit not only created a political base for
this class; it had an immediate impact on the overall economy. This was
felt in many ways: as a stimulus to the production of raw materials and
the mobilization of manpower, as a way of meeting a growing demand
which became a mass demand. But in addition, it made possible the
industry responsible for the creation of many external economies: roads,
flood control devices, parks.[213]

It is clear, too, that the sixteenth century saw a remarkable shift of
locus of the textile industry. During the late fifteenth and early sixteenth
centuries, these industries expanded in the "old" centers: northern Italy,
southern Germany, Lorraine, Franche-Comté, Spanish-Netherlands, and
in England only in the southwest and only in woolen cloth. Then, new
centers arose, principally in England and the northern Netherlands, in
countries that had been, as Nef observed, "industrially backward at the
beginning of the sixteenth century. . . ."[214]

We have sought to present the case in this chapter of the emergence
of a new economic framework of action in the sixteenth century—the
European world-economy based on capitalist methods. It involved a division
of productive labor that can only be properly appreciated by taking into

account the world-economy as a whole. The emergence of an industrial sector was important, but what made this possible was the transformation of agricultural activity from feudal to capitalist forms. Not all these capitalist "forms" were based on "free" labor—only those in the core of the economy. But the motivations of landlord and laborer in the non-"free" sector were as capitalist as those in the core.

We should not leave this theme without looking at the objections to this analysis. Ernesto Laclau has taken André Gunder Frank to task for arguing that sixteenth century Hispanic America had a capitalist economy. He argues that this is both incorrect and un-Marxist. Without diverting ourselves into a long *excursus* on Marxian exegetics, let me say simply that I think Laclau is right in terms of the letter of Marx's arguments but not in terms of its spirit. On the substance of the issue itself, Laclau's main argument is that Frank's definition of capitalism as production for profit for a market in which the profit does not go to the direct producer and feudalism as a closed-off subsistence economy are both conceptually wrong. He argues that Frank's definition, in omitting "relations of production" (that is, essentially whether or not labor is "free"), makes it possible not only to include sixteenth century Hispanic America but also "the slave on a Roman *latifundium* or the gleb serf of the European Middle Ages, at least in those cases—the overwhelming majority—where the lord assigned *part* [my italics] of the economic surplus extracted from the serf for sale.[215] He then suggests that, if Frank is right, "we would have to conclude that Elizabethan England or Renaissance France was ripe for socialism. . . ."[216] Finally he says far from feudalism being incompatible with capitalism, the expansion of the external market in Hispanic America served to "accentuate and consolidate [feudalism]."[217]

Laclau precisely beclouds the issue. First, the difference between the gleb serf of the Middle Ages and the slave or worker on an *encomienda* in sixteenth century Hispanic America, or a "serf" in Poland, was threefold: the difference between assigning "part" of the surplus to a market and assigning "most of the surplus;" the difference between production for a local market and a world market; the difference between the exploiting classes spending the profits, and being motivated to maximize them and partially reinvest them. As for Laclau's inference about Elizabethan England, it is absurd and polemical. As for involvement in a capitalist world market accentuating feudalism, precisely so, but "feudalism" of this new variety.

The point is that the "relations of production" that define a system are the "relations of production" of the whole system, and the system at this point in time is the European world-economy. Free labor is indeed a defining feature of capitalism, but not free labor throughout the productive enterprises. Free labor is the form of labor control used for skilled work in core countries whereas coerced labor is used for less skilled work in peripheral areas. The combination thereof is the essence of capitalism. When labor is everywhere free, we shall have socialism.

But capitalism cannot flourish within the framework of a world-empire. This is one reason why it never emerged in Rome. The various advantages merchants had in the emergent world-economy were all politically easier to obtain than if they had sought them within the framework of a single state, whose rulers would have to respond to multiple interests and pressures.[218] That is why the secret of capitalism was in the establishment of the division of labor within the framework of a world-economy that was *not* an empire rather than within the framework of a single national state. In under-developed countries in the twentieth century, K. Berrill notes that "inter-national trade is often much cheaper and easier than internal trade and . . . specialization between countries is often much easier and earlier than specialization between regions in a country."[219] This was also true in sixteenth-century Europe. We shall try to demonstrate how and why this worked in the course of this volume.

In summary, what were the economic accomplishments of the sixteenth century and how have we accounted for them? It was not a century of great technological advance, except for the introduction of coal as a fuel in England and northern France. A. Rupert Hall sees both industry and agriculture as "in the last phases of a series of changes, both technological and organizational" which had begun in the fourteenth century, with the "crisis." But, he notes, it was in the sixteenth century that there was a "diffusion of techniques from the core to the periphery of European civiliza-tion."[220]

Four things are striking about the sixteenth century. Europe expanded into the Americas. This may not have been determinative by itself, but it was important.[221] The crucial fact about the expansion was captured by Braudel: "the gold and silver of the New World enabled Europe to live above its means, to invest beyond its savings."[222]

To invest beyond its savings, and to increase its savings, by the price revolution and wage-lag. Whether or not the expansion of bullion was responsible for the expansion of production, and to whatever extent demo-graphic expansion was the cause or consequence, the bullion itself was "merchandise, and a general expansion of trade underlay the 'prosperity' of the sixteenth century which was neither a game nor a mirage, not a monetary illusion."[223]

The third striking change was the pattern of rural labor—the rise of coerced cash-crop labor in the periphery and of the yeoman farmer in the core. Takahashi may exaggerate when he calls the yeoman farmer the "prime mover"[224] in the end of feudalism, but it is doubtful that one could have had a capitalist system without him. But also not without the coerced cash-crop labor.

Jean Néré attacks Dobb for putting exclusive emphasis on the availability

of proletarian labor in explaining the rise of capitalism. He says one has
to put this factor together with secular price movements.[225] Braudel and
Spooner, on the other hand, caution against confusing accidental fluctuations (the price revolution) for structural changes.[226] What is clear is that
in the sixteenth century a "capitalist era"[227] emerges and that it takes the
form of a world-economy. No doubt, "the fragility of this first unity of
the world"[228] is a critical explanatory variable in the political evolution.
But the fact is that this unity survives and, in the seventeenth and eighteenth
centuries, did come to be consolidated.

One of the principal features of the European world-system of the sixteenth century is that there was no simple answer to the question of who
was dominating whom? One might make a good case for the Low Countries
exploiting Poland via Gdańsk, and certainly Spain exploiting its American
possessions. The core dominated the periphery. But the core was so large.
Did Genoese merchants and bankers use Spain or did Spanish imperialism
absorb parts of Italy? Did Florence dominate Lyon, or France Lombardy,
or both? How should one describe the true links between Antwerp (later
Amsterdam) and England? Note that in all these cases we deal with a
merchant city-state on the one hand and a larger nation-state on the other.

If we are to untangle the picture any further, we must look to the political
side, the ways in which various groups sought to use the state structures
to protect and advance their interests. It is to this question we now turn.

3

THE ABSOLUTE MONARCHY AND STATISM

Figure 4: "The Grand-Duke has the port of Livorno fortified," engraving by Jacques Callot from a collection called *The Life of Ferdinand I of the Medicis*. Ferdinand was Grand-Duke of Tuscany from 1587–1609. The engraving was made between 1614–1620.

It is evident that the rise of the absolute monarchy in western Europe is coordinate in time with the emergence of a European world-economy. But is it cause or consequence? A good case can be made for both. On the one hand, were it not for the expansion of commerce and the rise of capitalist agriculture, there would scarcely have been the economic base to finance the expanded bureaucratic state structures.[1] But on the other hand, the state structures were themselves a major economic underpinning of the new capitalist system (not to speak of being its political guarantee). As Braudel says, "Whether or not they wanted to be, [the states were] the biggest entrepreneurs of the century."[2] Furthermore, they were essential customers of the merchants.[3]

There are several different arguments about the role of the state in capitalist enterprise. One concerns its extent, a second, its economic impact, and a third, its class content. The third argument we shall discuss later. First, while there is much disagreement about the extent of state involvement in the world-economy of the nineteenth century, there seems to be widespread consensus that in the earlier periods of the modern world-system, beginning at least in the sixteenth century and lasting at least until the eighteenth, the states were central economic actors in the European world-economy.

But if most agree that the states did play this role, some feel it was an unnecessary and undesirable role. For example, Schumpeter, true to his belief in the long-range superior efficiency of private enterprise, denies that the state was good for business as purchaser of goods or credit. He says it is an "unpardonable [error] to think that in the absence of the extravagance of courts there would not have been equivalent goods from the peasants and the bourgeois from whom the corresponding means were taken."[4] Unpardonable it may be, but error perhaps not. Why is it not conceivable that, to meet tax demands, a peasant produces a surplus which he might otherwise either consume or not produce? Does Schumpeter really assume that in the sixteenth century the peasants of Europe were totally oriented to a commercial market?

As for the thesis that court expenditures were vital in the creation of credit, Schumpeter has two responses. One is that any benefit obtained in developing a "credit-engineering machine" must be weighed "against all the destruction wrought and all the paralysis of economic activity spread, both by the methods of raising that revenue and by the uses it financed."[5] This involves a tremendous counterfactual argument, whose validity can only be assessed in terms of the entire argument of this book. The view expounded herein will be that the development of strong states in the core areas of the European world was an essential component of the development of modern capitalism. His second response is that the counterpart of loans to courts was economic privileges which were most probably economically unsound from the perspective of the interests of the larger community.[6] No doubt this is true, but to me this seems a description of the essence of capitalism, not an accidental distortion of its operations, and hence an assertion which in fact provides a good part of the refutation of Schumpeter's previous one.

We have already reviewed previously the various aspects of the economic crisis of the fourteenth and fifteenth centuries which contributed to the slow but steady growth of state bureaucracies. We have also mentioned the evolution of military technology which made obsolete the medieval knight and thereby strengthened the hand of central authorities who could control large numbers of infantrymen. The main political objective of the monarchs was the restoration of order, a prerequisite to economic resurgence. In Génicot's succinct summary, "by revealing the evil effects of a breakdown in authority, the troubled times established the case for centralization."[7]

But why should such political regimes come to the fore at this particular time? One classic response is to talk in terms of the centrifugal phenomena of new states, an argument often used about twentieth-century new states.[8] The initial thrust of the fifteenth century "restorers of order" came out of the "crisis of feudalism." The economic squeeze on the seigniors had led to increased exploitation of peasants and consequently to peasant rebellions. It had also led to internecine warfare among the nobility. The weakened nobility looked to the kings to preserve them from the threats of greater disorder still. The kings profited from the circumstances to enhance their own wealth and power vis-à-vis this very nobility. This was the price of their provision of security, what Frederic Lane calls their "protection rent" and which he reminds us were at that time both "a major source of the fortunes made in trade [and] a more important source of profits . . . than superiority in industrial technique or industrial organization."[9]

Of course, the king's advance was not merely a function of opportunity but of the pressures he was under himself. Eisenstadt argues that what he calls "bureaucratic politics" come into existence when "the political rulers cannot rely on the facilities available to them through their own resources (e.g., the king's domains), or through the unquestioning commitments of other groups. . . ."[10] But were commitments ever unquestioning? And as for the availability of resources, the fact that the kings' personal resources were insufficient for their objectives was a function of more ambitious objectives. We must then look to the pressures that led rulers to seek to *implement* more ambitious objectives.

One suggestion comes from Archibald Lewis, who ties it to the availability of land: "When . . . the sovereign has given out all the free land and none remains, it is necessary for him to begin to tax—taking back in another form the wealth he earlier showered out upon his people."[11] This need for national taxation did not immediately lead to "absolutism." Rather, the sovereign had to create parliaments to obtain the assistance of the nobility in the taxation process but only "until such time as the rulers felt powerful enough to dispense with such assistance."[12] Dobb has a different emphasis. He sees the pressure on the king as having come not from the shortage of land but from "labor scarcity." The growth of the state machinery served to promote "control of the labor market."[13]

It might follow from this analysis that if economic crisis led to greater power for the monarchs, the economic expansion of the sixteenth century would have had the inverse effect. To a certain extent, as we shall see, this was true. The "first" sixteenth century was the era of imperial strivings, not of strong states, as we shall discuss in the next chapter. It was not until the "failure of empire," of which we shall speak then, that strong states once again came to the fore. And indeed it would only be the eighteenth century that historians would deem "the age of absolutism."[14]

In fact, however, despite fluctuations in the curve, we are faced with a secular increase in state power throughout the modern era. The capitalist world-economy seems to have required and facilitated this secular process of increased centralization and internal control, at least within the core states.

How did kings, who were the managers of the state machinery in the sixteenth century, strengthen themselves? They used four major mechanisms: bureaucratization, monopolization of force, creation of legitimacy, and homogenization of the subject population. We shall treat each in turn.

If the king grew stronger, it was unquestionably due to the fact that he acquired new machinery to use, a corps of permanent and dependent officials.[15] Of course, in this respect, Europe was just catching up with China. Hence we know that a bureaucratic state structure is by itself insufficient to demarcate the great changes of the sixteenth century, much less account for them. Nevertheless, the development of the state bureaucracy was crucial, because it was to alter fundamentally the rules of the political game, by ensuring that henceforth decisions of economic policy could not be easily made without going through the state structure. It meant that the energy of men of all strata had to turn in significant part to the conquest of the political kingdom. To be sure, we are still talking in this era of a relatively small bureaucracy, certainly by comparison with contemporary Europe.[16] But the difference of size and structure by comparison with the late Middle Ages represented nonetheless a qualitative jump.

How did a king acquire these men? He bought them. The problem of the king was not that he had no agents. There were persons who performed administrative and military functions in the realm, but they were not previously for the most part *dependent* on him, and hence were not bound to carry out his dispositions in the face of adverse pressure deriving from their own interests or from that of their peers and families. The king turned to persons, usually "of modest origin"[17] to become a paid, full-time staff. The major institution which made this possible has come to be known as the "venality of office." By contrast with bureaucracies based on a norm of financial disinterestedness and universalistic recruitment, no doubt these forms underline the *limited* power of the king, and the likelihood that state income would be diverted to increased payments to this venal bureaucracy. But by contrast with the preceding feudal system, venality made possible the relative supremacy of the state-system. As Hartung and Mousnier say, "Despite appearances, the venality of offices was most often favorable to the absolute monarch."[18]

The political choice was made by the king between realistic alternatives. In order to establish a rational bureaucracy, the state needed a sure source of prior funds other than that which the bureaucracy would bring in. K. W. Swart suggests that what monarchs lacked in the sixteenth century, unlike later governments, was the possibility to "issue loans without assigning a special part of their income as security for the interest."[19] They were caught in a cycle because in order to acquire this possibility they first had to create a stronger state machinery. Venality of office had the virtue of providing both immediate income (sale of office) and a staff. Of course this then went hand in hand with the development of a self-interested corporate group of venal officers.[20] To be sure, venality creates a "vicious circle" as Richard Ehrenberg points out, in which the increased bureaucracy eats up revenue and creates debts, leading to still larger fiscal needs by the state.[21] The trick was to transform the circle into an upward spiral wherein the bureaucracy was sufficiently efficient to squeeze out of the population a surplus larger than the costs of maintaining the apparatus. Some states succeeded at this. Others did not. The crucial distinguishing factor would be their role in the world-economy.

The upward spiral operated something like this: The momentary advantages acquired by the king in the late Middle Ages because of the economic squeeze on the nobility created the funds that made it possible to begin to "buy" a bureaucracy. This in turn made it possible both to tax more and to borrow more. In those areas of the world-economy where economic transformation was proceeding in such a way as to ensure a disproportionate share of the world surplus, states found it easier to tax and to borrow, a sheer reflex of future-oriented confidence of money-possessing elements. The states used these increased revenues to increase their coercive power which in turn increased what might be termed "confidence in the coercive potential" of the state.

This made it possible for national debts to come into existence, that is, deficitary state budgets. National debts were unknown in the ancient world, and impossible in the Middle Ages because of the weakness of

the central governments and the uncertainty of succession. It is only with
the regime of Francis I in France in the sixteenth century that we first
encounter this economic phenomenon.[22] For national debts can only exist
when the state can force people to delay collecting them or at opportune
moments refuse to pay them, while simultaneously forcing groups to lend,
in specie or by various paper transactions, the current excess. It is part
of the drive to ensure increasing revenues to the Crown. The Crown needed
money with which to build up its state machinery, and had enough state
machinery to obtain the money. The system employed was not yet mercantilism, a policy aimed at strengthening the long run tax base of the state,
so much as "fiscalism," in Martin Wolfe's phrase,[23] a policy aimed at increasing the immediate income of the state.

At this point in time, nonetheless the *lack* of serious financial state machinery was still striking, "another sign of weakness," as Braudel calls it, of
the sixteenth-century state, compared to later states.[24] Still, the weakness
of the State as financial manipulator does not detract from the fact that
national debts reflected the growing autonomous interests of the states
as economic actors, as actors however with a special ability to pursue their
economic ends.

Perhaps the most important use to which the surplus of money was
put, once one deducted the cost of the administrative machinery used
in collecting it, was in the creation of standing armies. Once again the
way states got personnel initially was to buy them. The counterpart of
"venal" bureaucrats was "mercenary" soldiers.

Who however was available to be purchased? Not just anyone, since
being a mercenary was a dangerous albeit occasionally rewarding
occupation. It was not an occupation generally speaking of choice. Those
who could do better did so with alacrity. It was consequently an occupation
whose recruitment was geographically and socially skewed, part and parcel
of the new European division of labor.

The population growth in western Europe led as we have mentioned
to the phenomenon of "vagabondage." There was a growth everywhere
of a "lumpenproletariat." They were a threat to the not too well established
order of the new states. Incorporating some of them into the armies served
multiple functions. It provided employment to some, and used this group
to suppress the others.[25] It gave the kings new weapons to control the
lords, but also to sustain them. V. G. Kiernan has indicated how many
of the mercenaries came from the "less-developed" corners of western
Europe: from Gascony, Picardy, Brittany, Wales, Corsica, Sardinia, Dal-
matia. "Altogether, a striking number of these recruiting-grounds lay in
mountainous regions on the fringes of Europe, inhabited by alien peoples
such as Celts or Basques."[26] And, it seems, above all, from Switzerland.[27]

Kiernan argues that this pattern of recruitment was not only directly
responsible for controlling the social explosion of the sixteenth century;[28]

it also had a second subtler impact, albeit one just as important, if we remember that, in our terms, we are dealing with a world-economy:

> The reservoirs of mercenary recruitment remained politically stagnant, compared with their neighbors, somewhat as Nepal and the Panjab, two great recruiting-grounds for the British army, long did. For Switzerland the three centuries of symbiosis with despotic France had evil consequences. Cantonal politics were corrupted by the fees received for licensing the export of soldiers, and rings of patricians increased their power at the expense of common people. . . . As Alfieri was to remark bitterly, these free-men of the hills became the chief watchdogs of tyranny. European history might have taken a different turn if the Swiss had still been as revolutionary a force in 1524, when the Peasants' War was fought, as fifty years earlier.[29]

The mercenaries were not even recruited directly by the state in most cases. The existing machinery did not permit it. Rather the state contracted with "military entrepreneurs," who sought profit. Redlich is dubious that this was an optimal means of capital accumulation since if their income was "extraordinarily high . . . typically their expenditures were tremendous."[30] But it is one more piece of evidence on how state building affected the rise of capitalism. In the short run at least, "in a society where there is chronic underemployment of resources, increased military expenditure has often stimulated more production of other kinds so that the amount of surplus rose in time of war."[31] But more than commerce and production was involved in the military enterprise. The system was credit-creating. For not only did princes borrow from bankers; so did the military entrepreneurs, whose capital was supplied by the large merchant bankers such as the Fuggers. This would remain true as late as the Thirty Years' War.[32]

Furthermore, it is not only that mercenary armies offered employment for the poor and entrepreneurial opportunities. Armies had to be fed. Typically, food merchants accompanied armies in the field, also serving as intermediaries for the booty.[33] Alan Everitt argues that army victualling was a major stimulus to regional grain specialization in Tudor England[34] and that it even stimulated the export trade.[35] This is all the more plausible if one takes into account that states also felt a responsibility to make sure that their growing bureaucracies had sufficient food as well.[36] The expansion of capitalism came thus to serve the short run needs of the state.

Here as with the civil bureaucracy the monarch was in a dilemma. The military entrepreneur was a necessary adjunct in the monarch's search for power. He also drained a goodly part of the surplus. No doubt the military entrepreneur was a more reliable agent of the prince than a noble vassal, but ultimately he too pursued his own interests primarily. Woe to the prince whose liquidity failed![37] The likelihood, however, of this happening was once again a direct function of the state's role in the world-economy.

Up to a point, in any case, the armies paid for themselves. For they made possible more taxes. Since the "weight of [these taxes] fell almost entirely on the people—especially those who lived in the country,"[38] the people chafed, and to the extent that they could, they rebelled.[39] The armies were then there to suppress these rebellions, to the extent that they could. The easiest form of rebellion, because the most difficult for the states to counteract, was banditry, which was of course the easier the more mountainous the region.[40] The police of the state was still too thin to do too much about it, except in central areas, and this banditry often found a resonant chord in the opposition of some traditional seigniors to the new states.[41]

No doubt, as Delumeau puts it, "banditry was often the insurrection of the country against the city."[42] But who in the country and most importantly when? It is clear that peasant involvement in banditry seems to be highly correlated with moments of grain shortage.[43] Of course when a food riot occurred, the very poor were involved, but in banditry as a movement, especially in the Mediterranean area, it was not the very poor who made up the heart of the movement. It was more clearly the nascent yeoman farmers, who in the late sixteenth century, found in banditry their form of protest against the "refeudalization" that was occurring, against the semiperipheralization of their countries.[44] In such countries, it was particularly the small entrepreneurs, like the *massari* of southern Italy, who having fewer means of resistance to poor harvest years than larger landowners, feared a precipitous fall into the ranks of the rural poor, and hence employed banditry against these large landowners whom they saw as their immediate enemy.[45]

The other element involved in banditry was a part of the nobility, but again which ones? It seems to be those who were squeezed out by the economic upheaval. In our discussion of mercenaries, we pointed out that the growth of population along with various thrusts toward enclosure created the problem of vagabondage, and that the rise of mercenary armies served, among other purposes, to employ some of these "vagabonds" to hold the rest in line. Mercenary armies strengthened the princes. By the same token, they weakened the traditional nobility, not only by establishing forces strong enough to enforce the royal will, but also by creating an employment vacuum for the lesser nobility.[46] There was of course an alternative for impoverished knights in many areas. They could join the king's service. Furthermore, where the king was stronger, banditry was more difficult. But in areas where the prince was weak, his weakness made banditry more profitable and alternative service less available. It is in this sense that banditry implicitly was a demand for a stronger state rather than a flight into "traditional" resistance. It was a form of opposition, in some cases "the greatest force of opposition existing within the kingdom,"[47] but an opposition *within* the framework of the modern state.

It would hence be a serious error to see banditry as a form of traditional feudal opposition to state authority.[48] It was the consequence of the inadequate growth of state authority, the inability of the state to compensate for the dislocations caused by the economic and social turbulence, the unwillingness of the state to ensure some greater equalization of distribution in times of inflation, population growth, and food shortages. Banditry was in this sense created by the state itself, both by depriving some nobles of traditional rights (and hence sources of wealth) and some peasants of their produce to feed the new bureaucracies, and by creating in the state itself a larger concentration of wealth such that it became more tempting to try to seize part of it. Banditry was a symptom of the dislocations caused by the tremendous economic reallocations resulting from the creation of a European world-economy.

Political organisms are always more stable to the extent that they achieve even partial legitimacy. There is much mystification in the analyses of the process of legitimation caused by an almost exclusive look at the relationship of governments and the mass of the population. It is doubtful if very many governments in human history have been considered "legitimate ' by the majority of those exploited, oppressed, and mistreated by their governments. The masses may be resigned to their fate, or sullenly restive, or amazed at their temporary good fortune, or actively insubordinate. But governments tend to be endured, not appreciated or admired or loved or even supported. So it surely was in sixteenth-century Europe.

Legitimation does not concern the masses but the cadres. The question of political stability revolves around the extent to which the small group of managers of the state machinery is able to convince the larger group of central staff and regional potentates both that the regime was formed and functions on the basis of whatever consensual values these cadres can be made to believe exist and that it is in the interest of these cadres that this regime continue to function without major disturbance. When such circumstances obtain, we may call a regime "legitimate."

Legitimacy furthermore is not a once-and-for-all matter. It is a matter of constant compromise. In the sixteenth century, the ideology which arose as a means of legitimating the new authority of the monarchs was the divine right of kings, the system we have come to call absolute monarchy. Since absolutism was an ideology, we must beware of taking its claims at face value. It would be useful to examine therefore exactly what were the claims and how they corresponded to the realities of the social structure.

First, to what extent did "absolute" mean absolute? The theory that there were no human agencies that could, under most circumstances, make any legitimate claim of refusing to implement the proclaimed will of the monarch was not altogether new. However, it did get more widespread exposition and intellectual acceptance in this era than in earlier and later epochs. "Absolute" is a misnomer, however, both as to theory and as to fact. In theory, absolute did not mean unlimited, since as Hartung and Mousnier point out, it was "limited by divine law and natural law." They argue that "absolute" should not be read as "unlimited" but rather as "unsupervised" *(pas contrôlée)*. The monarchy was absolute by opposition to the past feudal scattering of power. "It did not signify despotism and tyranny."[49] Similarly, Maravell says that "in neither the initial nor subsequent phases of the modern state did 'absolute monarchy' mean unlimited monarchy. It was a relative absoluteness."[50] The key operational claim was that the monarch should not be limited by the constraints of law: *ab legibus solutus.*

Whatever the claims, the powers of the monarch were in fact quite limited, not only in theory but in reality. In most ways, the power of the king was far less than that of the executive of a twentieth-century liberal democracy, despite the institutional and moral constraints on the latter. For one thing, the state apparatus of the twentieth century has a degree of organizational capacity behind it that more than compensates for the increased constraints. To understand the real power of an "absolute" monarch, we must put it in the context of the political realities of the time and place. A monarch was absolute to the extent that he had a reasonable probability of prevailing against other forces within the state when policy confrontations occurred.[51] But even the strongest states in the sixteenth century were hard pressed to demonstrate clear predominance within their frontiers of the means of force, or command over the sources of wealth,[52] not to speak of primacy of the loyalty of their subjects.

The rise of the state as a social force, and absolutism as its ideology, should not be confused with the nation and nationalism. The creation of strong states within a world-system was a historical prerequisite to the rise of nationalism both within the strong states and in the periphery. Nationalism is the acceptance of the members of a state as members of a status-group, as citizens, with all the requirements of collective solidarity that implies. Absolutism is the assertion of the prime importance of the survival of the state as such. The former is by definition a mass sentiment; the latter by definition the sentiment of a small group of persons directly interested in the state machinery.

No doubt the proponents of a strong state over time would come to cultivate national sentiment as a solid reinforcement for their objectives. And to some extent they had something to work with in the sixteenth century already.[53] But this collective sentiment was usually primarily geared, to the extent it existed, to the person of the prince rather than to the collectivity as a whole.[54] The absolute monarch was a "heroic" figure,[55] the process of deification getting ever more intense as time went on. This was the era in which the elaborate court ceremonial was developed, the better to remove the monarch from contact with the banal work (and incidentally the better to provide employment for court aristocrats, keeping them thereby close enough to be supervised and checked).

It was only in the late seventeenth and eighteenth centuries within the framework of mercantilism that nationalism would find its first real advocates amongst the bourgeoisie.[56] But in the sixteenth century, the interests of the bourgeoisie were not yet surely fixed on the state. Too large a number were more interested in open than in closed economies. And for state builders, premature nationalism risked its crystallization around too small an ethno-territorial entity. At an early point, statism could almost be said to be antinationalist, since the boundaries of "nationalist" sentiment were often narrower than the bounds of the monarch's state.[57] Only much later would the managers of the state machinery seek to create "integrated" states,[58] in which the dominant ethnic group would "assimilate" the outlying areas.

In the sixteenth century, a few states made substantial progress in centralizing power and achieving acceptance at least partially of the legitimacy of this centralization. It is not too difficult to outline the conditions under which this was likely to occur. Whenever the various cadres, the various groups who controlled resources, felt that their class interests were better served politically by attempting to persuade and influence the monarch than by seeking their political ends in alternative channels of action, then we can talk of a relatively effective monarchical system, a relatively "absolute" state.

"Absolute" conveys the wrong tone, the one of course kings hoped to convey. Absolutism was a rhetorical injunction, not a serious assertion. It might be perhaps wise to de-emphasize the concentration on the person of the king and simply talk of a strengthened state, or more "stateness."[59] We might better call the ideology "statism." Statism is a claim for increased power in the hands of the state machinery. In the sixteenth century, this meant power in the hands of the absolute monarch. It was a claim to power, the claim being part of the attempt to achieve it. Nobody, then or now, took it or should take it as a description of the real world of the time. This claim was validated up to a point in certain states, those that would make up the core of the European world-economy. It failed elsewhere, for reasons we shall elucidate later.

One of the major indications of success as well as one important mechanism in the process of centralizing power was the degree to which the population could be transformed, *by one means or another,* into a culturally homogeneous group. Once again it is less the masses that are relevant than the cadres in the broadest sense: the king, his bureaucracy and courtiers, the rural landowners (large and small), the merchants. In the sixteenth century, while core states are moving toward greater "ethnic" homogeneity among these strata, peripheral areas are moving precisely in the opposite direction.

Let us start by looking at the attitude of the state machinery toward the trader who belonged to a "minority" group. First, there were the Jews, a group which played a large role in trading activities throughout the Middle Ages. One of the things to note is that in both social and economic terms, there was "a steady deterioration of the Jewish status in the late Middle Ages."[60] On the one hand, as England, France, and Spain created stronger centralized structures, they began to expel the Jews: England in 1290, France at the close of the fourteenth century, Spain in 1492. But this phenomenon also occurred in Germany, where, if not expelled, the Jews were in many ways weakened in their role as trading groups. It was Jews who had conducted much of the international trade between western and eastern Europe along the northern transcontinental route between 800–1200 A.D., and were its mainstay.[61] During this period, in both regions, their legal status was reasonably favorable.[62] In the thirteenth and fourteenth century, there is a general decline in both the legal status and the economic role of the Jews *throughout* Europe.[63] However, by the sixteenth century, we can speak of a geographical *imbalance:* their virtually total absence in western Europe but, on the other hand, their presence in *increased* numbers in eastern and parts of southern Europe, that is an absence in the core and an increase in the periphery and semiperiphery.[64]

Although Jews played an ever increasing role in east Europe's economic life, they were permitted only the role of merchant among professions above the status of working-class. For them alone, the classic route of entrepreneur to rentier was impossible.[65] Similarly in northern Italy, as a result of the decline of the financial strength of the city-states, which was due in part to their small size with consequent small tax base and inability to protect their citizens outside the country,[66] the position of the Jews began to improve somewhat, once again playing principally the role of merchants.[67] The Jewish issue, as it presented itself to rulers, was a dilemma of "fiscalism" versus nascent "mercantilism." On the one hand, these Jewish merchants were an important source of state revenue; on the other hand, non-Jewish merchants saw them as competitors and landowners as creditors, both groups often combining in pressure on the ruler to eliminate the Jews. The former consideration prevailed at first, as often as the kings were in a position to arrange it.[68] As the indigenous bourgeoisie grew stronger in the core states, intolerance to Jews made substantial legal progress.

The Jews were an easy target for their competitors because an ideological cause could be made of them. One could argue against their economic role on religious grounds. One way monarchs handled this in western Europe was to expel the Jews, but substitute another group which was less vulnerable on religious grounds although, from the point of view of the indigenous merchants, an equal competitor. For example, P. Elman describes how, when the English monarch was finally forced to expel the Jews in 1290, he welcomed Italian moneylenders in their place. Since the king often did not repay loans, "for practical purposes, the Italian loans may not have differed greatly from Jewish tallages."[69] Still, by the sixteenth century, the Italians were ousted from their role as entrepreneurs inside England,[70] if not in Spain,[71] but the Jews were ousting Poles in Poland.[72] How was this possible?

In western Europe, the increasingly diversified agricultural base along with the nascent industries strengthened the commercial bourgeoisie to the point where the king was obliged to take them politically into account. The other side of it was that they were able to serve as fiscal underpinning of the monarchy—as taxpayer, moneylender, and commercial partner—as well, if not better than foreign merchants. The "nationalist" reflex was thus natural.[73] In eastern Europe, however, the issue presented itself very differently. The monarchs were weaker, the merchants weaker, the agricultural producers stronger. The issue in eastern Europe in the sixteenth century, as in all other parts of the capitalist world system who came increasingly to specialize in the production of cash crops, was not the existence or nonexistence of a commercial bourgeoisie. If there is a money economy, there must be people to serve as funnels for the complex exchange of goods and services which the use of money encourages. The issue was whether this commercial bourgeoisie was to be largely foreign or largely indigenous. If it were indigenous, it added an additional important factor in internal politics. If it were foreign, their interests were linked primarily to those of the emerging poles of development, what in time would be called metropoles.

Was not a critical reason for the "welcome" given to the Jews in eastern Europe in the sixteenth century the fact that the indigenous landowners (and perhaps also merchants in western Europe) preferred to have Jews as the indispensable local merchants in eastern Europe rather than an indigenous commercial bourgeoisie?[74] The latter, if it gained strength, would have a political base (totally absent for Jews) and might have sought to become a manufacturing bourgeoisie. The route they would doubtless have chosen would have involved reducing the "openness" of the national economy, which would threaten the symbiotic interests of the east European landowner–merchant. While we know that the early modern period was a time of *decline* for the indigenous bourgeoisie in eastern Europe,[75] "in the countryside, on the other hand, Jews played an increasing role as both the agents of the landlords and the traders and craftsmen in the small hamlets."[76] This illustrates a more general phenomenon of a world-economy. The class alliances *within* the political system of the state are a function of whether the ruling group is dominated primarily by those persons whose interest is tied to sale of primary products on a world market or by those whose interests are in commercial–industrial profits.

It is not the Jews alone who were the plaything of these transnational politico–economic alliances. Merchants in Catholic countries were often

"Protestants." The central pan-European ideological controversy of the sixteenth and seventeenth centuries—Reformation versus Counter-Reformation—was inextricably intertwined with the creation both of the strong states and of the capitalist system. It is no accident that those parts of Europe which were re-agrarianized in the sixteenth century were also those parts of Europe in which the Counter-Reformation triumphed, while, for the most part, the industrializing countries remained Protestant. Germany, France, and "Belgium" were somewhere "in between," the long-term result being an ideological compromise. Germany divided between Protestants and Catholics. France and "Belgium" came to have few "Protestants" but developed an anticlerical, free-thinking tradition to which certain groups could adhere.

This is no accident, not because, following Weber, we think Protestant theology is somehow more consonant with capitalism than Catholic theology. No doubt one can make a case for this argument. On the other hand, it seems to be true in general that any complex system of ideas can be manipulated to serve any particular social or political objective. Surely Catholic theology, too, has proved its capacity to be adaptable to its social milieu. There is little reason at the abstract level of ideas why one couldn't have written a plausible book entitled "The Catholic Ethic and the Rise of Capitalism." And Calvinist theology could be taken to have anticapitalist implications.[77] The point I am making is a different one. By a series of intellectually accidental[78] historical developments, Protestantism became identified to a large extent in the period of the Reformation with the forces favoring the expansion of commercial capitalism within the framework of strong national states, and with the countries in which these forces were dominant. Thus when such forces lost out in Poland, or Spain, or "Italy," or Hungary, Protestantism declined too and often rapidly. The factors which favored the expansion of export agriculture favored the reassertion of Catholicism.

One must look at the Reformation as it developed. As Christopher Hill notes:

> The Church had long been a source of power, patronage and wealth to rulers of major powers like France and Spain. Those governments which broke with Rome in the early sixteenth century were on the fringes of catholic civilization, secondary powers whose rulers had not been strong enough to drive so hard a bargain with the Papacy—like England, Sweden, Denmark, Switzerland, Scotland.[79]

There was clearly at this point an element of the chafing of northern Europe against the economic weight of the more "advanced" Christian Mediterranean world.[80] But as we know, by the end of the extended sixteenth century, northwest Europe had become the core of the world-economy, eastern Europe the periphery, and southern Europe slipping fast in that direction.

P. C. Gordon-Walker seeks to tie the evolution of Protestantism—first
Luther, then Calvin—to the two phases of the Price Revolution:
1520–1540/50—mild and limited to Germany and the Netherlands (Central
European silver production); 1545 on for about a century (American silver).
He argues that the paired phases are further linked to the successive struc-
tural needs of the new capitalist system:

> The social problem, presented by the Price Revolution, was really a problem with
> two parts. The first need was primary accumulation. . . . The second, subsequent,
> and really basic need was the acclimitisation of the classes of capitalist society into
> the new positions made necessary by the resources of primitive accumulation. . . .
>   These two phases controlled the importance of various parts of Europe. From
> 1520–40 the leading areas were Spain (which inherited no strong middle class
> from the Middle Ages)[81] and Germany (which had a strong feudal bourgeoisie).
> From 1545–80, both Spain and Germany fell away, and the lead was taken by
> England, the Netherlands, and parts of France and Scotland. The parallelism
> between these areas and the areas of the Reformation is striking; as also the parallel
> in time between the first phase of the Price Revolution and Luther (both about
> 1520–40); and between the second phase and Calvin (both about 1545–80).[82]

One does not have to accept all the historical details to see that it is a
relevant hypothesis.

What is more, we have further evidence on the close tie of religious
and politico–economic conjunctures when we turn to the triumph of the
Counter-Reformation in Poland. Stefan Czarnowski makes a careful analysis
of why Poland shifted *back* to Catholicism from a Reformation that seemed
to be gaining ground, and why it shifted with great rapidity. He notes
a synchronization between the moment when the landed nobility *(noblesse
territoriale)* took over political power in what he terms a "class dictatorship"
and the moment of the Catholic offensive. In his analysis, he distinguishes
between the aristocracy, the landed nobility, and the lesser *(petite)* nobility.
He argues that it was in the ranks of the aristocracy (as well as the bourgeoisie) that the partisans of the Reformation were located. He sees the
aristocracy as lusting after Church lands. The smaller landowners found
it more difficult to fight the local curate, supported as he was by the still
powerful Catholic episcopacy. So there was less advantage to them in
embracing Protestantism and, hence they tended not to do so. Czarnowski
and others point out that in Poland while it was the seigniors who favored
Calvinism, the king and the bourgeoisie were inclined to Lutheranism.[83]
This is quite a twist on the Weberian theme, but reminds us of the argument
of Erik Molnar who saw an alliance of the monarchy, lesser nobility, and
bourgeoisie against the aristocracy. Czarnowski further argues that the
"bourgeoisie" was in this case split. The "upper bourgeoisie" of the towns,
especially of Cracow (an "old" commercial center), was allied to the aristocracy. He is speaking here of the town patriciate, those who from the
end of the fifteenth century to about the middle of the sixteenth century

"were part of that class of money-handlers and merchants which came into existence with the rise of nascent capitalism."[84] But Poland was not destined to take the path of England as a locus of the bourgeoisie of the European world-economy. The great crisis of 1557, of which we shall speak later, ruined not only financiers in Lyon, in Antwerp, in southern Germany, but the bankers of Cracow as well:

> [From] that moment on, the elan of the aristocracy and of Calvinism was weakened.
> . . . The goods which allowed the great commercialism of previous times to flourish:
> the silver of Olkusz, Hungarian copper, industrial products, continuously declined
> in value. The money with which the peasants paid their rent depreciated with
> a despairing rapidity. Meanwhile the international demand for Polish wheat, potas-
> sium, oak bark, skins, and horned beasts grew greater. The more that the producer
> of these latter goods could do without coins, use forced unpaid labor of serfs,
> and barter his products against those he needed, the better he resisted [the effects
> of the financial crisis]. This was precisely what the small and medium-sized land-
> owners/nobility were able to do.[85]

This did not mean, notes Czarnowski, that there was no bourgeoisie in Poland. The Cracovian bourgeoisie may have been ruined, but they were replaced by Italians, Armenians, and Germans. In 1557, one international network fell and the Polish bourgeoisie–aristocracy who were tied into it fell with it. After that, another came into existence. The Poles who worked with it—the "nobility"—accepted Poland's new role in the world-economy. They gave their children to the Jesuits to educate, to keep them out of the influence of the old aristocracy: "Thus the Church of Poland ended by being, one might say, the religious expression of the nobility."[86] And this nobility now triumphant could define Polish "national" sentiment as virtually indistinguishable from Catholic piety.

Thus it was that Poland became securely Catholic because she became definitively a peripheral area in the world-economy. The Counter-Reformation symbolized (not caused) the "social regression" that Protestants viewed it as being. But their pious shock was misplaced. For the social advance of northwestern Europe was made possible by the "regression" of eastern and southern Europe as well, of course, as by the domination of the Americas. The Counter-Reformation was directed not merely at Protestantism but at all the various forces of humanism we associate with the Renaissance. This is illustrated by the tensions between Venice and Rome in the sixteenth century. The controversy culminated in 1605 when Venetian actions in limiting certain rights of the Church led to an excommunication by Rome of the Venetian Senate. The Counter-Reformation was in Italy a Counter-Renaissance,[87] and its triumph there was a function of the transformation of northern Italy into a semiperipheral arena of the world-economy.

It is because the Church as a *transnational* institution was threatened by the emergence of an equally transnational economic system which found its *political* strength in the creation of strong *state* machineries of certain (core) states, a development which threatened the Church's position in these states, that it threw itself wholeheartedly into the opposition of modernity. But paradoxically, it was its very success in the peripheral countries that ensured the long-run success of the European world-economy. The ultimate abatement of the passions of the battle of the Reformation after 1648 may not have been because both sides were exhausted and there was a stalemate, but rather because the geographical division of Europe was the natural fulfilment of the underlying thrusts of the world-economy. As to the role of the Protestant ethic, I agree with C. H. Wilson:

> If Protestantism and the Protestant ethic seem to explain less of economic phenomena than they seemed at one time to do, it also appears there is, in the Reformation era, less to be explained. . . . Leadership in economic matters passed slowly from the Mediterranean to the north, and as the Italian cities declined, those of the Netherlands rose; but there was little in the way of business or industrial technique in use in northern economies that would have been unfamiliar to a Venetian merchant or a Florentine clothier of the fifteenth century.[88]

In the sixteenth century, some monarchs achieved great strength by means of venal bureaucracies, mercenary armies, the divine right of kings and religious uniformity *(cuius regio)*. Others failed. This is closely related, as we have suggested, to the role of the area in the division of labor within the world-economy. The different roles led to different class structures which led to different politics. This brings us to the classic question of the role of the state vis-à-vis the leading classes of the new capitalist era, the capitalist landlords and the capitalist merchants, sometimes not too helpfully abbreviated as aristocracy and bourgeoisie, since some aristocrats were capitalists and others not. Unfortunately, what role the state played, whose agent it was, the degree to which it could be thought to be a third force all are questions upon which no consensus exists. Pierre Vilar has well stated the basic underlying theoretical issue:

> A question of particular relevance is how feudal revenues were divided, by means of a system of "adjudications" and in other ways, between an idle aristocracy and an intermediary class of "merchant-cultivators" or similar types who transformed seigniorial revenues and held them ready for new types of investment; in other words how feudal revenues came to be mobilized for capitalist investment.[89]

One aspect of this is the degree to which the absolute state should be seen to be the last resort of a feudal aristocracy facing the "crisis" of feudalism, the reduction of seigniorial revenues, and the onslaught of other classes (the commercial bourgeoisie, the yeoman farmers, the agricultural laborers). One view is that of Takahashi, who sees absolutism as "nothing but a system of concentrated force for counteracting the crisis of feudalism arising out of this inevitable development [in the direction of the

liberation and the independence of the peasants].”[90] This view is substantially shared by Christopher Hill,[91] V. G. Kiernan,[92] Erik Molnar,[93]
and Boris Porchnev.[94]

A second point of view argues that the politics of the absolute monarchy
is one upon which the aristocracy had a considerable, perhaps determining,
influence, but one in which the monarch was more than a simple extension
of the needs of this aristocracy. For example, Joseph Schumpeter argues:

> Thus the aristocracy [under the absolute monarchs] as a whole was still a powerful
> factor that had to be taken into account. Its submission to the crown was more
> in the nature of a settlement than a surrender. It resembled an election—a com-
> pulsory one, to be sure, of the king as the leader and executive organ of the no-
> bility. . . .
>
> The reason [the nobles did not resist, even passively, the regime] was, in essence,
> because the king did what they wanted and placed the domestic resources of the
> state at their disposal. . . . It was a class rather than an individual that was actually
> master of the state.[95]

Braudel similarly insists that the conflict of king and aristocracy was a
limited one, which included an effort by the king, on the one hand, to
bring the nobility under his discipline, but, on the other hand, to protect
its privileges against popular pressure.[96] The position of A. D. Lublinskaya
seems very close to Braudel.[97] J. Hurstfield emphasizes the dilemma of
the monarchies which “found it hard to rule without the nobility; but
they found it equally difficult to rule with them.”[98]

A third point of view, perhaps the most traditional one, is that of Roland
Mousnier, in which the monarchy is viewed as an autonomous force, often
allied with the bourgeoisie against the aristocracy, occasionally mediating
the two.[99]

But is there a necessary conjuncture of these two propositions, that
of the relatively autonomous role of the state machinery and that of seeing
the class struggle as one between aristocracy and bourgeoisie? Molnar does
not seem to think so. In the first place, he uses more categories. He talks
of a feudal aristocracy to whom the monarch was in clear opposition. In
addition, there was a “nobility” and a bourgeoisie, both potential allies.
The nobility seems to be smaller landowners and those more oriented
to capitalist agriculture, but it is not entirely clear. He points out that
while absolutism seemed to involve heavy taxation upon the peasantry,
it is less clear how the money was distributed. On the one hand, the increased
state budget was used to pay the tax collectors and the bureaucracy, pay
off the state loans, and purchase military equipment, all of which benefited
the bourgeoisie. But on the other hand, all the current expenses of the
state—that is, the maintenance of court and army—were payments to the
nobility. He sees this as a tactic of “maneuvering . . . between the nobility
and the bourgeoisie.”[100] Engels similarly points to the ways in which the

state machinery comes to play, in some ways against its inner will, a mediating function, at least during "exceptional periods."[101]

One source of this unclarity about the relationship of monarch and aristocracy is the vagueness that exists about the composition of the nobility. No doubt family membership in the nobility varies over time; the situation is one of perpetual mobility in all societies with a nobility. But the sixteenth century was an era in which there was not only family mobility but occupational mobility. For example, the status of noble was presumably incompatible in Western feudalism with the occupation of entrepreneur. This was probably already a myth to a considerable extent in the municipalities of the late Middle Ages. By the sixteenth century, this was simply untrue in the whole of Europe, and in both urban and rural areas. Everywhere—in Italy, Hungary, Poland, East Elbia, Sweden, England—members of the nobility had become entrepreneurs.[102] This was so much the case that the nobility successfully sought to eliminate any formal impediments to this occupational role wherever it existed, as happened in Spain.[103] Nor should we forget that, although in Protestant countries the Church was seeing its lands confiscated, the sixteenth century was an era of the Church as a capitalist agricultural entrepreneur, especially in Italy.[104]

The other side of this coin was that the successful bourgeois was constantly becoming a landowner and a noble, and thirty years later, it surely became difficult to draw clear lines separating the two. R. H. Tawney sees it as a normal process which was however much accelerated in the sixteenth century.[105] Both Braudel[106] and Postan[107] agree with the perception of a continuing pattern of transition from entrepreneur to rentier for those of non-noble status and see in it a search for long-run security. What is crucial, however, is to appreciate that despite this occupational mobility, the strength of the landowning class did not disintegrate. As Marc Bloch put it: "The seigniorial regime had not been undermined. Indeed it would soon take on a renewed vigor. Rather seigniorial property, to a large extent, changed hands."[108] It was the absolutism of the monarch which created the stability that permitted this large-scale shift of personnel and occupation without at the same time, at least at this point in time, undoing the basic hierarchical division of status and reward.

What then of the presumed key role of the state in assisting the commercial bourgeoisie to assert itself, to obtain its profits and keep them? The liaison was surely there, but it was a question of degree and timing, the mutual support of the early liaison developing into the stifling control of later years. It is no accident that the symbiotic relationship of merchant and king would come in the seventeenth and eighteenth centuries to seem one of direct opposition. Hartung and Mousnier see signs of this tension already in the sixteenth century.[109] Douglass C. North and Robert Paul Thomas, in seeking to outline the rise of various judicial and economic institutions which had the effect of encouraging entrepreneurial activity based on rising productivity as opposed to forms of commerce which merely redistributed income,[110] try to elucidate the conditions under which it made sense to have emphasized the institutional role of the state. They argue that alongside the economic distortions that state intervention brings to the market and hence to the likelihood of innovation, one must place the fact of "coercive power which permits government to undertake policies even though they may be strongly objected to by a part of the society."[111] This way of formulating the issue alerts us to seeing the functions of statism for capitalism in terms of a cost-benefit analysis. Whereas for the aristocracy the absolute monarchy represented a sort of last-ditch defense of privilege, for those deriving their income through the maximization of the economic efficiency of the firm the state machinery was sometimes extremely useful,[112] sometimes a major impediment.

We have now outlined the two main constituent elements of the modern world-system. On the one hand, the capitalist world-economy was built on a worldwide division of labor in which various zones of this economy (that which we have termed the core, the semiperiphery, and the periphery) were assigned specific economic roles, developed different class structures, used consequently different modes of labor control, and profited unequally from the workings of the system. On the other hand, political action occurred primarily within the framework of states which, as a consequence of their different roles in the world-economy were structured differently, the core states being the most centralized. We shall now review the entire sixteenth century in terms of a process, one in which certain areas *became* peripheral or semiperipheral or the core of this world-economy. We shall thereby try to give flesh and blood to what has risked thus far being abstract analysis. We shall also hopefully thereby demonstrate the unity of the whole *process.* The developments were not accidental but, rather, within a certain range of possible variation, structurally determined.

4

FROM SEVILLE TO AMSTERDAM:
THE FAILURE OF EMPIRE

Figure 5: "Massacre of the Innocents," oil painting by Pieter Brueghel, the Elder. It was painted about 1565 as a protest against Spanish atrocities in the Netherlands.

The European world-economy in creation was a great prize, and it is understandable that men should seek to control it. The route of imperial domination was the classical route, familiar to the men of the era. Many dreamed of the possibility. The Hapsburgs under Charles V made a valiant attempt to absorb all of Europe into itself. By 1557, the attempt had failed. And Spain steadily lost not only its political imperium but its economic centrality as well. Many cities aspired to be the hub of the European world-economy. Seville, Lisbon, Antwerp, Lyon, Genoa, and Hamburg all had aspirations if not claims. But in fact it would be Amsterdam, an unlikely candidate in 1450, which by 1600 had achieved preeminence. We turn now to this story of the failure of empire, entailing the decline of Spain and all of her allied city-states in favor of the successful rebels of Amsterdam.

The upward economic swing beginning circa 1450 created a buzzing prosperity first of all in all the old centers of trade, in what has been called the dorsal spine of Europe—Flanders, southern Germany, northern Italy—and, of course, as a result of the discoveries, Spain. It is striking how precisely these areas came to make up the Hapsburg empire under Charles V. In this expansion, the newest significant element was the sixteenth-century transatlantic trade of Spain, centering on Seville and her *Casa de Contratación de las Indias,* a trade which became so important that "all of European life and the life of the entire world, to the degree that there existed a world, could be said to have depended [on this traffic]. Seville and her accounts . . . should tell us the rhythm of the world."[1]

How did Spain come to play such a central role? After all, as we discussed in Chapter One, it was Portugal, not Spain, which took the lead in the fifteenth century overseas expansion of Europe. Furthermore, the fifteenth century was not a tranquil era in the history of Spain. Indeed, Jaime Vicens Vives says that "the word crisis sums up the history of Spain in the fifteenth century."[2]

The crisis was political (a period of rebellion and of internal warfare) and economic (the Europe-wide recession). Spain's reaction to the crisis in economic terms was to develop her sheep industry and to gain, as a result of low prices, a considerable share of the (reduced) world market.[3] The strength of the combine of wool producers in Spain, the *Mesta,* was such that attempts by potential Castilian bourgeois to have the king adopt protectionist policies in the fourteenth and fifteenth centuries all failed.[4] Even under the Catholic Monarchs, Ferdinand and Isabella, presumed partisans of industrial activity, Vicens finds that the industries mentioned produced "either luxury items or had only a local market."[5] Unlike England, Spain was not moving toward developing an important textile industry.[6] Ironically, it may have been the very fact of Castilian competition,

115

combined with the depression of the late Middle Ages, that encouraged England to move on the road to industrial growth. The fact was, however, that Spain did not take this road.

But then, if the Spanish economy was structurally so weak, how do we explain the central *economic* position of Spain in the first half of the sixteenth century? Partly because the weaknesses were long-term, not short run, and partly because at some levels the political system was strong. Castile had a clear "national" task throughout the Middle Ages. On the one hand, there was the *Reconquista,* the gradual expulsion of the Moors from the Iberian peninsula, which culminated in the fall of Moslem Granada and the expulsion of the Jews from Spain, both in 1492, the year of Columbus. On the other hand, there was the drive to unify the Christian states of Hispania. This drive culminated in the union at the summit only, Aragon retaining a separate legislature, state budget, and socio–legal system.

Because Spain was built on a reconquest, feudalism as a *political* form was weak.[7] Consequently, as José Maravell states it, "having a political and social order which was not based on the feudal structure provided favorable terrain for the development of 'state' forms."[8] A first-rate road system made political and economic liaison of the center and the periphery relatively easy.[9] Ferdinand and Isabella aided the *Mesta* to create a strong system of *national* markets.[10] They provided a system of individual mobility, albeit within a context of maintaining the values of rank and hierarchy.[11] They strengthened the bureaucracy, making of it one that was "rooted in the community . . . of which it is . . . 'pars rei publicae.' "[12] They nationalized, so to speak, the Catholic clergy.[13] Above all, they created "conditions in which Castile's existing economic potential could be amply realized."[14]

If the bullion flowed through Spain, if Castile could soar into the center of the European sky, it was, says Pierre Vilar, "consequence as well as cause."[15] But consequence of exactly what? Of in fact a long series of facts centering around the economic role of metals: the weak bullion base of the Mediterranean world, the previous centrality of the Sudan as supplier of gold, the impact of Portuguese expansion on the northern African intermediaries of the Italian city-states, the role of the Genoese in Spain, and the Genoese drive to find a non-Portuguese source of bullion (a drive which only Spain was in a position to implement).

Let us trace this complex story. We have already spoken of the role of bullion in medieval trade, and how Sudanic gold came to Europe via North Africa to the Christian Mediterranean world. Suddenly in the middle of the fifteenth century, the North African role diminished greatly. The extent of this diminution seems to be a matter of some debate. Braudel speaks of a collapse of the North African position.[16] Malowist acknowledges reduction but calls it not catastrophic.[17] The sudden shortage of bullion aggravated the Spanish state's financial burden, which had been rising steadily because of growing military and court expenses, by leading to a fall of value in the money of account, the *maravedi*.[18]

The financial crisis was serious, and it caused the Genoese of Spain to react, both because they were Spain's bankers and the purchasers of the gold. We have already spoken of Genoa's role in Spanish commerce. The Genoese were involved in many ways, not only as financiers.[19] But why could not the Genoese have gotten their gold via Portugal? Perhaps Portugal's strength, as the lead country in exploration, meant that its terms were not as advantageous for Genoa as those Spain would offer.[20] Perhaps also because its very strength led to a lack of imagination. Imagination is usually nothing but the search for middle run profits by those to whom short run channels are blocked. When channels are not blocked, imagination suffers. Portugal was already doing well enough with navigation down the African coast. It felt no pressure to set out on risky westward navigational ventures.[21] Chaunu eloquently argues the sensible proposition that it was not luck that accounts for Spain's discovery of America. She was the country best endowed in the context of the times "not only to seize opportunities that were offered, but to create them for herself."[22] England employed the Italian, John Cabot, but his second "English" expedition required *Spanish* support. It was not until the seventeenth century that France and England became countries of overseas exploration and not until the eighteenth that they really succeeded.[23]

Spain succeeded, however, in the sixteenth century in creating a vast empire in the Americas, one as large as the cost of maritime transport would permit.[24] It meant a lightning growth of transatlantic trade, the volume increasing eightfold between 1510 and 1550, and threefold again between 1550 and 1610.[25] The central focus of this trade was a state monopoly in Seville, which in many ways became the key bureaucratic structure of Spain.[26] The central item in the transatlantic trade was bullion. At first the Spaniards simply picked up the gold already mined by the Incas and used for ritual.[27] It was a bonanza. Just as this was running out, the Spaniards succeeded in discovering the method of silver amalgam which enabled them profitably to mine the silver which existed in such abundance, and which represented the truly significant inflow of bullion to Europe.[28]

The "lightning growth" of trade was accompanied by a spectacular political expansion in Europe as well. Upon the coronation of Charles V as Holy Roman Emperor in 1519, his domain in Europe included such varied and noncontiguous areas as Spain (including Aragon), the Netherlands, various parts of southern Germany (including Austria), Bohemia, Hungary, Franche-Comté, Milan, and Spain's Mediterranean possessions (Naples, Sicily, Sardinia, the Balaerics). For a moment, this empire, parallel in structure to the contemporaneous Ottoman Empire of Suleiman the Magnificent

and the Moscovite Empire of Ivan the Terrible, seemed to be absorbing
the political space of Europe. The nascent world-economy seemed as though
it might become another imperium. Charles V was not alone in the attempt
to absorb the European world-economy into his imperium. Francis I of
France was trying to do the same thing,[29] and France had the advantages
of size and centrality.[30] But France had less resources for the attempt,
and the election of Charles V over Francis I as Emperor was a great setback.
Nonetheless France, located "in the heart"[31] of the Spanish Empire, was
strong enough to make the story of the following 50 years one of virtual
constant warfare between the two imperial giants, Hapsburg and Valois,
a struggle that would result eventually in the exhaustion of both in 1557,
and the end for a long while of dreams of imperium in Europe.

The long struggle of the two giants, France and Spain, was fought
out in military terms principally on the Italian peninsula, first in the Franco-
Spanish wars of 1494–1516, and then in the Hapsburg–Valois rivalry
that continued until 1559.[32] The reason for the struggle over Italy, from
the viewpoint of the empires, was clear. The northern Italian city-states
had been in the late Middle Ages the centers of the most "advanced"
economic activities, industrial, and commercial, on the European continent.
If they no longer monopolized long-distance trade they were still strong
in their accumulated capital and experience,[33] and an aspiring world-empire
needed to secure control over them. In the scattered political map of Italy,[34]
only Lombardy had developed a relatively strong state machinery over
a medium-sized area,[35] but one apparently still too small to survive
politically.[36]

We are in fact speaking of a relatively small area, "a narrow urban quad-
rilateral, Venice, Milan, Genoa, Florence, with their discordances, their
multiple rivalries, each city having a somewhat different weight. . . ."[37]
The political problem for these city-states (as for those of Flanders) had
long been to "[emancipate] themselves from feudal interference and [at
the same time to keep] at bay the newer threat of more centralized political
control offered by the new monarchies."[38] One of the ways they kept the
monarchies at bay was to be linked to an empire.[39] So although Gino Luzzatto
describes what happened between 1530 and 1539 as Italy coming under
the "domination direct or indirect of Spain over the largest part of the
peninsula,"[40] and Paul Coles similarly says that "the dominant theme of
international history in the first half of the sixteenth century was the struggle
for Italy between French and Spanish imperialism,"[41] it is not clear that
the city-states resisted this form of "domination" all that much. They may
well have considered it their best alternative. We should remember that
this was a world-economy and that the economic loci of activities and the
"nationalities" of key economic groups were not related in any one to
one fashion with the foci of political decision-making. Within such a
framework, the linkup of the city-states and the empire was primarily

a "marriage of interests."[42] Whereupon metaphor became reality. Ruth Pike points out that the greatest increase of Genoese in Seville occurs between 1503 and 1530 and that by the middle of the century they "largely controlled the American trade and exerted a powerful influence over the economic life of Seville."[43] However, as the Portuguese had done to an earlier wave of Genoese, the Spaniards dissolved them by absorption: "With naturalization came stability and assimilation, which in sixteenth-century Spain could only lead to the abandonment of trade by their descendants."[44]

In addition to controlling three of the four main Italian city-states (Venice remained outside its dominion), the empire of Charles V had two other economic pillars: the merchant-banking houses of southern Germany (in particular the Fuggers), and the great mart of the European world-economy of the "first" sixteenth century, Antwerp.

The situation of the merchant cities of southern Germany, on the other side of the Alps, was not really too different from those in northern Italy. R. S. Lopez, for example, notes that: "In the fifteenth century, the most rapidly advancing region lay in the towns of Southern Germany and Switzerland."[45] From 1460 to about 1500 or 1510 silver mining grew at a very rapid rate in central Europe, providing a further source of economic strength.[46] The sixteenth-century expansion of trade only seemed to reinforce the German role as a conduit of trade between northern Italy and Flanders.[47] At first not even the growth of Atlantic trade and the relative decline of Mediterranean trade seemed to affect their economic prosperity, especially once they were able to participate in the benefits of the Atlantic trade within the framework of the Hapsburg Empire.[48]

This was the era of the flourishing of those most spectacular of all modern merchant-capitalists, the Fuggers. The apogee of their strength, the era of Charles V, has sometimes been called the Age of the Fuggers. The Fuggers bought Charles' imperial throne for him.[49] They were the financial kingpins of his empire, his personal bankers par excellence. A contemporary chronicler, Clemens Sender, said of them:

> The names of Jakob Fugger and his nephews are known in all kingdoms and lands; yea, among the heathen, also. Emperors, Kings, Princes and Lords have sent to treat with him, the Pope has greeted him as his well beloved son and embraced him, and the Cardinals have risen up before him. All the merchants of the world have called him an enlightened man, and all the heathen have wondered because of him. He is the glory of all Germany.[50]

The Fuggers and Charles gave each other their power and their base. But this also meant that they rose and fell together. For, in reality, the activity of the Fuggers was "limited to the confines of the Empire of Charles, and was international only to the extent . . . that empire can be regarded as international. . . ."[51] When Charles and his successors could not pay, the Fuggers could not earn. In the end, the total loss of the Fuggers in unpaid debts of the Hapsburgs up to the middle of the seventeenth century "is certainly not put too high at 8 million Rhenish gulden."[52]

But even more important than northern Italy or the Fuggers was Antwerp, which "played in the economic life of the sixteenth century a leading role."[53] J. A. van Houtte has traced the great difference between Bruges in the fourteenth century, a "national" market center (that is, primarily for Flanders) and Antwerp in the sixteenth century, an "international" market center, which linked the Mediterranean and Baltic trades with the transcontinental trade via southern Germany.[54] Not only did Antwerp coordinate much of the international trade of the Hapsburg Empire, but it was also the linchpin by which both England and Portugal were tied into the European world-economy.[55] It served among other things as England's staple.[56] If it was able to play this role despite the fact that Anglo–Italian trade, for example, would have been less expensive in transport costs had it transited via Hamburg, this was precisely because it offered the multiple side advantages to merchants that only such an imperial mart had available.[57]

In addition, at this time, Antwerp became the supreme money market in Europe, "caused mainly by the increasing demand for short-term credit, chiefly occasioned by the Emperor Charles V's world policy. . . ."[58] Antwerp not only served as the securities exchange of the empire; the city itself as a collectivity became one of Charles's chief moneylenders.[59] Since empires had no firm tax base, they found it difficult to obtain the kind of credit modern states manufacture with relative ease. A sixteenth-century empire had credit to the extent that its sovereign did.[60] Thus he had to turn to the cities as "centers of public wealth"[61] to guarantee his loans. But cities too were limited in credit, and they in turn needed the guarantee of some large house such as the Fugger, as this account by Lonchay illustrates:

> The credit of the towns, as that of the provinces, as those of the receivers, was limited. That is why some financiers demanded the guarantee of a solvent commercial house, preferably that of a large bank, before agreeing to a loan to the government. Thus, in 1555, the merchants asked as a guarantee for a loan of 200,000 pounds letters of obligation from the states or the "responson" of the Fugger. Maria of Hungary asked Ortel, the factor of that house to give his approval and promised to give him in exchange a counter-guarantee of income from taxes (*le produit des aides*).[62]

Thus Charles V, Castile, Antwerp, the Fuggers were all imbricated in a huge creation of credit laid upon credit, cards built upon cards, the lure of profits based on hope and optimism.

From the 1530s on, the growing trans-Atlantic trade gave Antwerp a new phase of expansion.[63] The combination of the two foci of commercial expansion—the transcontinental trade in which southern German merchants were so central and the Atlantic trade of the Spanish (*cum* Genoese), both coming together in the Antwerp market which was also a money market created the atmosphere of "a feverish capitalistic boom."[64] This boom had its own dynamic which overwhelmed the politico-administrative framework of the Hapsburg putative world-empire. Beset by the incredible financial strains caused on the one hand by the social crisis that was raging in the Germanies and the military expenditures resulting from the desire to encompass the rest of Europe, either the empire had to go bankrupt or the capitalist forces. The latter turned out to be stronger. Let us review the two strains under which the empire operated.

In political terms, the years 1450–1500 were a time of "consolidation of the principalities" of Germany, a difficult task but one which succeeded in part. Geoffrey Barraclough writes: "The princes . . . raised Germany out of its inherited anarchy. . . ."[65] The consolidation was however too partial. When the Reformation and the Peasants' War of 1525 came along to perturb the new prosperity, the political divisions made it impossible to contain the turmoil, as other countries could do at this time.[66] The failure of the German "nation" has been variously explained. Napoleon once said that it was the failure of Charles V to put himself as the head of German Protestantism.[67] Engels has argued at length that it was the fear of Luther and the middle class of the revolutionary aspirations of the peasantry.[68] Tawney has pointed out the contrast with England where the peasants (that is, the yeomen) found significant allies among other classes and were considered sufficiently important "to make them an object of solicitude to statesmen who were concerned with national interests."[69]

What caused the social crisis with its politically self-defeating qualities, not too different in consequences from the outright subjection which large parts of Italy suffered? Probably the same factor: lack of *prior* political unity, that is, the absence of even an embryonic state machinery. "Germany" in the early sixteenth century is an excellent illustration of how deeply divisive "nationalist" sentiment can be if it precedes rather than grows within the framework of an administrative entity. Charles V could not lead German Protestantism because he was involved in an empire. German statesmen could not take into account the needs of the yeomen within the framework of national interests when no state existed within which to register whatever political compromise might be achieved. Men turned to the political arenas in which they might achieve their ends. These were the principalities and, since these were too small to be economically meaningful, they turned to outside benefactors. The result was floundering and disaster.

The critical moment seems to have been in the early years of Charles V's rule. A. J. P. Taylor argues somewhat dramatically but not unpersuasively:

The first years of Charles V were the moment of Goethe's phrase which, once lost, eternity will never give back. The moment for making a national middle-class Germany was lost in 1521 perhaps forever, certainly for centuries. By 1525, it was evident that the period of national awakening had passed, and there began from that moment a steady advance of absolutism and authoritarianism which continued uninterruptedly for more than 250 years. . . .[70]

In any case, the turmoil went on in a very acute form until the Treaty of Augsburg in 1555 and its solution of a divided Germany, based on *cuius regio eius religio.* Nor was the turmoil to end even then. In the early seventeenth century, Germany became the battleground of the Thirty Years War, and underwent severe regression, both demographically and economically.

The social turmoil of the Germanies was however only one problem for Charles V and not perhaps the greatest. It is surely insufficient to explain the collapse of his empire. Why then did it split apart? Why was it ultimately reduced essentially to Spain plus Hispanic America? And why did this latter Spain lose its preeminence and become part of the semiperiphery of Europe? Pierre Chaunu sees the rise of the economic importance of Hispanic America, its centrality to the economic life of the Hapsburg Empire, and indeed all of Europe, as "not the consequence but the cause of the partition of the states of Charles V."[71] J. H. Elliott and Ramón Carande similarly argue that the European imperialism of Charles V came to be unduly expensive for Spain, especially for Castile.[72] Indeed, Braudel argues that even the reduced empire (Spain and the Netherlands without central Europe) would turn out to be "too vast" in terms of its ability to keep its financial head above water, given the great price inflation.[73] The argument seems to be that the political extremities are a financial burden in moments of inflation that are greater than their value as income, especially perhaps in this early stage of capitalism.[74] Spain was an empire when what was needed in the sixteenth century was a medium-size state. The bureaucracy was inadequate because imperial Spain required a larger one than it could construct given its resources, human and financial. This is the fundamental cause of what historians have called the "slownesses" of the Spanish bureaucracy.[75]

Once again, the structural advantage of the world-economy as a system over a world-empire as a system seems to thrust itself upon us. For example, H. G. Koenigsberger describes Spain's inability to exploit its Sicilian colony, attributing it to an absence of a political theory.[76] This seems to me to invert horse and chariot. Spain had no theory that encouraged her to establish a trade monopoly in Sicily because, bureaucratically, she was already spread too thin to exploit her empire properly. She devoted primary energy to maintaining an empire in the Americas, as well as conducting wars in the Netherlands and governing Hispania. To maintain her empire in America, she had to invest in a growing bureaucracy to keep the Spanish colonists and their allies among the Indian nobility under control.[77]

Could the Spanish empire have worked? Perhaps if it was structured differently. As Koenigsberger says: "Its fundamental weakness was ... the narrowness of its tax base. Castile and the silver financed and defended the empire; the other dominions were, to a greater or lesser degree, onlookers."[78] Ferran Soldevila documents how the Castilians deliberately excluded even such a "close" group as the Catalans from the Hispano–American trade.[79] But if it were structured differently, it would not have been an empire, which is precisely our point. If the Catalans were incorporated into a single state with the Castilians, which they were not, and if Charles V's imperial ambitions had not both drained Castile and drew him into inevitable conflicts of interest with portions of his empire, conflicts that were self-defeating,[80] then Spain might indeed have had some chance of becoming a core state in the European world-economy. Instead, overextension merely exhausted Charles V and his successors.

In 1556 the empire split apart. Charles V abdicated. Philip II of Spain, son of Charles V, received the Netherlands, but the lands in central Europe became a separate realm. In 1557 Philip declared bankruptcy. Within the Spain–Netherlands, the center of political gravity then shifted back to Spain when Philip moved there in 1559. Thereupon came the Netherlands Revolution[81] which ended, some eighty years later after much ado and to and fro, in the division of the area into the northern, Calvinist, independent United Provinces (more or less contemporary Netherlands) and the southern, Catholic, so-called Spanish Netherlands (more or less contemporary Belgium). But this crisis was more than a Spanish crisis, or a Hapsburg imperial crisis. It was a turning point in the evolution of the European world-economy. For a crucial element in this revolution was the peace of Cateau–Cambrésis entered into by Spain and France in 1559. To understand the import of this treaty we first must look at the other aspirant to imperial rule, France.

No country illustrates better than France the dilemmas of western European states in the "first" sixteenth century. On the one hand, probably no European state emerged from the late Middle Ages with a relatively stronger monarchy.[82] We have already reviewed in a previous chapter Bloch's explanations of the differences between France, England, and eastern Europe in terms of the tenure arrangements as they emerged in the sixteenth century, based on the differing dynamics of their juridical structures in the late Middle Ages. While the English system permitted, as we saw, a legal redefinition of tenure to satisfy the new needs of landowners in the fourteenth to sixteenth centuries, these definitions were more frozen in France. Hence the nobility had to be politically more militant to retain their advantages. Thus whereas Bloch rightly points to the "decadence of seignorial justice"[83] in France by the sixteenth century, it is also true, as Rushton Coulbourn points out, that the political strength of the nobility led to an economic structure which was less able to maneuver in the new world-economy.[84]

The consequences of the fact that there was not the relative merger of the nobility and the new merchant-gentry in France as in England were many. For the moment, let us concentrate on its implications for state policy in the world-system. Edward Miller points out that the political strength of trading interests was greater in England than in France. As a consequence, French trade policy was far more open in the late Middle Ages.[85] The end result was that, despite a stronger bureaucracy, France in the early sixteenth century had acquired fewer "powers of economic direction"[86] than England. The pressures of fiscalism in such a situation pushed the French monarch to imperial ambitions, a fortiori because the Hapsburgs also had them. They could have tried overseas expansion as did Spain, but they lacked the backing of international capital, that is northern Italian capital, for that.[87] The alternative was imperial expansion within Europe itself, directed precisely against northern Italy.

France had a competing international network of finance and trade, which centered on Lyon. In the High Middle Ages, the fairs of Champagne were for a while the great meeting point for the merchants of northern Italy and Flanders. They also served as an international financial center. Then in the late thirteenth, early fourteenth centuries, decline set in.[88] In the fifteenth century, the French monarchs carefully nurtured the growth of Lyon[89] and encouraged its links with Florence[90] who were the great bankers of the time.[91] By bringing together enormous amounts of capital in the early sixteenth century, both Lyon and Antwerp "reduced the power of the individual financiers within bearable limits ⌊and thus⌋ made it possible to raise large masses of capital at moderate rates. . . ."[92] Lyon was not quite the international center Antwerp was because the French kings sought simultaneously to make it "their financial arsenal."[93] Nor did Lyon ever match Antwerp as a commercial center. It was in short a second best.

Nonetheless, France tried. The Hapsburg and Valois empires both failed and fell together. Not only Spain but France also declared itself bankrupt in 1557. The Hapsburg however were first as if to emphasize their primacy even in defeat. The two financial failures led very rapidly to the cessation of military fighting and the treaty of Cateau-Cambrésis in 1559, which was to change the political terms of reference of Europe for a hundred years. These bankruptcies thus were more than a financial readjustment. A whole world had come tumbling down.

What tumbled was not merely a particular state structure. It was more than the tragic abdication of Charles V amid the tears of his knights. What tumbled was the world-system. For a hundred years, Europe was enjoying a new prosperity. Men had tried to profit from it in the ways of old. But technological advance and the upsurge of capitalist elements had already progressed too far to make it possible to recreate political empires that would match the economic arenas. The year 1557 marked, if you will, the defeat of that attempt, and the establishment of a balance of power in Europe which would permit states which aimed at being nations (let us call them nation-states) to come into their own and to batten on the still flourishing world-economy.

Crises are symbolic turning points. As many historians have pointed out, many of the organizational features of the "first" sixteenth century do not disappear until much later: 1576, when the Spanish authority collapsed in the Netherlands, or 1588 with the defeat of the Armada, or 1598 with the Peace of Vervins (and the Edict of Nantes). It is not worth debating the most appropriate date, since a shift in organizational emphasis is always gradual, because the underlying structural factors move glacially.

But shift there was, and it is worth our while to spell out the implications this had for the European world-economy. Let us start with R. H. Tawney's description of the organizational emphasis of the "first" sixteenth century:

> In its economic organization the machinery of international trade had reached a state of efficiency not noticeably inferior to that of three centuries later. Before the most highly-organized economic systems of the age were ruined by the struggle between Spain and the Netherlands, and by the French wars of religion, there were perhaps ten to twelve commercial houses whose money-markets were the financial power-houses of European trade, and whose opinion and policy were decisive in determining financial conditions. In the Flemish, French, and Italian cities where it reached its zenith, and of which England was the pupil, the essence of the financial organization of the sixteenth century was internationalism, freedom for every capitalist to undertake every transaction within his means, a unity which had as its symptoms the movement of all the principal markets in sympathy with each other, and as its effect the mobilisation of immense resources at the strategic points of international finance. Its centre and symbol was the exchange at Antwerp, with its significant dedication, "*Ad usum mercatorum cujusque gentis ac linguae,*" where, as Guicciardini said, every language under heaven could be heard, or the fairs at Lyons which formed, in the words of a Venetian, "the foundation of the pecuniary transactions of the whole of Italy and of a good part of Spain and of the Netherlands."[94]

Tawney says that this system collapsed because of ruinous wars. This is true, but the causal sequence is too immediate. We suggested in the last chapter that the efficient cause was the inability to make an imperial system viable given the economic thrusts of sixteenth-century Europe but its structural limitations, that is, the relatively low level of productivity and thinness of bureaucratic framework faced with an expanding economy based on scattered medium-size enterprise.

One crucial bottleneck became the growing financial demands of imperial state machineries and the consequent inflation of public credit which led to the imperial bankruptcies of mid-century. Charles V had run through states and their merchants as sources of finance: Naples, Sicily, Milan, Antwerp, Castile.[95] The classic exposition of this argument was made by Henri Hauser who argued that the European financial crisis of 1559 "probably hindered the evolution of commercial capitalism, and gave the impetus to the transformation of economic geography."[96] Hauser argues that the war between Spain and France that began in 1557 simply stretched the state credits too thin, led to defaults, and forced both states to make a hasty peace at Cateau-Cambrésis in 1559.

The consequences for the extended Hapsburg Empire were great. It led directly to the beginning of Spain's decline.[97] The crisis would lead to a definitive break of Antwerp and England, leaving the latter free to develop its new and winning economic alliance with Amsterdam.[98] In Antwerp itself, the boom which was based on the axis with Spain ended. "The bankruptcy of Philip II of 1557 brought the rupture which finally decided Antwerp's fate."[99]

Throughout Flanders, the crisis would lead to a reinforcement of Calvinist tendencies, especially among the skilled workers. In 1567, the Spanish sent the Duke of Alva to repress the new socio–political unrest but this simply resulted in the long run in an exodus of the Calvinist merchants and craftsmen to Protestant countries,[100] and by 1585 there was a collapse of Flemish industry and commerce, which "were at a standstill for years."[101] The Netherlands revolt, combining social and political unrest consequent on this disaster, created a viable political base in the northern half of the Low Countries for its role as the center of world commerce beginning in the late sixteenth century.[102]

Southern Germany was hard hit too. Luzzatto points out that "the most severe blow came to them from first the insolvency then the bankruptcy of the Spanish crown which swept totally away the personal fortunes not only of the Fuggers but of the larger part of the great merchant-bankers of southern Germany."[103] As the situation worsened economically, the former commercial allies of southern Germany and northern Italy, began to invade each other's territory in competitive search of business, which was a mutually destructive affair.[104]

The political consequences of this collapse for the Germanies were enormous. What Barraclough calls the "revolutionary ferment of Protestantism which, in reaction against the decline of the empire . . ., was strongly national in character"[105] swept Germany. But, as we have already mentioned, Charles V's involvement in his empire meant that he could not invest his political fortunes in German unification, no more than he could take the perspective of a Spanish nationalist. The compromise of *cuius regio* entrenched the German principalities, undermined the German bourgeoisie, and put off all hope of unification for centuries. Germany would come to be largely divided into a Lutheran north and northeast, the latter at least economically part of the eastern European periphery, and a wealthier, Catholic southwest (including parts of the Rhine country). As A. J. P. Taylor says: "Both developments were a retreat from the flourishing days of the Renaissance, which had embraced all Germany. . . ."[106] Even in the relatively wealthier southwest, there would come to be a reversion to handicraft industries by the seventeenth century.[107] Taylor may exaggerate the extent of Germany's prosperity and economic leadership in the early sixteenth century, but he is undoubtedly correct in noting the dramatic collapse of nascent economic development.[108]

The effort of Charles V to dominate politically the European world-economy thus redounded negatively upon Spain and upon the Germanies, upon the cities of Flanders and of northern Italy, and upon the merchant houses which linked their fate to empire. The construction of an empire had seemed a reasonable thing to attempt, even a possible one. But it was not.

We have already told in large part the story of the Spanish colonial enterprise in the Americas. It would be best simply to describe here the situation as a phenomenon internal to the Spanish empire, in order to measure the impact of Spanish decline upon the Americas. Spain had established colonies in the Caribbean and some of the littoral surrounding it (contemporary Mexico, Guatemala, and Colombia) as well as in Peru and Chile. These colonies were conceived as economic complements not only of Europe as a whole, but of Spain in particular.[109] Spain did not have the administrative energy to create a large bureaucracy in the Americas. Therefore they used the old expedient of empires, the cooptation of local chieftains into the political system as intermediary agents of the Crown and the Spanish settlers.[110]

Nor did Spain have the energy to control entirely its own settlers. To keep their political loyalty, it made many economic concessions. One of these was to forbid Indians independent bases of economic power by barring them from raising cattle, the one activity in which they might have been able to compete effectively in the new capitalist economy.[111] Furthermore, not only were the Indians barred from this profitable activity, but its very success weakened them economically, for sheep ate men, in middle America just as in England.[112] The settlers were nonetheless dependent on continued Spanish support, not so much against Indian and African slave rebellions, as against English and other intrusions into their trade and hence their profit margins.[113] Hence, though they were occasionally unhappy with the Crown and its bureaucracy, they did not organize as an autonomous force. Besides, the settlers, many of humble origin, profited from the fact that the colonies were export economies.[114]

Indeed, as often happens, in imperial structures, subimperialisms grew up—layers within layers. We can speak of the ways in which Mexico (that is, the Spaniards in Mexico) "colonized" Peru. Mexico had a far larger population. There was a constant disparity in price levels throughout the sixteenth and seventeenth centuries. Mexico exported manufactures, luxuries, and slaves to Peru and received in return specie and mercury.[115] When the Philippines entered the Spanish trading sphere, the Spaniard in Mexico became the middleman between Manila and Lima, cutting out the Spanish Manileños.[116] This re-export of Chinese wares via Manila from Mexico to Peru became the mainstay of the intercolonial trade.[117] The Spanish Crown tried unsuccessfully to break Mexico's role, as it was cutting into the profits of Castile.[118] "No one will contest," says Chaunu, "that during the 16th century Mexico behaved towards Peru as a metropole towards its colony."[119]

One of the effects of political overextension in Europe combined with economic contraction in the "second" sixteenth century was that there was an increased emigration of Spaniards to America.[120] It provided a job outlet for Spaniards who needed it and an immediate source of income for the Spanish state, since positions in the American colonial bureaucracy were sold.[121] On the other hand, the growing population of Spaniards living off the land in America in the face of economic contraction, along with the disastrous demographic decline of the Indians under early Spanish rule, combined to create a "century of depression" in Hispanic America[122] and as a result gradually to give rise to the system of haciendas based on debt peonage.[123] But the hacienda was oriented to a smaller economic world than the plantation,[124] one of relative self-sufficiency of a settler elite.[125] Spain itself found the developing system of lessening economic benefit to her and of increasing political difficulty. It would be easy later for other European states to obtain the economic benefits of Hispanic America while Spain continued to bear its imperial political costs.[126]

Hence, in the post-1557 era, Spain not only lost the central European parts of her empire and after a long struggle the northern Netherlands. She was losing some of the benefits of her remaining colonies. Furthermore, the very fact that the Americas had become such an important source of revenue for Spain, as much as 10% of the total, led to Spain's slowing down the process of expansion in order to consolidate the gains already won.[127] But the slowdown turned out to be more than temporary.

The decline of Spain has been one of the great topics of modern European historiography. The cause, in our terms, seems to be that Spain did not erect (probably because she could not erect) the kind of state machinery which would enable the dominant classes in Spain to profit from the creation of a European world-economy, despite the central geographical-economic position of Spain in this world-economy in the sixteenth century. This indicates that the "core" areas need not be those that are most "central," either in geographical terms or in terms of trade movements.

Spain already suffered from some underlying faults of economic structure as she entered the sixteenth century. First, as we previously mentioned, the relative organized strength of the migratory sheepherders was an important barrier to the rise of a yeomanry, because they were able to retain their prerogatives against enclosures of arable land. In England, sheep raising was less migratory and more compatible with an enclosures system which permitted the slow rise of copyhold.[128] Second, there was the lack of a significant industrial sector, and such as there was (cloth and silk industries in Castile) would collapse in the crisis of 1590.[129] Vicens attributes this a bit mystically to "Castile's failure to comprehend the capitalist world."[130] In any case, his empirical description of what happened after the crisis indicates that the pattern of expenditure represents at least an intervening variable of decline:

> Precisely those who did possess money (aristocrats, gentry in Andalusia and Extremadura, and retired government officials) petrified it in construction (churches, palaces, and monasteries) or sanctified it in works of art. But none of them succumbed to the temptation to engage in industry, or even simply in commerce.[131]

A similar shift in investment pattern affected the Catalan bourgeoisie who were far more oriented to the new capitalist economy. Braudel notes their increasing shift away from commerce to investment in cultivable land. "Is this not one of the aspects of the economic drama of Barcelona? The bourgeoisie of Barcelona began to place its money in land rather than continuing to risk it in maritime enterprise."[132] Does this not cause us to reflect: How is it that in a center of the most important empire in Europe at this time its bourgeoisie is turning from overseas investment to grain growing, instead of building up their industrial base?[133] There is another puzzle. Many writers make statements similar to Vilar: "For the metals which enriched Spain parasitically . . . flowed out into those countries *where its purchasing power was greatest.*"[134] Or Vicens: "True, Castile did rely upon the injection of precious metals from America at critical moments in the struggle with the rest of Europe."[135]

Surely one factor here was the continued key financial role of foreigners: Genoese, Dutch, Portuguese Jews, French.[136] Another was the unwillingness of Charles V to take a Spanish *nationalist* perspective and adopt a mercantilist policy[137] before the Castilian bourgeoisie was overwhelmed by the impact of rising prices, luxury expenditure of the aristocracy, and the inflationary and antiprotectionist effects of the Emperor's borrowings,[138] all of which were tied to Spain's involvement in the pan-European Hapsburg empire. The results of these two factors, the large role of non-Spanish financial interests within Spain and the unwillingness (or inability) of the government to take appropriate protective measures, led to an inversion of Spain's economic role.[139]

Instead of moving against foreign merchants, Spain pursued the path of expelling Spanish non-Catholics, a self-destructive course. Spain's international position as the leading opponent of the forces of Protestantism in Europe and of Islam in the Mediterranean, led, once having suffered the defeat of the Great Armada in 1588,[140] to follow through on the logical internal conclusions of international policy. Having expelled Jews in 1492, Moors in 1502 and 1525, and having persecuted *marranos* and "Erasmians" throughout the sixteenth century, Spain expelled the last pseudo-religious minority, the so-called *Moriscos* in 1609.[141] The Moriscos numbered 300,000 and were mostly agricultural workers, disproportionately located in Valencia and Andalusia.[142] The explusion of the Moriscos tore at the internal social structure of Spain. It originated as a consequence in part of the economic setbacks of the first decade of the seventeenth

century,[143] in part as a result of the declining international situation of
Spain.[144] It was a move aimed at the landed aristocracy of the *latifundias*
by the bourgeois elements of Spain, a last effort as it were to break the
hold of this class not geared to capitalist growth.[145] But the aristocracy
saved itself by finding a compensation for its lost income in a refusal to
pay its loans owed to the bourgeoisie, a move in which the state supported
them.[146] Pierre Vilar sums up the result by saying: "Instead of hurting
the feudal economy, it thus boomeranged on their creditors: well-to-do
yeomen (*laboureurs riches*), and bourgeois."[147] The net result was twofold.
On the one hand, "the expulsion of the Moriscos had the consequence
of disequilibrating for more than a century the Iberian peninsula. Decided
in Castile, it broke the back of Valencia and Aragon."[148] On the other
hand, it deepened the economic difficulties still more[149] and sent Spain
looking for ever more ephemeral scapegoats of its decline.[150]

Meanwhile, the government found itself ever more indebted abroad,
ever more prone to meet budgetary crisis by debt repudiation (1557, 1575,
1596, 1607, 1627, 1647) and finally "unable to raise more money and
therefore unable to go on fighting."[151] And at home, the "fantastically
expensive foreign policies of Charles V and his dependence on credit to
finance them" had the consequence, argues J. H. Elliott, not only of establishing "the dominance of foreign bankers over the country's sources of
wealth" but also of ensuring that "within Castile the brunt of the burden
was borne by those classes which were least capable of bearing it."[152] The
resulting dilemma of Spain was captured as early as 1600 by a
lawyer-theologian named Martin González de Cellorigo: "Thus it is, that
if there is no gold or silver bullion in Spain, it is because there is; the
cause of her poverty is her wealth."[153]

The growing economic difficulties of Spain combined with the inability
to create a strong state machinery led to extensive brigandage with which
the state was not coping well.[154] The "slowness" of the bureaucracy got
worse, not better, as these very difficulties created a structural rigidity
in which "Spanish kings were able to go on and on, and rule with a minimum
of change and reform."[155] And despite the decline in state income, the
state maintained, perhaps even increased, the high level of luxury expenditures of a parasitical court bureaucracy.

The crowning blow may have been demographic (which enters, when it
does, as an intervening variable, as we have argued). If in the "first" sixteenth
century, Spain's population (or at least that of Castile) was large and growing,[156] this ceased to be true in the "second" sixteenth century for multiple
reasons: emigration to the Americas, military deaths, famine and plague
in 1599–1600 in Andalusia and Castile, and, as we have seen, expulsion
of the Moriscos in 1609. It was not therefore that Spain was somehow
less entrepreneurial than other parts of Europe.[157] It is that, for reasons
we have adduced, the state machinery was not adequately and properly
constructed, and hence that "adverse circumstances proved too strong,"

in Elliott's phrase,[158] and that Spain demonstrated a "hypersensitivity . . . to the phenomenon of secular contraction," in Chaunu's phrase.[159] In any case, Spain did not become the premier power of Europe. On the contrary, she was destined to become first semiperipheral and then peripheral, until in the twentieth century she tried slowly to begin to move back upward. Nor had Spain declined alone. She had brought down in her wake all those parts of Europe that had been linked to her ascension: northern Italy, southern Germany, Antwerp, Cracow, Portugal. With the exception of Portugal, all of these were essentially city-states servicing both the Hapsburg (and Spanish) empires as well as the world-economy as a whole. Their prosperity did not long survive the restructuring of the world-system in the "second" sixteenth century.

The new system was to be the one that has predominated ever since, a capitalist world-economy whose core-states were to be intertwined in a state of constant economic and military tension, competing for the privilege of exploiting (and weakening the state machineries of) peripheral areas, and permitting certain entities to play a specialized, intermediary role as semiperipheral powers.

The core-states themselves had drawn a salutary financial lesson from the economic catastrophes of the Hapsburg and Valois empires. They were determined not to get caught out again in a financial maze out of their control. First, they sought to create the kind of import controls which would enable them to maintain a favorable balance of trade, a concept which came into currency at this time. [160] But the states did more than worry about the balance of trade. They worried also about the gross national product, though they did not call it that, and about the share of the state in the GNP and their control over it. The result was that, by the end of the "second" sixteenth century, as Carl Friedrich points out, "the state itself had become the source of credit, rather than the financial houses which had hitherto loaned funds."[161]

Thus began a period of turning inward. Overall, the following period may perhaps be considered, as R. B. Wernham does, "one of the most brutal and bigoted in the history of modern Europe,"[162] but the conflicts at first were more within than between states. Between the states, there reigned for the moment a relative calm, born of weariness—"a bickering and still explosive co-existence."[163]

This political turning inward of the state—that is, statism, because it was not necessarily nationalism—was intimately linked to the nature of economic development. It is important to start by remembering comparative demography. France in 1600 was estimated at 16 million population, the largest in Europe, although the various German principalities added up to 20 million. Spain and Portugal (united after 1580) were about 10 million, England and Wales 4.5 million. Densities are in quite a different order. The areas with the traditional merchant–industrial city-states headed the list: Italy with 114 per square miles and the Low Countries with 104.

France had 88 and England and Wales 78. Spain (and Portugal) had only 44.[164]

The meaning of both absolute figures and densities is ambiguous. Numbers meant strength in war and industry. They also meant people to rule and mouths to feed. The optimal size is far from clear, as our previous discussion already indicated. For the "second" sixteenth century, Frank C. Spooner registers skepticism about the economic benefits of expanding population. He speaks of "diminishing returns."[165] At first after Cateau-Cambrésis, "the economic activity of western Europe enjoyed a period of prolonged ease and recuperation."[166] This was the period of silver inflation which undercut German mining, appreciated gold, and stimulated Europe's economy.[167] One consequence of the silver inflation was that, as Tawney observes, "by the latter part of the sixteenth century, agriculture, industry and foreign trade were largely dependent on credit."[168] A second consequence is that it definitely shifted the economic center of gravity from central Europe to the new Atlantic trade to the west. Spooner says of the Treaty of Cateau-Cambrésis that it "was not so much the closing of a period as an opening on the future," and he adds: "The path of the future lay . . . across the Atlantic and the seven seas of the world."[169]

Economically, the most striking event of this time was however not located in the Atlantic but to the north. Astrid Friis argues it was rather "the exceptional expansion of the sea trade in the Netherlands and England coeval with a rapid rise in the imports of Baltic goods, especially grain, into other parts of Europe."[170] In her view, crises in bullion, credit and finance are not the motor of economic (and political) change, but its consequence.[171] In this case, she says, it was the grain penury that was the immediate cause of the strain on the money market.[172] One of the outcomes of this was to strengthen enormously the hand of Amsterdam which was already at that time the pivot of the Baltic grain market and which, thereby, was able to remain more solvent than Antwerp and other cities of the southern provinces.

Thus we go from Seville to Amsterdam. The story of the "second" sixteenth century is the story of how Amsterdam picked up the threads of the dissolving Hapsburg Empire, creating a framework of smooth operation for the world-economy that would enable England and France to begin to emerge as strong states, eventually to have strong "national economies."

These developments were for the most part the consequence of the fact that the first expansionist phase of the European world-economy was drawing to its close in this period. It was the moment when the "great tide began to ebb, as if its rise lacked the requisite momentum to overcome the obstacles and impediments which it itself had raised."[173] We shall turn now to the responses of the traditional centers of population and finance, the Low Countries and northern Italy. Then, in the next chapter we shall deal both with the emergence of England not only as the third political power of Europe (alongside France and Spain) but as the one most rapidly advancing in the industrial sphere, and with the ways in which France, in making the shift from an imperial to a statist orientation, was constrained from obtaining the full benefits of the organizational shift.

How important were the Low Countries at this time? Lucien Febvre, in his introduction to Chaunu's *magnum opus* on the Atlantic trade, suggests—no, affirms—that the trade to and from the Netherlands pales in comparison:

> From the point of view of an economic history seen from on high, from the point of view of world and cultural history on a grand scale, what is there in common between this coastal trade of bulk goods, useful, but in no ways precious, going from North to South and from South to North . . . this coastal trade of foodstuffs, the barter, the modest purchases, the short-haul transport to which it gave rise—and, considering only the trade going from America to Europe, the contribution of precious metals in quantities theretofore unknown, which was to revive both the economy and the polity, the "grand policies" of European powers and, thus, to precipitate and accelerate social upheavals of incalculable scope: enrichment of a merchant and financial bourgeoisie rising, as did the Fuggers and so many others, to princely rank; progressive decadence of a nobility which maintains its status and its brilliance only by exploiting parasitically the benefits acquired by the creators of wealth; the long supremacy in Europe of the Hapsburgs, masters of the overseas gold and silver: Beside so many great things, what is the importance of this local trade *(trafic casanier)*, this potluck trade of the Sound and its barges, dragging prudently their fat stomachs under foggy skies?[174]

What indeed? This is the question. Even if Febvre's facts were totally correct—and there seems reason to believe that he has seriously underestimated the northern trade[175]—we should hesitate before accepting the intimidating flourish of Febvre's prose. For this potluck local trade carried raw materials for the new industries and food for the townsmen.[176] As we have seen, it ensconced and codified a new European division of labor. Precious metals after all must be used to buy real goods, and as we have also seen, the precious metals may not have done too much more for Spain than pass through its ledgers.

Nor was it only a question of the *economic* centrality of the trade which revolved around the Low Countries. It was also a question of specialization in the new skills required to run a financial and commercial focus of the world-economy. It was the command of such skills that enabled the Dutch to seize control of the world spice trade from the Portuguese as we move from the "first" to the "second" sixteenth century.[177]

The importance of the Low Countries for intra-European trade is of course nothing new. As S. T. Bindoff reminds us, "from the eleventh to the seventeenth century the Netherlands . . . were one of the nodal points of European trade. . . ."[178] We have noted the key role of Antwerp in the "first" sixteenth century.[179] Antwerp fell in 1559,[180] and the important thing to note is that the succession was by no means obvious. As we know, Amsterdam stepped into the breach, but Lawrence Stone argues that one way to read this fact is to see it as the failure of England as much as the success of the Dutch, a failure that would "retard" England's ascendancy in the world-system.[181]

Amsterdam's success then was politically as well as economically important. But what was the political framework that made this success possible? The last five decades of the sixteenth century mark not only the rise of Amsterdam but the so-called Netherlands Revolution, whose boundaries in time and space are as amorphous (or rather as contested) as its social content.

To begin with, was it a revolution? And if it was a revolution, was it a national revolution or a bourgeois revolution? And is there any difference between these two concepts? I shall not now begin a long excursus on the concept of revolution. We are not yet ready in the logic of this work to treat that question. I should like merely to underline at this point that it seems to me this question is no more ambiguous (and to be sure no more clear) in the case of the Netherlands "Revolution" than in the case of any other of the great "revolutions" of the modern era.

The historical literature reveals one very great schism in interpretation. Some consider the Revolution essentially the story of the "Dutch" nation—that is, of the northern Netherlanders, Calvinists, struggling for liberty and independence against the Spanish crown, the latter aided and abetted by the "Belgian" (southern Netherlander) Catholics. Others consider it essentially a revolt of the all-Netherlands ("Burgundian") nation, supported by persons from all religious groups, which succeeded in liberating only half a nation. J. W. Smit ends a survey of the historiography with this very sensible comment:

> These problems, however, can only be resolved if we stop treating the Revolt as a *bloc* and if we become aware that there were a number of revolts, representing the interests and the ideals of various social, economical and ideological groups: revolts which sometimes run parallel, sometimes conflict with one another, and at other times coalesce into a single movement.[182]

From the point of view of the world-system as it was developing we must ask why it was the Netherlands and in the Netherlands alone that a complex national-social revolution occurs in the "second" sixteenth century, an era of relative quiet and social order elsewhere (except, most importantly, for France) and how it was that the revolt was largely successful.[183]

During the era of Charles V, Netherlands internal politics was not remarkably different from the politics of other parts of Europe. The nobility was in an ambivalent relationship to its prince, fearing his growing political and economic power, seeing him as a protector of their interests both against the bourgeoisie and popular revolt, finding service for the prince a financial salvation for the "younger sons" or distressed peers, ultimately siding with the prince.[184] Then, suddenly, we get a situation in which "the frustrated prosperous bourgeois of the booming towns joined the desperate declassed craftsmen and thriving or declining nobles, and local riots coalesced into a general revolution."[185] How come?

I think the key to the *outbreak* of revolution is not in the social discontent of artisans and urban workers, nor in the bourgeoisie who were doubtless to be the great beneficiaries of the revolution, but in the fact that large parts of the "Netherlands" nobility were suddenly afraid that the prince was not *their* agent, that his policies would in the short and medium run threaten their interests significantly and that it was outside their political possibility to persuade him to make alterations in his policy, since his political arena (the Spanish empire) was so much larger than one which, if established, they might control.[186] In short, they had a reflex of "nationalist" opposition.[187]

Let us look at some of the evidence. The nobility there, as elsewhere, was in increasing debt. Furthermore, the Emperor was steadily cutting into their sources of current income.[188] When Philip II came to power, he discovered sudden resistance to his fund raising.[189] The last years of Charles V were trying ones—great financial demands of the Emperor combined with a decline in real income of the nobility caused by the price inflation. The bankruptcies and the economic difficulties resulting from the peace treaty of Cateau-Cambrésis made the situation suddenly worse.[190]

Then, on top of the economic grievances, Philip II obtained Rome's permission in 1559 to create new bishoprics. The move was intended to rationalize political and linguistic boundaries, increase the number of bishoprics, and require that bishops be technically skilled (that is, theologians rather than sons of great lords). For good measure, the plan required that the funds to endow the new bishoprics were to be taken from the revenues of certain historic and hitherto financially independent abbeys, the new bishops replacing the abbots in the various political assemblies. No doubt, as Pieter Geyl remarks tersely it showed Philip to be a "diligent" state builder.[191] Still, "it is not to be wondered at that there arose a storm of opposition to a plan which involved such a strengthening of the King's authority at a moment when his designs were viewed with mistrust on all sides."[192]

In the other direction, the nobility sought to transform the Council of State into "an exclusively aristocratic executive body."[193] Philip refused but compromised by withdrawing Spanish troops, leaving his government in the Netherlands with only forces supplied by the local nobility and the urban centers to maintain order. If one adds to this picture the general grievances of the lower classes and middle bourgeoisie brought on by the recession of the 1560s[194] and the general weakness of the Church under attack now for forty years, a revolt became possible:

> Religiously indifferent mobs attacked prisons, the hated symbols of oppression, and freed Protestants. Toleration became the general slogan and in conjunction with the demand for a free Estates-General, became the core of the opposition's

political program. For some time these slogans worked as perfect generalized beliefs
of a national, or interprovincial, scope; they were simple principles and above all
were socially neutral.[195]

We must not forget that this is shortly after the peace of Cateau-Cambrésis,
that this peace permitted the sessions of the Council of Trent to resume,
and thus for the Counter-Reformation to become institutionalized.[196] Hence
Catholicism and the Spanish Crown were more closely identified than previously.

The "Revolution" went through a number of phases: the first uprising
(in both north and south) and its suppression (1566–1572); the second
uprising (more "Protestant") of only Holland and Zeeland in the north
(1572–1576) ending in the Pacification of Ghent; a radical uprising in
Flanders in the south (1577–1579); a division of the country into two from
1579 on (United Provinces in the north, a loyalist regime in the south);
an attempted reunification in 1598; conclusion of a lasting truce in 1609.

Over this period, what should be noticed is that the conflict—amorphous
and multisided in the beginning—took on an increasingly clear form as
the struggle of the Protestant, or rather "Protestantized," north for national
independence of the north with a regime in the latter consonant with
the needs of the commercial bourgeoisie, whose strength on a worldwide
scale grew throughout the struggle and subsequently in the seventeenth
century. Once started, there probably was very little that Spain, given "the
failure of empire," could do to stop it,[197] especially given, as we shall see,
the new European balance of power. Indeed, the constraints on Spain
are clearly indicated by the fact that virtually every major political turning
point in the Spanish–Netherlands relationship from 1557 to 1648 was
immediately preceded by a financial crisis in Spain.[198]

Though the Netherlands Revolution was a "nationalist" movement, it
involved a religious component from the beginning. While the nobility
sought in the beginning to monopolize the form and nature of the quarrel
with the King, the Calvinist community broke through their prescribed
passive role into a frenzy known as the Breaking of the Images which
swept the country, north and south. Geyl describes the authorities as
"paralyzed with fright" and the Calvinist leaders themselves showing
"surprise and discomfiture."[199] It was religion that added the note of
ideological passion to the Revolution and enabled I. Shöffer to compare
the Breaking of the Images to the storming of the Bastille and the street
riots in Petrograd in March 1917.[200]

Though this phase quickly passed, the strength of the Calvinists as a
revolutionary party, as sixteenth-century Jacobins in the analogy of H. G.
Koenigsberger,[201] meant that they had the stamina to persist when others
fell by the wayside, to use a policy of "terrorizing the population,"[202] and
to be able "to mobilize the mob at strategic moments."[203] When in the
Pacification of Ghent, the authorities tried to solve the conflict by religious
partition, they merely entrenched the Reformed party in Holland and

Zeeland and reinforced the identification of the political and religious cause,[204] which led eventually to the "Protestantization" of areas under Protestant control. The division of the country in 1579 led to a consolidation on each side and thus to a lasting religious polarization.[205] The actual lines of administrative division were the result of geo–military factors. The southern Netherlands was open country where Spanish cavalry could prevail. The northern part was covered with waterways and other barriers to cavalry movement. It was, in short, ideal guerilla country.[206] In the course of time, those to the north *became* Protestant, those to the south *became* Catholic.

Hence it is not that, as many have already argued, Protestantism is particularly consonant with social change—no more with nationalism than with capitalism. It is rather, as Sir Lewis Namier is quoted, "religion is a sixteenth-century word for nationalism."[207] Protestantism served to unify the northern Netherlands. We noted in the previous chapter how and why Catholicism became linked with Polish national sentiment. And Catholicism did the same thing for Ireland.[208] Wherever a religion was not firmly linked to the national cause, it did not prove capable of surviving, as Calvinism in France.[209]

What was going on was that, in the maelstrom of conflicting interests, new organizational structures could only be built by strange and unstable alliances. Men sought to secure these alliances. H. G. Koenigsberger captures the point precisely:

> Religion was the binding force that held together the different interests of the different classes and provided them with an organization and a propaganda machine capable of creating the first genuinely national and international parties in modern European history; for these parties never embraced more than a minority of each of their constituent classes. Moreover it was through religion that they could appeal to the lowest classes and the mob to vent the anger of their poverty and the despair of their unemployment in barbarous massacres and fanatical looting. Social and economic discontent were fertile ground for recruitment by either side, and popular democratic tyranny appeared both in Calvinist Ghent and Catholic Paris.[210]

If religion then serves as a national cement, it tells us little about the social content of the resulting state structures. J. W. Smit argues that the Netherlands Revolution was essentially, despite the ambiguities, a bourgeois revolution, bringing the bourgeoisie to power, and the partition of the Netherlands and the resulting state boundaries are a measure of the degree of its strength in the face of its enemies.[211]

To be sure, the nobility were involved at various places and times, particularly in the beginning, but they were frightened away from the nationalist cause by the recurring undercurrents of social radicalism.[212] But if radical social movements had a sufficient base in the lumpenproletariat of the towns born of economic expansion *cum* recession, as exemplified by the brief control of Ghent by Jan van Hembyze from 1577–1579,[213] they were rapidly isolated and destroyed themselves by losing sight of the national theme and turning against the bourgeoisie, and hence, paradoxically, toward alliance with the king's forces.[214]

Thus, slowly, emerged a confederation of town governments who quickly shed any "democratic" trimmings but who also were free from the economic burdens which their participation in the old Spanish system inflicted.[215] The merchants created for themselves a loose confederation without the administrative apparatus of most other states. Many have termed this a weakness but Smit is closer to the point when he reminds us that the state machinery of the Dutch Republic "permitted the achievement of a higher degree of economic integration than any of the monarchies of Europe. The bourgeoisie of Holland had carried through exactly the degree of reform it needed to promote economic expansion and yet feel free from overcentralization."[216] Thus, the Netherlands Revolution may never have started without the defection of many nobles from the established order. It may never have gotten a second wind without the radical currents from below. But in the end it was the bourgeoisie who held firm to the reins and emerged the beneficiaries of the new social order.

Why, however, the Netherlands and not elsewhere? We said that the "second" sixteenth century was the era of turning inward, the rejection of the imperial ideal in favor of seeking to create the strong state. There was still, however, during part of this period one arena in which all the great powers intervened, one arena of general entanglement. It was the Netherlands. One way to interpret the Netherlands Revolution is to see it as the effort of the local dominant groups to achieve the same exclusion of outsiders from political interference, the same control of self, that Spain, France, and England at least were striving to enjoy.

Another way to interpret it is to say that because after 1559, Spain, France, and England balanced each other off, the Netherlanders had the social space to assert their identity and throw off the Spanish yoke. This was particularly true after the defeat of the Spanish Armada in 1588.[217] It was not that any of these countries stood for the independence of the Netherlands. Spain did not want to lose part of her dominions. France, although it wanted to weaken Spain, vacillated because of the implications for the internal religious struggle in France. England wanted to get Spain out but not let France in, and preferred therefore Netherlands autonomy under nominal Spanish sovereignty.[218] The point however is that this conflict within the world-system, this weakening of Spanish world dominance, made it possible for the bourgeoisie of the United Provinces to maneuver to maximize *its* interests. By 1596, they could enter as equals in a treaty with France and England, when only shortly before they had offered themselves as subjects to the one or the other. As Geyl comments: "Once more the mutual jealousies of France and England where the Low Countries were concerned proved a benefit."[219]

The significance of the Netherlands Revolution is not that it established a model of national liberation. Despite the romantic liberal historiography of the nineteenth century, the Dutch example did not serve as a generator of ideological currents. The importance lies in the economic impact on the European world-economy. The Netherlands Revolution liberated a force that could sustain the world-system as a system over some difficult years of adjustment, until the English (and the French) were ready to take the steps necessary for its definitive consolidation.

Let us recall the prior economic history of Amsterdam and other towns of the northern Netherlands. The Dutch had been playing an increasing role in Baltic trade.[220] They gained a footing in the late Middle Ages and by the early sixteenth century were replacing the Hanseatic cities. Their total Baltic trade was on a rising curve in the sixteenth century, reaching a point, in about 1560, when they controlled about 70% of the trade. Although the Revolutionary period interfered somewhat with the level of Baltic trade, the Dutch recouped their temporary decline by 1630.[221]

The effect of the Revolution was not only to ensure the economic decline of Flanders but to strengthen the north in personnel because of the migration of many Flemish bourgeois north. "If Holland and Zeeland flourished, it was partly because they fed on the best vital forces of Flanders and Brabant."[222] Furthermore, the principle of religious toleration proclaimed by the United Provinces in 1579 led to the arrival of Sephardic Jews beginning in 1597. "Bringing their riches and business acumen to supplement the prosperity of the mercantile states of the north, such an emigration became by definition a European phenomenon."[223]

As soon as the political struggle within the Netherlands seemed to stabilize, the Dutch surged forward from being merely a center of Baltic trade to being a center of world trade.[224] Furthermore, the new trade increased rather than decreased the importance of the Baltic trade, which the Dutch themselves called the "mother trade." After all, eastern Europe supplied both the grain to feed Dutch cities and the naval supplies essential to Dutch fishing interests and shipbuilding.[225] Shipbuilding in turn was a key to Dutch success elsewhere.[226]

This illustrates once again the cumulating quality of economic advantage. Because the Dutch had an edge in Baltic trade, they became the staple market for timber. Because they were the staple market for timber, they reduced shipbuilding costs and were technologically innovative. And in turn they were thus still better able to compete in the Baltic trade. Because of this edge, they could finance still further expansion.[227] On this basis Amsterdam became a threefold center of the European economy: commodity market, shipping center, and capital market, and it became "difficult to say which aspect of her greatness was most substantial, or to dissociate one from dependence on the other two."[228] This process of cumulating advantage works most in an expansionist stage of economic development before the leading area suffers the disadvantages of out-of-date equipment and relatively fixed high labor costs.

There was another reason for the ability of the Dutch to prosper. Braudel poses the question of why, after 1588, the English did not come to dominate the seas, as they would eventually. He finds it in the Dutch economic ties with Spain, relatively unbroken despite the political turmoil.[229] Could not England have created the same link with Spain's American treasure? Not yet, England was still too much of a threat to Spain to be permitted this kind of relationship.[230] And Spain was still strong enough to resist England. The Empire may have failed, but control of the European world-economy still depended on access to Spain's colonial wealth. Holland, albeit in revolt against Spain, was still part of her. And in any case, Holland was no political threat, unlike France and England.

Holland thus profited by being a small country. And she profited by being a "financially sound" state.[231] She offered the merchants who would use her arena maximum advantages. Her route to riches was not that of the incipient mercantilism of other states[232]—essential for long-run advantage but not for maximizing short-run profit by the mercantile and financial classes. Her route was the route of free trade.[233] Or rather this was her route in the "second" sixteenth century when she predominated on the seas. When Amsterdam was still struggling for a place in the commercial sun, she had been protectionist in policy.[234]

From the point of view of the European world-economy as a whole, with its era of expansion coming to an end, Dutch world trade becme a sort of precious vital fluid which kept the machine going while various countries were concentrating on reorganizing their internal political and economic machinery. Conversely, however, the success of the Netherlands policy was dependent on the fact that neither England nor France had yet pushed their mercantilist tendencies to the point where they truly cut into the market for Dutch merchants operating on free trade assumptions.[235] This may be because the Dutch still were too strong because of their relative control of the money market by their continuing Spanish links.[236]

If Amsterdam succeeded Seville, if the northern Netherlands became the commercial and financial center of the European world-economy in the "second" sixteenth century, how may we describe what happened to the city-states of northern Italy, particularly Venice and Genoa which seemed to expand, rather than diminish, their commercial and financial roles at precisely this time? What we may say is that this expansion was short-lived and masked a process of decline hidden beneath the glitter so that, by the end of the "second" sixteenth century, these areas were relegated to the semiperiphery of the European world-economy.

The true forward surge of Amsterdam did not occur until 1590. Between the crisis of 1557 and 1590 came the Netherlands Revolution. The Netherlands role in world commerce was necessarily less during that period. As a result, Genoa picked up some of the functions formerly played by Antwerp and, in banking, by the Fuggers.[237] Curiously, England which had most to lose by the fall of Antwerp, because it threatened to deprive England of access to American bullion,[238] engaged in impetuous short run military seizures of treasure that led the Spaniards to ship the bullion through Genoa.[239] Genoa's strength thus partly derived from the turmoil of the Netherlands, partly from its total devotion to the primacy of economic considerations,[240] partly from their continuing close ties with the Spanish monarchy and commercial system,[241] ties whose origins we spelled out previously.

As for Venice, whereas the "first" sixteenth century was an era of the decline of Mediterranean trade (the impact of the Turkish conquest of Constantinople and Egypt, and the new Portuguese sea routes to the east), the "second" sixteenth century saw a great revival of its trade, especially in the eastern Mediterranean.[242] This revival had already begun about 1540 and was due in part to Portuguese inability to control the Indian Ocean trade,[243] in part to some competitive advantages of Venice over Portugal,[244] and in part to Portuguese weakness in Europe[245] as well as Spain's crisis in the Netherlands.[246]

But the revival of northern Italy could not last. Neither its agricultural nor its industrial base were sound, unlike the northern Netherlands and a fortiori England, and by the seventeenth century, we talk of the decline of Italy.

The weakness of the agricultural base was multifold, given the growth of population in the sixteenth century, particularly accentuated in the period 1580–1620.[247] We have already mentioned the relative difficulty of soil conditions. It is true that, during the "first" sixteenth century, as profits from trade declined, there was a shift of investment to agriculture, particularly wheat.[248] This was especially true of monastic orders which were not permitted to engage in urban commerce. This trend was accentuated, particularly in the Terraferma around Venice[249] between 1570 and 1630, as local investors responded to the rise in agricultural prices and the decline in industrial profits.

Nevertheless, despite increased production, there was famine. Part of the explanation lies in a factor which, from the point of view of the social system, is accidental and external: a sudden increase of rain and cold in the last decades of the sixteenth century which led to the increase of swampland, and hence of malaria.[250] The latter was particularly serious since Italy was already suffering from its increase as a result of the extension of land cultivation in the process of internal colonization.[251] Still one would have thought that a region having so much bullion would have imported wheat. This seems to have happened to some degree, enough to spread the effects of the famine by creating shortages elsewhere,[252] but not apparently enough to maintain an agricultural base for industrial production. Why not? One can speculate that the new large agricultural producers (such as the monasteries) did not lend their political weight to expanded grain imports.[253] There was of course the cost factor. Baltic grain was

far, and Egyptian and Syrian grain was often unavailable, either because
they too were suffering shortages or because of a state of war with the
Turks.[254]

Furthermore, to the extent that they were importing grain, it was under
the worst bargaining conditions possible and via their commercial rival,
the Dutch. For Amsterdam controlled the Baltic stocks and could dole
them out at its pleasure.[255] This conjunctural advantage of Holland over
northern Italy could then be transformed into something more permanent
because of the linkages created by the world-economy. Spooner notes the
role of the new sophisticated credit techniques—endorsement of bills of
exchange, *patto di ricorsa* (a form of short-term credit), and public banks—all
of which were emerging just at this point. This credit system was international, and, as northern Italy began to decline, the locus of these activities was
shifted without ado.[256] For the merchant financiers saved themselves, in
Genoa as elsewhere, without too much worry about geographical loyalties.

But industry? Was not northern Italy an industrial center, and indeed
one that was infused with new life, especially in Venice? J. H. Elliott mentions
new investment between 1560 and 1600, and a moment of "opulent splen-
dour."[257] The opulence however did not last. From being one of the most
advanced industrial areas in Europe in 1600, northern Italy became a
depressed agricultural region by 1670. We have already suggested that
the prosperity was deceiving. Domenico Sella says of Venice's economic
prosperity in the late sixteenth century that it could not "conceal the fact
that the base on which it rested was somewhat narrower than in the past
and that, accordingly, her economy had become somewhat more vulnerable."[258] There are two main considerations here. One is the loss of France
and England as customers because of the rise of their own textile industries.
Hence the market was now confined more or less to northern Italy and
Germany. The second is that sea transport was now more and more in
the hands of non-Venetian ships. As Carlo Cipolla puts it: "The whole
economic structure of the country was too dependent upon its ability to
sell abroad a high proportion of the manufactured articles and the services
that it could offer.[259]

What does it mean to be *too* dependent on sales of manufactured goods?
After all, the secret of the success of core areas of a world-economy is
that they exchange their manufactures for the raw materials of peripheral
areas. But that simple picture leaves out of account two factors:
politico–economic ability to keep down prices of raw materials imports
(which we argued was more possible for the Netherlands than for northern
Italy), and ability to compete in the markets of *core* countries with the
manufactured products of other core countries.

The story here was quite simple. While the Dutch could undersell the
English in England, the Italians by contrast were probably outpriced[260]

and old-fashioned.[261] The Italian guilds kept the labor costs up. State taxation was comparatively high. The Italians produced for the quality market. Others came along with lighter and more colorful cloths—less durable, of inferior quality, but cheaper. The secret of modern industrial success was revealing itself early. When the Thirty Years War interfered with the German market as well, disaster followed: decline in production of textiles; disinvestment of capital; migration of industries to the rural areas to escape guild labor costs and the tax collector. Since the industries were noncompetitive, they died out.[262]

Could northern Italy at least have played the role of the northern Netherlands? Possibly, but there was probably not room for them both, and Holland was better suited for the task for a host of reasons than Venice or Milan or Genoa. Nor could Italy follow the path of England and France, for one thing for lack of political unity.[263] When the plague hit Italy in 1630,[264] it reduced the pressure on food supply, but it also drove wages up still higher. It served as a last straw. Northern Italy thus completed the transition from core to semiperiphery. We already noted previously that Spain had been making the same transition at this time. No doubt northern Italy never fell as far as some other Mediterranean areas like southern Italy[265] and Sicily,[266] but this was to be a small consolation in the centuries ahead. R. S. Lopez in recounting all the things that went wrong for the Christian Mediterranean since 1450, concludes sadly: "Obviously the primacy of the Mediterranean peoples could not survive so many adversities."[267]

L. Bloud excud.

Bellange fec.

5

THE STRONG CORE STATES: CLASS-FORMATION AND INTERNATIONAL COMMERCE

Figure 6: "Two Beggars Fighting," etching by Jacques Bellange, official painter, engraver, and decorator of the Court of Lorraine at Nancy from 1602 to 1616. The etching was made between 1612–1617 (Washington, D.C.: National Gallery of Art, Rosenwald Collection).

One of the persisting themes of the history of the modern world is the seesaw between "nationalism" and "internationalism." I do not refer to the ideological seesaw, though it of course exists, but to the organizational one. At some points in time the major economic and political institutions are geared to operating in the international arena and feel that local interests are tied in some immediate way to developments elsewhere in the world. At other points of time, the social actors tend to engage their efforts locally, tend to see the reinforcement of state boundaries as primary, and move toward a relative indifference about events beyond them. These are of course only *tendencies* and not all actors are bound to observe the dominant tendency, nor is consistency obligatory or likely for the actors.

I should stress that I am talking of an organizational tendency, not a structural one. The issue is not whether the world-economy is more or less integrated, whether the trends are inflationary or deflationary, whether property rights are more or less concentrated. These structural variables underpin the organizational options but the correlation between the two is long run, not middle run. Organizational options are political choices, are decisions men make about the forms which are most likely to support their interests.

In the "second" sixteenth century, after the peace of Cateau-Cambrésis, the economic balance would swing. Northwest Europe became the economic heartland of the European world-economy. It is now time to look at what gave England and France such fundamental strength. Since the rise of the industrial sector is an important element in this picture, let us see what kind of industrial transformation was going on and how it was that England especially seemed to benefit from it so greatly.

The most important aspect of the industrial transformation of the "second" sixteenth century is not in the novelty of its technology (although there was some), nor in its social organization. The factory and mass production were still essentially unknown. Nor did the overall level of industrial production of the European world-economy rise that much. Domenico Sella reminds us that despite all the economic development of the "long" sixteenth century, "Europe's industrial sector as it stood in 1700 bore far greater resemblance to its medieval antecedent than to its nineteenth century successor."[1]

The key change was in the geographical distribution of industry. Up to about 1550, there were nodes of industrial activity in various parts of Europe. The "industrial backbone of Europe ran . . . from Flanders to Tuscany,"[2] but there was some industry everywhere. From about 1550, industrial activity began to concentrate in certain states of "northwest" Europe and decline in other European states. It is striking the extent to which this decline hit one area after another of the territories that made up Charles V's empire.[3]

As industry drastically declined in some areas, it seemed to divide itself into two varieties in the remaining areas of Europe. John Nef distinguishes between northern Italy, France and Switzerland on the one hand and the "north" of Europe (England, the Dutch Republic, Sweden, Denmark, and Scotland) on the other. According to Nef:

> In the [former] there was a notable growth in the products of the artistic and the luxury industries, a fresh development of art and artisanry, but only a slight increase in the output of the heavy industries, and consequently no remarkable change in the volume of output. In the [latter] there was an expansion of the heavy industries, and consequently of output, for which there had been no precedent.[4]

Sella draws his geographical lines a bit differently. He includes Flanders and southern Germany along with northern Italy among the areas of decline, for which as we have seen he has good reason. He makes no mention of Switzerland. He distinguishes rather between Sweden and France which show some gains and England and the Dutch Republic where the gains achieved were "far more remarkable"[5] and in each of which was established "a broad spectrum of industrial activities."[6]

Both authors agree however on the great rise of England. This is all the more startling when we recall that many describe the relation of medieval England to the European continent as "colonial,"[7] and that Nef contends that as late as 1547 England was "industrially in a backwater compared with most continental countries, including France." Yet, because of England's industrial expansion, particularly between 1575 and 1620, "the positions of the two countries [came to be] reversed. . . ."[8]

The late Middle Ages saw a major shift in the composition and hence destination of England's export trade. She started out as a supplier of raw materials—cereals, wood, and to a lesser extent metals and leather. By the sixteenth century, the export of these items had declined relatively, and in the case of cereals absolutely, and cloth had become the major export of England.

Cereals (in particular wheat) played a diminishing role from the fourteenth century on. This was due, partly, to the fact that eastern Europe began to export grain and came to absorb a very large part of the international grain market. This may have served to dampen any tendency to expand English production unduly.[9] Instead, as we also know, England moved toward the breakup of the demesnes, a factor usually explained by demographic decline, fall in the price level (especially of cereals), and high cost of living. To be sure, the growth of the London market in the fifteenth and sixteenth centuries led to a new demand for wheat,[10] but by that time the English demesnes were broken up and the grain was supplied in part from abroad.[11] Ireland and Norway became economic "colonies" of England although England was still a "colony" of the continent.[12] This was the period too of the legal incorporation of Wales into the English Crown which provided England with an internal colony, devoted at this time in particular to raising cattle.[13]

The wool export trade was "already steadily declining"[14] in the fifteenth century, because of Spanish competition, the rise of textile exports, and the absorption of the wool by the cloth industry in England itself. In particular, the export taxes on wool, used as a fiscal device by the state, "acted as a tariff shelter for the nascent English cloth industry."[15] By 1614, the export of wool was formally prohibited, at which time England attempted to regulate Ireland's trade in wool, turning Ireland into an exporter of wool but not cloth, and only to England.[16]

The English textile industry had two features very important for the emergent world-economy. It was more and more a *rural* industry in England, and it involved England in a search for widespread export markets.

We have referred, in a previous chapter, to the theory of Marian Malowist that in England, as in some other parts of Europe, the recession of the fourteenth and fifteenth centuries, which had caused a sharp reduction in agricultural income, led to the creation of rural textile industries to supplement income. From the point of view of the capitalists, rural industries also had the virtue of avoiding the high wages imposed by city guilds[17] and taking advantage of the cheaper water power to run fulling mills.[18] These rural industries produced textiles "not of the highest quality but . . . cheaper and therefore within the reach of the impoverished nobility and other less well-to-do customers."[19] This expansion of the rural textile industry in England more than compensated for any decline in the urban centers.[20] But in time of economic contraction, the internal market was far too small to sustain the industry. "Hence, this industry had to look for markets abroad. This . . . it did not fail to do in England and Holland from the second half of the fourteenth century on."[21]

Thus, textiles became the hub of English export trade, a shift from the thirteenth century when grain export played a larger role, and this within the context of what Postan calls "precocious mercantilism."[22] One aspect of this was the squeezing out of alien merchants, the Italians in particular, a process that was carried out in the fifteenth century,[23] not to be sure without difficulty.[24] It was even harder to squeeze out the Hanseatic merchants, but that too was accomplished by the sixteenth century.[25]

The cloth trade created great difficulties for England. The need to sell in many markets meant that England was subject to more loss as a result of competition and political difficulty than from the relatively sheltered wool trade.[26] In fact, the cloth industry received a number of setbacks in the fifteenth century because of its exposed position. Both Postan and S. T. Bindoff see these setbacks as the major explanation of the creation of the new commercial organization of overseas traders, the Fellowship of Merchant Adventurers of London, formally created in 1486 and monopolizing the export links with Antwerp.[27] But what the English lost in breadth of market, they made up in quantity. Furthermore, they were pressed to rationalization and efficiency since, as Bindoff notes, "the new situation meant not only an increased demand for cloth, especially for the particular lines favoured by the foreign buyer, but—what was more important—a demand for more cloth to be delivered at an overseas market at a particular time."[28] In addition, the English side was more unified than the Netherlands side which was beset by intercity competition, and hence the Merchant Adventurers could engage in a "calculated avoidance of any commitment to a sole use of one of the towns,"[29] remaining thereby in an economically advantageous bargaining position.

There is one further positive aspect to England's trade position. Her taxation was less oppressive than that of some of the older centers of commerce (Flanders, northern Italy) and her technical organization was up-to-date and hence more economical, thus giving her competitive advantages as early as the beginning of the "first" sixteenth century.[30] So it was that in the beginning of the "second" sixteenth century, England had a flourishing export trade, two-thirds of it going to Antwerp, the other third to France and the Iberian peninsula. Its net deficit with France was covered by the bullion resulting from its favorable balance with the Hapsburg areas. At the beginning of the Elizabethan era, England's overseas trade could already be described in glowing terms.[31]

England had political as well as economic advantages as the "second" sixteenth century began. It could be argued that England internally was exceptionally unified and from a relatively early period.[32] We shall not review here the reasons for this, which we discussed to some extent previously, except to notice that the explanations fall into two main camps: The form of medieval social structure was said to have lent itself particularly well to the development of a strong monarchy,[33] and the natural geography of insular England posed fewer obstacles to the centralizing thrust of the monarch than areas on the continent.[34]

Given such explanations, let us see in what ways did the Tudor monarchs make the most of these "natural" opportunities, and thus explain England's ability to pursue its tentative industrial advantages in the "second" sixteenth century.

One factor was what is sometimes called the Henrician or Tudor "administrative revolution" which G. R. Elton put forward as having occurred between 1530–1542 under the genius of that "most radical of modernizers,"[35] Thomas Cromwell. Elton argues that this period was one of real change, one which saw the creation of the modern sovereign state: "The Tudor state was a national monarchy to a degree new in England, and while the apparent emphasis lay on the monarch the real stress was already on its national character."[36] The administrative revolution was a concomitant of the greater coordination required by emerging capitalist interests. If

England were to be a coherent entity within the framework of the world-economy, it could no longer be several somewhat separate economies.[37]

Elton sees a series of new procedures instituted—a new mode of managing finances, the centralization of administration under the principal secretary, the organization of the privy council as a sphere of coordination, the rationalization of the king's household—each of which involved a reorganization "in the direction of greater definition, of specialization, of bureaucratic order."[38] Elton's work has given rise to one of those endless controversies in which historians debate, without the aid of quantitative data, the degree to which some "differences" add up to a qualitative jump.[39]

Was the Henrician Reformation really new or not? Was the administrative change truly revolutionary, or was it simply one more step in a process going on continuously from the fourteenth to the seventeenth centuries? Christopher Hill seems to me to hold a sensibly balanced view of what was going on:

> Throughout the Middle Ages [the] see-saw continued: more "bureaucratic" government under baronial control when the king was weak or a minor; "Household" government under the king's personal control when he was strong. But in the sixteenth century this cycle was broken. Departments "went out of court" without the king's losing control over them. . . .[40]

This period of administrative strengthening of the state was at the same time, as Hill also reminds us, "the only period in English history since 1066 when the country had no overseas possessions (except Ireland)."[41] So the administrative talent could all be focused inward. The results are very straightforward and very important.

England was able to develop a strong capital city as a cultural and economic unifying force.[42] And England was able to maintain internal peace at a time of turmoil on the continent, without a standing army, which accounts in part for its industrial advance.[43] Why should England have escaped the religious wars of the continent when it could be argued, as R. B. Wernham does, that in the period following the treaty of Cateau-Cambrésis, "the internal instability of the British Isles [caused largely by the uncertainty of the English succession] made them . . . the danger area and focal point in the rivalries of Western Europe."[44] Mainly it was this very rivalry and the relative exhaustion of the French and Spanish empires (which we already spelled out) combined with the boldness of the Act of Supremacy of 1559 in establishing England as an Anglican state[45] that "made possible the emergence of a third great power in western Europe and the eventual supersession of the twin imperialisms of Hapsburg and Valois by a multiple balance of powers.."[46]

Relative internal peace and no standing army also meant a lower need for taxation and of a bureaucracy swollen beyond its efficient size by the sale of offices.[47] The expansion of central power was by means of a more efficient bureaucracy more than through a much larger (and more burdensome) one. It was also made possible by the economic position of the monarch himself, England's greatest landowner.[48] But as greatest landowner in a relatively isolated and unified national economy whose strength was to be built on the new industries, where lay the interests of the king? No doubt the king's interests were ambiguous, since as landowner the king sought to maximize his income from his lands, and as king he sought to maximize his income from the landowners.[49] One way to try to solve the dilemma was for the Crown to try to reduce its role as a landlord. But then the monarchy had to find a substitute source of income. Toward this end, in 1610, the Crown offered Parliament the "Great Contract"—an exchange of its feudal rights for an annual allowance.[50] This proposal failed because of disagreement about the size of the annual amount. As the amount of income from royal rent was then diminishing, this failure was to contribute to the political strains of the era.

Internal instability and internal peace, an administrative revolution but a relatively small bureaucracy, a national network of markets and the king as a great landowner—a curious combination, leading to G. E. Aylmer's "paradox and truism that early Stuart England was at one and the same time a 'much-governed' country and a country with very little government."[51] This paradox is in fact the secret of England's relative success. To understand it, we must turn to a central debate of modern English historiography: the nature of the English upper classes in the century preceding the English Revolution, and the role of the much disputed "gentry."

Going through the literature of this debate, what J. H. Hexter has called "the storm over the gentry"[52] gives one the sensation of watching a fast and seemingly endless pingpong volley, where each play is brilliantly riposted ad infinitum. It requires distraction rather than concentration to realize that there are two debates intertwined: one over the substantive issues of English history in the "second" sixteenth century, and the other over the fundamental lines of battle in modern social science. Armed with this insight, it then requires concentration to notice that some people are in fact switching sides very fast in the middle of the debate, thus creating the illusion of a single straightforward ball game.

If the debate is difficult to unravel, it is because the story itself is so complex. Let us start by seeing what is thought to have happened in terms of landownership.

Frank C. Spooner argues that the profound economic crisis that shook Europe from about 1540 to 1560 "was particularly severe in the case of England...."[53] This was no doubt one of the factors that led to the official proclamation of the Reformation which made possible the confiscation of the monasteries and of other church properties. The Crown then sold most of this land, both to provide immediate income and as a means of political consolidation, giving the purchasers what Christopher Hill calls "a vested interest in Protestantism."[54] This political decision dramatically expanded the amount of land available on the market, which accelerated the whole process of extension of capitalist modes of operation in a way and to a degree that no other European country (except possibly the northern Netherlands) was experiencing at that time.[55] The lands once sold were sold again (and often a number of times over). Where did this all lead to over the next 75 years? This seems to be one of the cornerstones of the debate.

There seems to be relatively little debate about two arguments that R. H. Tawney put forward in his initial essays. One argument was "that the tendency of an active land-market was, on the whole, to increase the number of medium-sized properties, while diminishing that of the largest."[56] Note however that this does not necessarily say anything about who, peers or "gentry," own these "medium-sized" properties.[57] The second point that Tawney makes is that this land shift resulted in "a more business-like agriculture."[58] Again, relatively little argument here.

But what was the social classification of those who controlled the land? There is the storm. It is far more than a semantic issue but semantics plays its role, as everyone proceeds to give varying meanings to aristocracy, gentry (upper gentry, lower gentry, mere gentry, gentlemen), and yeomen. It is no accident that the scholars debate furiously here, because the whole point is that this period in English history is not only a moment of economic change and great individual social mobility, but of the change of categories. Not only are we unsure how to designate the meaningful social groupings; the men of the time also were.[59] To point however to the fluidity of a concept in a given epoch is not to point to its uselessness. It should urge the scholar on to skeptical boldness.

To untangle the threads, we must start by following the terms of discourse. Let us go successively through aristocracy, gentry, and yeomen. But as we do it, let us remember that "economic changes were hurrying the more enterprising among [those who controlled the land, whatever their designation,] into novel methods of estate management. . . . They stood to gain much if they adapted their farming to meet the new commercial conditions. They stood to lose much if they were so conservative as to adhere to the old methods."[60] It seems fairly clear that there was no across-the-board correlation of social status and adaptability to the demands of capitalist agriculture. Lawrence Stone paints a picture of the aristocracy as guilty of "incompetent management" on large estates and with a "spreading taste for conspicuous waste," such that "the gap between income and expenditure grew from a tiny crack to a vast chasm."[61] In addition, the aristocracy had to bear the high costs of litigation and public service, for "the Tudors operated through an unpaid bureaucracy."[62] But their efforts to increase income were to no avail: they traded away long leases for quick cash returns;

they overborrowed; they depended on state favors until the state could or would give no more. All to no avail:

> The process of attrition of the economic resources of the aristocracy . . . was one that continued without interruption throughout the Elizabethan period. . . . By 1603, it would seem as if the whole hierarchic structure of Tudor society was on the verge of imminent dissolution.[63]

Yet it is this same author who, a few years later, sings the imagination and enterprise of these same aristocrats in this same Elizabethan era:

> [I]n this period the peerage fulfilled a role that no other class, neither the gentry nor the merchants, was able or willing to rival. . . . The importance of the aristocracy at this period is due rather to their willingness to encourage and finance new ventures, which were regarded as risky and therefore failed to secure the backing of more cautious social groups. Since large-scale mining and metallurgical industries were still novelties in the Tudor period they took the lead in their expansion. Since oceanic trade and exploration were novelties they again played a prominent part.[64]

Nor was this initiative, it seems, absent on their demesnes:

> [T]he older nobility showed a surprising readiness . . . to develop new resources on their own estates. . . . The economic and social decline of the peerage relative to the gentry between 1558 and 1642 is certainly not due to any lack of entrepreneurial initiative.[65]

It is hard to reconcile the two portraits by Stone. Since Stone's statistics on the degree of financial crisis of the aristocracy have been subject to so much attack, and since he has partially but not wholly retreated,[66] we may well ask with H. R. Trevor-Roper:

> If "over two-thirds of the English aristocracy were in 1600, not merely living above their means but poised on the brink of financial ruin," . . . how are we to explain the fact that they not merely recovered from this imminent ruin, but survived the far greater crisis of the next sixty years? Their extravagance did not diminish in those years. . . . How did they do it?[67]

Trevor-Roper's explanation is that the predicament of the aristocracy, "though genuine, was nothing like so serious as Mr. Stone, with his swollen figures, supposes," that they "clung" to their lands, and that the rise in value of land after 1600, did "more than King James did, or any king could do," to sustain their fortunes.[68] It turns out, however, that Stone does not disagree. Although he dates it from 1620, he says that:

> Even the most incompetent [member of the landed classes] could not fail to profit from the massive rise in average rents in the early seventeenth century, and thereafter the levelling off of prices reduced the importance of inefficient estate management.[69]

As for J. H. Hexter who attacks both Stone and Tawney on the one hand and Trevor-Roper on the other, he argues:

> Around the 1580's the land market began to boom, and it seems to have continued to boom for the next half century. . . . [O]n the whole a general increase in land values is likely to be most profitable in gross to the men who have the most land to profit from, that is, to the very segment of the landed class which both Tawney and Trevor-Roper have consigned to economic debility.[70]

Aside, however, from a quibble about dates, the position Hexter takes on this item is *not* at variance with Stone and Trevor-Roper. Finally, let us turn to a fourth point of view, differing in many ways from the three others, that of Christopher Hill. On this question, he says:

> So for a section of the aristocracy the Reformation brought economic loss, though not for the class as a whole. We should be careful not to see anything "anti-feudal" in this process [of land transfers]. Indeed, in a sense the dissolution [of the monasteries] led to an intensification of feudalism, since it multiplied tenures in chief. . . . The ecclesiastical property which passed to [the monarchy] was soon dissipated. . . . In the short run, then, the Reformation strengthened the position of the lay landed ruling class as a whole, though it weakened some of those members of it hitherto powerful.[71]

If then there turns out to be less argument about the aristocracy than it seemed on first glance, can we say the same about the gentry who were the original focus of the debate? Gentry is of course a much vaguer term. Cooper spells out some of the difficulties:

> The peerage is a group of individuals enjoying a legally defined status which belongs . . . to only one male member of each family. Thus the younger sons of peers and their descendants will appear as gentry in Professor Tawney's classification. Great landowners, whenever they could afford it, were usually more generous to their sons in cash or land than is sometimes supposed. . . . Such provision certainly influenced the distribution of property. . . . [T]he gentry were not only, like the peerage, recruited from below, they were also recruited from above. . . . Furthermore, the groups are non-compatible in another respect: the peerage is a group strictly defined by legal status, while the gentry is not definable in any such fashion. It is a classification by wealth and to some extent by mode of life. . . . Although peerages were sold after 1603, entry to the peerage was never by a simple test of wealth and style of life.[72]

Who then are the gentry? The gentry are not yet peers, and are more than "yeomen," the latter a term as difficult to define as gentry. But then we discover that included among "gentry" are not only younger sons of peers, but various categories such as knights, esquires, and gentlemen. ✓ This should make it clear what is happening. In the hierarchical order of feudal society a large number of categories evolved which prescribed rank, duties, privileges, and honors. The ranks were constantly evolving, the family continuity of course unstable, the income correlates of rank varying. The expansion of capitalist agriculture was reflected in the stratification system by a new category of "landowner" (which to be sure might be subdivided by size of holding). Gentry emerged as a term covering capitalist landowners. The other terms did not disappear. But the "gentry" was a group label which expanded slowly to absorb and obliterate other terms. In the Elizabethan period, there were still "aristocrats" and "yeomen" in addition to "gentry" at the very least. In the twentieth century, there are only really "farmers." We get nowhere if we reify "gentry" be defining it either as it was defined at a certain moment in time or as we determine the social reality to have been at that moment in time. The whole point about "gentry" is not only that it was a class in formation but a concept in formation. It was, however, a case of new wine in old bottles. F. J. Fisher seems to me to put it exactly right: "The effect of the economic changes of the new sixteenth and seventeenth centuries was less to create new categories of men than to offer the existing categories new opportunities and to inspire them with a new spirit."[73]

Christopher Hill, by contrast, seems to me to add to the confusion in this formulation of the problem:

> We must surely start from the fact that "the gentry" were not an economic class. They were a social and legal class; economically they were divided. The inflationary century before 1640 was a great watershed, in which, in all sections of the community, economic divisions were taking place. Some yeomen were thriving to gentility; others were being submerged. Some peers were accumulating vast estates; others were on the verge of bankruptcy. It is easy to argue that "the gentry" were either "rising" or "declining" if we take samples of the class; for some families were doing the one and others the other.[74]

Though the empirical description of the social facts seems to me faultless, the theorizing seems to me to miss the point, precisely the Marxist point. "The mark of the gentry," says Julian Cornwall, "was the ownership of land."[75] The term gentry was *coming* to cover a group of men all in the same relationship to the means of production: owners of unentailed land producing for the market. The clarity of this process was confused by the fact that men still valued the social perquisites of an older legal category[76] but it was the common *economic* thrust that was the dominant unifying theme of this category in the sixteenth century and later. Within an economic class, some can be more wealthy than others, more successful than others in the market. Variation in income does not demonstrate that a group is not a class.

What light does this then throw on the now classic debate on the gentry? Tawney's essential point was that the gentry were a group with a style of life better adapted to survival in the age of inflation than the spendthrift peerage and the fly-by-night speculators. "Compared with the adventurers who dealt in properties they had never seen, the local gentry was a settled population confronting mere marauders."[77] Their advantage over their French counterparts was that they were "kept few and tough by the ruthlessness of the English family system, which sacrificed the individual to the institution.[78] They were politically far stronger than their Dutch counterparts, "wholly severed from their rural roots"[79] because they "combined the local and popular attachments essential for a representative role with the aristocratic aroma of *nobiles minores,* and played each card in turn with tactful, but remorseless, realism."[80] Hence they epitomize the process of succession of elites which Pirenne argues was the essence of the social history of capitalism.[81] The outcome was that "political institutions [were not in] accord with economic realities," which led inexorably to an English Revolution led by the "rising" gentry and caused by "impersonal forces too strong for both [Parliament and ruler to control]."[82]

The basis of Trevor-Roper's attack, as is well-known, aside from challenging Tawney's statistics and coding operations,[83] was to suggest that the basic model of the political arena was off base:

> I have already suggested that office rather than land was the basis of many un-doubtedly "rising" families. I would now go further. Instead of the distinction between "old" and "new" landlords, between peers and gentry, I would suggest as the significant distinction of Tudor and Stuart landed society, the distinction between "court" and "country," between the officeholders and the mere landlords. . . .
>
> What fortunes were made by the officials of Henry VIII who carried out the nationalization of monastic property! Naturally the best bargains went to them and to their local agents, the office-holding gentry in the counties. . . .
>
> But what of the mere gentry who had no such positions? As each prize came more valuable it moved farther away from their reach.[84]

Hence, the English Civil War can be seen, at least in part, as the rebellion of the overtaxed "mere" gentry against a Renaissance court.

Finally J. H. Hexter insists that there is a "third group of English landlords."[85] He says a look at the Parliamentary opposition to the Stuarts shows they are drawn not from the "power-hungry rural middle class" of Tawney, for they are "rich country gentry" (is that really so different from Tawney?); nor are they the "angry hard-pressed yokels" of Trevor-Roper, for they were an "unusually well-educated group of men" (is that really incompatible with Trevor-Roper?)[86]

However if we follow Hexter's positive assertions, we shall in fact be led to a fairly clear picture of the social role of the gentry, though not to the one he apparently thinks he leads us. He says at one point in his critique: "We are still left with the problem that started Tawney on his quest. . . . Why at this particular historical juncture did the 'country' find its leadership in social strata beneath the top? Why among the gentry rather than among the nobility?"[87] Hexter's answer is essentially that the political rise of the gentry is to be explained by the growing military power

of the king and concurrent decline of the military power of the territorial
magnates. "Consequently the gentry of the Tudor period acted with greater
independence than their predecessors in the days of Lancaster and York.
. . ."[88] As many have observed, who ever said otherwise? And as Stone
pointedly remarks: "Mr. Hexter's deus ex machina to explain the rise
to political power of the gentry is altogether too superficial: he says that
the aristocracy lost military control. Of course; but why did this happen?"[89]
We are thus returned to those central variables we have been discussing
(as have Tawney and Trevor-Roper): the growth of a bureaucratic state
machinery and the development of capitalist agriculture—and the link
between the two.[90]

Hexter next takes off against "the myth of the middle class." But here
he is really challenging nineteenth-century liberalism and not the "un-
conscious" Marxism which he suggests underlies so much of modern
economic history.[91] In fact his own analysis is not in reality so far away
from that of Tawney and Trevor-Roper. The Tudors, he says, were not
promiddle class, except for "a small inner coterie of Tudor merchant-
bankers," a group of "Court-bound capitalists."[92]

Tudor policy was really very consistent:

> [It] was usually quite tender of vested interests. It protected old ones and created new
> ones in the emergent forms of enterprise. . . . It was not the policy of the Tudors
> either to stand mulishly athwart the path of change, or to allow it free rein, but to
> guide it, to bring it as they said to some rule conformable with good order.[93]

And, for good measure, Hexter adds, "the Tudors regarded the middle
✓ class as the milch herd of the commonwealth."[94]

But it was precisely Lawrence Stone who emphasized the degree to
which the Tudors exercised economic control, favored a handful of
entrepreneurs, but not the bourgeois classes as a whole, and placed the
strengthening of the state's military power at a premium,[95] and it is the
essence of Trevor-Roper's argument that the gentry rebelled against
being a milch herd.

Finally, says Hexter, it is not the case that the capitalist spirit only emerged
in the sixteenth century for it had long been in existence, nor that "the
sixteenth-century landowners waited for the example and inspiration of
town merchants"[96] to engage in capitalist agriculture. Precisely so. But then
we are back to the picture of an emerging capitalist class recruited from
varying social backgrounds.[97]

Why should this be strange? It was, as we have seen, happening throughout the European world-economy.[98] No doubt, there were varying political
expressions of different subgroups within the "gentry." Barrington Moore
for example has a suggestion about the political opposition of Trevor-
Roper's "declining gentry" which makes that phenomenon totally compat-

ible with the political opposition of Tawney's "rising gentry." He quotes Tawney: "There are plenty of gentry who stagnate or go downhill. It would be easy to find noble landlords who move with the times, and make the most of their properties."[99] Moore then says of those who "stagnated":

> These "growlers and grumblers" may have supplied a portion of the radical element behind Cromwell and the Puritan Revolution, though this impetus had its main origins farther down the social scale. Thus, under the impact of commerce and some industry, English society was breaking apart from the top downward in a way that allowed pockets of radical discontent produced by the same forces to burst temporarily into the limelight. . . . In this process, as the old order breaks up, sections of society that had been losing out due to long-run economic trends come to the surface and do much of the violent "dirty work" of destroying the *ancien régime,* thus clearing the road for a new set of institutions. In England the main dirty work of this type was the symbolic act of beheading Charles I.[100]

Probably Hexter is right in suggesting there were three types of landlords—"rising," "declining," and others. And it's very plausible that political opposition tends to correlate with the first two types more than with the third. In an explanation of the politics of the early Stuart era these details are crucial.[101] In assessing the trends of social change, it is far more important to see the rise of the gentry not as an economic force nor as a political entity but as a social category.

Concentration on detail, while it often lays bare the vacuousness of weak generalization, can also obscure secular change. Lawrence Stone, after making just such a detailed analysis of the complexities of social mobility in England at this time, points out that the form of this analysis tended to drop from view two important shifts of English society:

> The first was a polarization of society into rich and poor: the upper classes became relatively more numerous, and their real incomes rose; the poor became relatively more numerous and their real incomes fell. The second a greater equality among the upper classes: firstly the wealth and power of the greater gentry increased relative to that of the aristocracy; and secondly members of the trades and professions rose in wealth, number and social status relative to the landed classes.[102]

J. Hurstfield makes a similar point with emphasis on its impact on the politics of the "second" sixteenth century:

> In England the aristocracy never became a caste and the landed gentry never became a lesser nobility. Hence the middle and upper classes stood in much closer relation to each other than they did to the monarchy; and, in times of crisis, had much more in common with each other than they had with the Crown.[103]

Stone and Hurstfield are both demonstrating the crucial point here: the process of emergence of a new class category within which the "old" distinction of aristocrat–gentry was losing its significance. As Perez Zagorin sums up the situation, the general tendency of the long sixteenth century in

England, "was to give to men . . . in a position to deploy capital in agriculture, trade, and industry . . . the command of social life."[104] And this combined class gained at the expense of the peasantry.[105] The English situation is a good illustration of Lattimore's generalization: "[I]n any gradually changing society it is always those who rule that hang onto the best of what is left of the old order, and at the same time take the best of what is offered by the new, [leading in time to] a considerable diversification. . . ."[106]

If the "gentry" were simply the name for the capitalist farmers as they became a class, what are yeomen? Yeomen is a term just like gentry, a pre-existing socio–legal term whose content was evolving in the sixteenth century. Mildred Campbell, in her book on the English yeomen, sifts through the various uses of the word and its relation to such terms as farmer, gentleman, freeholder, husbandman, and laborer, noting acerbically: "There is nothing, one may say at the outset, as explicit as the distinction just discarded."[107] Her conclusion is that

> yeomen status viewed in terms of its relationship to other groups in the social structure assumes a fairly definite character. They were a substantial rural middle class whose chief concern was with the land and agricultural interests, a group who lived "in the temperate zone betwixt greatness and want," serving England, as it was given a "middle people" . . . in condition between the gentry and the peasantry to serve.[108]

To appreciate the role of this group we must return to a theme discussed in a previous chapter, the evolution of the tenure system in English agriculture. Marx in his discussion of the genesis of capitalist ground rent makes a crucial point which is often overlooked in the exegesis of his views:

> [A]s soon as rent assumes the form of money-rent, and thereby the relationship between rent-paying peasant and landlord becomes a relationship fixed by contract —a development which is only possible generally when the *world*-market, commerce and manufacture have reached a certain relatively high level—the leasing of land to capitalists inevitably also makes its appearance. The latter hitherto stood beyond the rural limits and now carry over to the country-side and agriculture the capital acquired in the cities and with it the capitalist mode of operation developed—i.e., creating a product as a mere commodity and solely as a means of appropriating surplus-value. This form can become the general rule *only in those countries which dominate the world-market* in the period of transition from the feudal to the capitalist mode of production.[109]

The relevance of Marx's point is that the process of transformation in the land tenure system is not unique to England, as is obvious. But as England (and the Dutch Republic) become more and more the core territories of the European world-economy in the "second" sixteenth century (and even more in the late seventeenth and eighteenth centuries), the process goes further and faster in these areas precisely because they are the core. It is crucial that resources be used more efficiently in order to benefit from the central trading and financial position in the world-economy. In England, it paid the landed classes to move to a system of fully alienable land just as it paid the landed classes in Poland (and even say in southern France) to restrain moves in this direction.

To make land fully alienable, to have production for commodity sale as the overriding consideration of agriculture, one has to eliminate not only various kinds of feudal tenure systems. One has to eliminate also the peasant farmer, for the peasant may hold on to the land and engage in marginal kinds of production activities for considerations that do not maximize short-run profitability. How was in fact such elimination accomplished?

H. John Habakkuk points out that there are three ways of expropriating peasants: chasing them from their tenures and incorporating their land into the domain; forcing them to yield life tenures for limited rentals; whittling away at the communal rights of the peasants. He argues that in the "second" sixteenth century only those peasants who were tenants for a limited term or for life without right or renewal were effectively subject to such forms of expropriation, and he estimates that this added up to only about 35% of the peasantry.[110] As for the sale of lands, the picture is far from one-sided:

> During [this] period . . . there were certainly lords (*seigneurs*) who bought land from the peasants; there were also some peasants who accumulated so much goods that they were elevated to the rank of gentry. In both cases, the result was a diminution of peasant property. But there were also peasants who bought the great domains when they were put on sale, or who obtained copyhold lease. The net result of these transactions is not known. But it is altogether possible that those acquisitions added up to a gain rather than a loss for the peasantry; whereas, on the one hand, the lords expropriated the peasants, on the other the peasants, in acquiring goods nibbled at the domains of the lords.[111]

The full capitalization of agriculture was yet to come in England. In the sixteenth century, the yeoman still had his role to play. The increasing commercialization of agriculture at this time offered the small landowner not only "dangers" but "opportunities." Campbell, who waxes a bit romantic, sees the yeomen as rather heroic:

> Scheming landlords and land-hungry neighbors were ever ready to take advantage of a man's misfortunes. Though prices in the main steadily went up, there were sometimes fluctuations that came without warning and in uncertain sequence. Other evils added to the insecurity of the times. Uncontrolled epidemics were a constant dread. Loss by fire was common, and insurance of any kind practically unknown. Either a man must have savings in hand for such rainy days or else go in debt. . . .
>
> But when it is a case of sink or swim, unless the odds are too great against a man he usually tries to swim. . . . And despite the uncertain conditions depicted above, more than ever before in the history of English landholding the little man who had industry and an abundance of enterprise was getting his opportunity.

> Those who could weather the storms found in the higher prices and better market opportunities for profit that urged them on to still greater effort. Gain begets the desire for more gain.[112]

If the yeomen was not the direct beneficiary of the dissolution of the monasteries, he might eventually get a piece of the pie.[113]

As many have pointed out, there were two kinds of enclosure going on in that era: enclosure of large domains for pasture, and small land consolidation for more efficient tillage. It is in this latter process that the yeomen played the central role, a role all the more important because it had important social consequences in terms of increasing food supply without incurring the kind of political opposition which pasturage enclosures encountered.[114] Part of the improvements came from other factors that increased efficiency of labor. Thirsk attributes it to:

> the use of more intensive rotations, accompanied by heavier manuring; the use of improved varieties of grain; and, probably most important of all, the impressive increase in the total acreage of land under the plough as a result of the reclamation of waste and the conversion of pasture. . . . Heavier manuring of the arable, of course, was made possible by keeping larger numbers of animals, which resulted in a great increase in the supply of meat and wool and other animal products. Heavier rates of stocking were made possible by the improvement of pastures and meadows by fertilizers, by the improved supply of spring grazing, through the watering of meadows in the west country, the growing of tares elsewhere, and by the increased supply of summer grazing through the use of bogs and the reclamation of coastal marshland and fen. *Thus improvements in arable and pastoral husbandry went hand in hand,* each helping the other, and *both serving to promote the specialization and interdependence of regions.*[115]

The inclusion of Wales in the English division of labor at this time aided this process of agricultural improvement. For one thing, the imposition of English legal forms, particularly primogeniture, led to great uncertainty about the land tenure system. This was propitious for the creation of large domains in Wales. "From one end of Wales to the other it was a time of estate-building and the laying of family fortunes."[116] This was particularly true in the "anglicized lowlands" which showed "marked inequality in the size of holdings. . . ."[117] I would suspect the landlords were disproportionately English. The degree of agricultural improvement brought about by enclosures in Wales seem to have been greater than in England. Wales had still been suffering until that time from "predatory techniques."[118] This meant, however, even greater displacements of population, who migrated to England, there most probably to become part of the lumpenproletariat, and many of them ending up as mercenaries as we have already mentioned.

Campbell says that the age was an age of "land hunger."[119] "[A]mong the land hungry none were more avaricious than the yeomen."[120] It obviously paid off by the evidence we have from rural housing in England from 1570 to 1640, the period of "The Great Rebuilding," the work, according to W. G. Hoskins, of "the bigger husbandmen, the yeomen, and the lesser gentry, all largely of the same social origin in medieval centuries."[121] Lawrence Stone cites this same fact, however, as further evidence of the "rise of the gentry,"[122] an indication once again of the fluidity of the designations we are using. Are not these yeomen simply the less well-capitalized version of the gentry who are capitalist farmers?[123]

This becomes clearer if we see who in fact loses out in the process of enclosures (of both varieties). As the enclosures proceeded—whether the large-scale enclosures of sheepherders or the small-scale enclosures of improving yeomen—a number of men who formerly lived on and off the land were forced to leave it, and others were reduced to the status of landless rural laborers working for wages.[124] This has long been considered to be a central element in the creation of the labor surplus that is a critical element in the "commercialising of English life."[125] This shift occurred between 1540 and 1640. In the economic squeeze, some small men gained but many more lost.[126] Indeed, the very process of fulfilling the liberation of the peasant from the constraints of feudalism may have served as an additional mode of impoverishment. Alexander Savine, in his article on the remains of feudal villeinage in Tudor England, notes the paradox "that for the bondman of the sixteenth century his personal dependence upon the lord became most burdensome at the moment he got his freedom."[127] The paradox is very simple to unravel. Manumission was not free. It was bought. Indeed, it must have bought high, because Savine notes:

> Manumission of bondmen was regarded as a regular source of seigniorial income. . . . The enfranchisement of the last bondsmen was a paying policy. The thing was done so openly in the sixteenth century that Elizabethan courtiers could receive as a special sign a favour from the sovereign a commission to enfranchise a definite number of villein families on the Crown manors; that is to say, they were enabled to repair their fortunes with the payments for enfranchisement.[128]

Villeins no longer gave work-week service to the lord on the demesne.[129] Rather, the "personal dependence of the bondman became a mere pretext for extortion."[130] Thus, in the process, no doubt, many became landless paupers.

We find further evidence of this pauperization in the virtual disappearance of the husbandman category. On the one hand, some husbandmen were "rising to be yeomen and the distinctions between husbandmen and yeomen were being blurred."[131] And on the other hand, the poorer husbandman was getting to be worse off than many rural laborers who were cottagers, and needed to engage in part-time wage labor to make ends meet.[132] Might not husbandmen spasmodically employed have thought it desirable to become laborers regularly employed?

In any case, both these categories of farmworkers were those vulnerable to enclosure and encroachment on their commons' right. Encroachment, in particular, led to abandonment of villages and migration.[133] Everitt points out that the growing distinction between the peasant–yeomen and the "poor squatters and wanderers, virtually landless, often lately evicted from elsewhere" was a phenomenon to be observed particularly in the more recently-settled forest areas of the countryside[134] and that "it was from this latter group, in consequence of their semi-vagrant origins, that the growing army of seasonal workers was largely recruited, called into being by the needs of commercial farming."[135]

Thus arose the crucial political problem of begging and vagabondage, a notorious feature of Elizabethan England.[136] Frank Aydelotte sees three separate factors combining to explain the upsurge of vagabondage in Elizabethan times: enclosures to be sure and most importantly; but also Tudor peace and hence the disbanding of enormous bands of retainers kept by nobles; and also the dissolution of the monasteries and the disappearance of their role as dispensers of charity. Aydelotte's view of these vagabonds, which cannot be far different from that of the rulers of the day, is to see them as a *social* problem:

> Far from being either an impotent or a harmless class, the vagabonds of the sixteenth century represented much of the solid strength of medieval England. Many of them came from good stock, but in the economic scheme of modern England they found no useful place. They had brains to plan villany and audacity to execute it. Their ranks contained political, religious and social malcontents and agitators. Hence it was that they were a danger as well as a pest in the England of Elizabeth. The vagabonds were menace enough to cause the lawmakers, from Henry VII onwards, to give their best thought to a remedy, both by framing statutes and providing for their execution, until the problem was finally solved, as far as legislation could solve it, by the admirable poor laws of 1572, 1597, and 1601.[137]

Admirable? Perhaps, although doubtless not in the simple sense Aydelotte wants us to admire them.

These laws do however throw light on the role the state machinery was playing. First let us note that "social welfare" legislation, previously unknown in Europe, appears on the scene in *many* places at this time. Furthermore, it is not even a matter of simultaneous invention, but of conscious cultural diffusion.[138] Second, the relationship of such legislation to economic transformation is ambiguous. It was to be sure a response to a social crisis brought on by economic change, a means of averting political rebellion.[139] But its economic meaning was not one of straightforward support for the capitalist classes. It was a form of political stabilization whose effect was as constraining to the employers as to the laborers, perhaps even more.[140] This policy of monarchical constraint on the free play of capitalism in the sixteenth century is in marked contrast with the collaboration of the state to intervene in the process of the great and definitive enclosures of the eighteenth century.[141]

The Tudors and early Stuarts are often thought to have "failed," because the ultimate outcome of their policy was the English Revolution. But perhaps the English Revolution should be viewed as a measure of the "success" of the Tudor–Stuart monarchs, in that they held off rebellion so long. Let us look at the reactions of sixteenth-century English peasants under stress. Many chose vagabondage. Another possibility was peasant rebellion, and rebellions there were, to be sure. But it should be noticed that there were fewer in England at this time than earlier, and fewer at this time in England than in France or elsewhere on the continent.

Each of these contrasts is worth looking at. R. H. Hilton argues that the sixteenth-century enclosures had a "pre-history." The process of leaving the land goes back to the thirteenth century. There was of course the phenomenon of depopulation, but Hilton feels that poverty was a more basic explanation for the rural exodus.[142] Then came the inflationary, "long" sixteenth century. Whereas in eastern Europe the landlords forced the laborers back onto the land because the expanded cash-crop production required it, England took a route of pasturage (which required less labor) and increased efficiency of arable production (which required less labor). Far from wanting to farm estates directly, large landowners sought tenants, and preferred "capitalist farmers" as tenants to "peasants."[143] Since this was to the disadvantage of many in the rural areas, why did the peasants not resist more than they did? Hilton argues that they were too weak to resist.[144] Further confirmation is to be found in the observation by C. S. L. Davies that there was relatively *more* peasant resistance in the "first" sixteenth century than in the "second," whereas if harshness of conditions were sufficient to explain peasant outbreaks, the opposite would have occurred. It is only after 1590 that rent rises surge ahead of price increases. Davies gives two kinds of explanations for this. On the one hand, the concept of variable rent was relatively new and therefore outrageous in the "first" sixteenth century, whereas by the "second," the peasants were habituated to this concept.[145] And second, and perhaps more importantly, the "yeomen" were not negatively affected by the enclosures.[146]

Let us now turn to a comparison of the lot of the "yeomen" in England and France at this same period. Here Davies notices that it was the burden of taxation which led most directly to rebellion against the central authority, and that this burden was less in England than in France because of the smaller size of the state, the relatively less venal and hence less extractive bureaucracy, and the institutional weakness of the regions which reduced the weight of state machinery as well as eliminating foci of rebellion.[147]

Finally, let us look at one last contrast, peasant revolts in sixteenth-century England and those of the eighteenth century. Tawney points out that this is a contrast between their "prevalence . . . in the middle of the sixteenth century" and their "comparative rarity two hundred years later," although the same potential cause, the enclosures, was there.[148] Tawney argues that

the agrarian disturbances of the sixteenth century "mark the transition
from the feudal revolts of the fifteenth century, based on the union of
all classes in a locality against the central government, to those in which
one class stands against another through the opposition of economic interests."[149]

What then is it we are saying? It seems that the sixteenth century, particularly the period between 1540–1640, is a period of class *formation*, a
capitalist agricultural class (whose wealthier members are called "gentry"
and whose lesser members are called "yeomen"). The social process of
land consolidation in England at this time is one of increasing income
to this class as a whole including to the lesser members of it, while it
involves the beginnings of the creation of a proletariat, most of whom
was still not firmly settled in the towns but rather were "vagabonds," seasonal
wage workers with subsistence plots, and lumpenproletariat in the towns.

The state machinery was not a coherent strong independent force but
a battleground of two conflicting trends—those persons of high traditional
status who were at best partially adapting to the new economic possibilities,
and those rising elements (whatever their background in terms of traditional
status and whatever their relative wealth in the present) who pushed toward
the full commercialization of economic life.

While both these elements sought and from time to time received the
assistance of the state, neither was sure that it stood to profit from a greatly
strengthened state machinery, largely because both sides feared that the
other side would dominate the state bureaucracy. A policy of "social welfare"
served the interests of preserving order and interfering with the full play
of market forces. It eased the transition, and thus had advantages for
all the forces in play.

England's position in the world-economy precisely made this balancing
game possible. It was sheltered from too much outside interference by
the struggle of the two great military powers: Spain and France. It was
unencumbered by imperial obligations.[150] It was free therefore to pursue
its economic specialization, especially with the assistance of eastern Europe's
raw materials, fed to it in part by its commercial alliance with the Dutch
Republic, which also wanted shelter from the military giants, and which
"paid the costs" of keeping the world trade machinery operating. The
English state machinery was just strong enough to fend off baneful outside
influences, but still weak enough not to give too great an edge either
to "traditionalist" elements or to the new parasites of the state bureaucracy,
so that neither the one nor the other were able to eat up totally the surplus
of the most productive forces. In short, it was a question of optimal position:
relative political insulation while having the economic advantages of the
world-economy, a relative balance of forces internally which maximized
internal peace, but minimized the errors of an overbearing state machinery.

How come, then, one might properly ask, the English Revolution? It might be said now that we are arguing that the proof of the "success" of England during this era is that the English Revolution occurred when it did—neither earlier nor later—and that the forces of modern capitalism emerged clearly triumphant, despite their presumed "defeat" and a presumed "Restoration" of the old. To appreciate this issue of timing, we should look at three related phenomena: the politics of alliance in this era, the patterns of migration, and the so-called commercial crisis of the early Stuart era. This will enable us to talk about the "real issues" that were the background to the English Revolution.

H. R. Trevor-Roper insists that the essential conflict is that of court and country. If this is his key point, then he has won, because this presumed opponents—for example, Stone and Hill[151]—have conceded the case. The issue however is not there. It is what political game was the Court playing, how was this game related to the social and economic transformation going on, and in what ways was it consequence and cause of England's role in the European world-economy.

The state-machinery, the Court, was at one and the same time a protagonist of the drama and a mediating agency, a vector of different forces. This was true of all the so-called absolute monarchies. They balanced forces; they served as power brokers; they effected compromises. But one of the outcomes they hoped for was to strengthen themselves, to become absolute in deed rather than merely in theory and in aspiration.

Given the ambiguity of its role and its objectives, the Court was ambivalent about the onsurge of capitalist elements. On the one hand, the Crown courted the "bourgeoisie," that is to say, the conglomerate of landed capitalist proprietors and well-to-do farmers, professional men (lawyers, divines, and medical practitioners), the wealthier merchants.[152] "Haunted by the fear of feudal revolts,"[153] as Tawney puts it, the State saw in them allies for its own ends. But the Court, when all is said and done, was dominated by the aristocracy, the king first among them—old aristocrats, men newly come to the titles and valuing them all the more for it, others in the service of the king aspiring to the peerage—and the Court could not be sanguine about the undermining of the hierarchical status system of which it was the apex. Nor was it sanguine. It cherished this system, reinforced it, elaborated it, paid for it. The Renaissance Court outshone all others that Europe had known.

Its need for money and political allies led the Court to further commerce and commercialization. Its need for stability and deference led it to be uneasy about the aggressive successes of the new class. To the extent that it was competent, the Court sought to apply a slow brake to an accelerating process of capitalist transformation while at the same time increasing the political centrality of state institutions. This was no different in Tudor England than in Valois France or Hapsburg Spain. What was different was both the historical background and the international position in the sixteenth century which made the new English capitalist class both relatively stronger and more able to absorb within it very large elements of the old aristocracy.

Many writers note that, about 1590–1600, there was a critical moment in the politics of England. Tawney writes:

> Few rulers have acted more remorselessly than the early Tudors on the maxim that the foundations of power are economic. They had made the augmentation of the royal demesne, and the protection of the peasant cultivator, two of the keystones of the New Monarchy. By the later years of Elizabeth, the former policy was crumbling badly, and the latter, always unpopular with the larger landowners, was encountering an ever more tenacious opposition.[154]

Over time the weight of the Crown's decisions was leaning toward the capitalist farmers, as opposed to the aristocracy as such.[155] The latter, in order to survive, became more and more like "rising gentry" and hence, from the point of view of the peasantry, more and more exploitative.[156] Hence the ties grew thinner between lord and peasant, and the latter were no longer likely to respond to regional vertical appeals of loyalty in national conflicts.[157] The Crown bureaucracy itself however was becoming overblown and "wasteful," a process which had its natural limits, as Trevor-Roper argues.[158] Then, agree Stone and Trevor-Roper, by 1590, overexpenditure led to cutback. Peace in Europe (the interval between 1598 and 1618) reduced the costs for all the states.[159] In England, the sale of titles by James I increased the income[160] and crisis was thereby averted. Crisis averted but extravagance increased, because of the logic of the Crown's dual-stranded policy.[161]

A century of Tudor rule may not have caused a sharp decline in the ownership of land by peers as Tawney originally thought. It seems in the end that all that happened is that the royal demesne was partially parceled out to non-peer capitalist farmers.[162] The beneficiaries of Tudor rule were doubtless both peers and non-peers who were able to master the new economy.[163] Tudor juggling kept them on top of the situation. But the "long" sixteenth century was nearing its end. And the strains of its contradictions would be felt under the early Stuarts. This is the point which Trevor-Roper makes:

> Even in the 1590's, even a far less expensive, more efficient bureaucracy had been saved only by peace: how could this much more outrageous system [of the Stuarts and other European monarchs of this time] survive if the long prosperity of the sixteenth century, or the saving peace of the seventeenth, should fail?
>
> In fact, in the 1620's they both failed at once. In 1618 a political crisis in Prague had set the European powers in motion. . . . Meanwhile the European economy . . . was suddenly struck by a great depression, the universal "decay of trade" of 1620.[164]

So we are once more back to the workings of the world-system. England's reaction to the so-called "crisis of the seventeenth century" was somewhat different from that of others. This is why she could enter the era of mercantilism with so much greater strength. One aspect of this strength was the high degree of commercialization of her agriculture, a process we have been describing. The other side was her "industrialization."

John Nef argues that England underwent an "early industrial revolution" in the period 1540–1640, and that by comparison France did not.[165] He asserts there were three main developments in England. A number of industries previously known on the Continent but not in England were introduced (paper and gunpowder mills, cannon foundries, alum and copperas factories, sugar refineries, saltpeter works, brass making). New techniques were imported from the Continent, especially in mining and metallurgy. Finally, the English made their own positive contribution to technology, especially in connection with the substitution of coal for wood.[166] Furthermore, Nef argues that "capital investment along with technical inventive ingenuity, was being oriented as never before in the direction of production for the sake of *quantity*."[167] If, however, one asks of Nef, why this sudden shift of England from being an industrial "backwater" to being relatively advanced, Nef offers principally a geographical explanation. The large internal market, a prerequisite for industrial concentration, was made possible "by the facilities for cheap water transport which Great Britain, by virtue of her insular position and good harbors, enjoyed to a greater degree than any foreign country except Holland."[168] No doubt this is true, but since the geography was the same in earlier centuries, we are left uncertain as to why the sudden spurt.

What does seem to be clear is that there was a spurt: in industrial technology, in degree of industrialization, and correlatively in population. K. W. Taylor, in observing the doubling of the English population under Tudor rule, offers two explanations: domestic peace and the new geography of world trade which changed England's location in the "world" and hence ended the concentration of its population in the south and east. "Like a potted plant, long left undisturbed on a window-sill and then transferred to an open garden, the economy of England threw out new leaves and branches."[169] Taylor's geographical explanation, because it speaks of England's position relative to the world-economy as opposed to Nef's argument of internal geographic advantages, is more satisfying since it deals with an element that precisely changed in the sixteenth century. Furthermore, if we remember the new importance of the Baltic as well as of the Atlantic trade, the argument is further strengthened. Still by itself, it is not enough to explain the discrepancy with France. Perhaps we shall have to look to factors within France that prevented her from taking as much advantage of the new geography as did England.

Let us further note that England's doubling of population was selective, because it involved not only demographic growth but quality immigration and helpful emigration. On the one hand, there is the oft-noted influx of continental artisans—Flemish clothiers, German metallurgists, etc.—whose arrival is usually attributed to the upheavals of the religious wars. But, if they went to England, it is because, as G. N. Clark argues, England had become "the place where capital and management could earn a better remuneration."[170] Let us however remember that the end of the Elizabethan era was a moment of economic and social strain—too great expenditures of the court, plus population growth combined with enclosures and hence the rise of vagabondage. As F. J. Fisher reminds us, contemporaries thought of Elizabethan England "as a country in which population pressure was gradually reducing many to poverty and possibly diminishing the national income per head."[171]

There are two ways to handle the problem of surplus population within a country: remove them from the cities (that is, geographically segregate them), or remove them from the country altogether. In Tudor–Stuart England, both were tried. On the one hand, the poor laws, the "laws against the poor" as Braudel calls them,[172] pushed them to the rural areas to exist in a borderline fashion. On the other hand, it is just at this time that England begins to think of overseas colonization—to Ireland first from about 1590, then to North America and the West Indies. In the case of external emigration, the temptation for the emigrants was social mobility.[173] Malowist suggests we look to an explanation of the second wave of European expansion which begins in the end of the sixteenth century—that of England, Holland, and to a lesser extent, France—not only in the commercial factors often cited, but in the need to dispense with surplus population. He notes that many see demographic expansion as a stimulus of economic expansion, but he reminds us that there is an optimal point. "Difficult economic situations and certain social situations unfavorable to economic progress seem therefore to create conditions which favor emigration, even the most risky."[174] Once again, only optima can be considered in a country "prematurely overpopulated."[175] Like England, France exported its population, to Spain in the sixteenth and seventeenth centuries (to replace the expelled Moriscos), later to the "islands" of America, and killed many off in the persecutions of the Protestants.[176] By the end of the eighteenth century, to be sure, France's population was once more balanced.[177] But it took far longer to arrive at this balance than England. And it was only at a price of internal warfare which strengthened some of the wrong forces and expelled some of the right ones—wrong and right, that is, from the point of view of industrial transformation. These pluses of English development become clear in the outcome of the European economic crisis of the 1620s. Before however we deal with that, we must look at what happened in France between Cateau-Cambrésis and the crisis.

For Frank C. Spooner, "the decade 1550–1560 is decisive [for France]."[178] It is marked by a sudden gold shortage which turns France's attention to African exploration and leads to a development of the western maritime regions. It marks the rise of Paris as a financial center (as against Lyon which definitively declines by 1580).[179] Furthermore, it is marked by the outbreak of the religious civil wars which were to preoccupy France for the rest of the century. This double development (of the maritime regions and Paris) and the religious wars are not unconnected.

The inflation affected the income of the nobility, particularly the lesser nobility who lived on fixed rents. But the peasants did not benefit, as might normally be expected, because of the devastations wrought by civil war. One major consequence was the vastly increased importance of the state machinery not only because of the vast expansion of tax farming that occurred at this time, but also because nobles who wished to survive economically sought financial refuge in attaching themselves to the court.[180]

France at this time was faced with one major problem in seeking to reorient itself to the new European world after Cateau-Cambrésis. It was neither fish nor fowl, no longer empire, but not quite a nation-state. It was geared half to land transport, half to sea transport. Its state machinery was at once too strong and too weak.

There are two arenas in which this ambiguity of option can be seen most clearly. One is in the arena of trade, the other is in politics and religion. The facts of the economic trading zones did not mesh with the political boundaries. This was to some extent true everywhere in Europe of course (and to some extent always true), but it was particularly glaring for France, especially if one compared France with what is the case for her great economic rivals-to-be: England and the northern Netherlands. Emile Coornaert describes the situation at the beginning of the sixteenth century in this way:

> In the region which, in rapid outline, runs from Paris and the bend of the Loire to the Mediterranean, France was part of an economic zone which still was heavily under the influence of the Italians, the principal men of affairs, masters of commercial techniques, since the last of the Middle Ages in all of western Europe. Thanks especially to them, this zone was the most developed from the point of view of organization and modes of work. In France, the pole and, at the same time, the port of exit in this part of the country was Lyon, which put it in contact with the south and centre of the continent and contributed rather actively to its links with the north-west. The latter which included the north of France and the French maritime front of the Ponant, the Low Countries, England, and the Rhenish fringe of the Empire constituted another zone. Its pole was Antwerp, which controlled contacts with northern Europe and, in large part, with Germany. From the point of view of techniques, it was on the way to reaching the level of the Southern European zone.[181]

This economic split meant that France was further from having a *national* economy than England, far closer in this regard to Spain. But whereas Spain's problem was that Spain was part of a larger Hapsburg Empire which, at least under Charles V, she did not really control, France's problem was that, after 1557, she was attracted in at least three different directions. The political heart of the country—roughly the northeast and including the capital—was attracted to a continental land mass, the economy that had been dominant in the "first" sixteenth century, that is, linked to Antwerp even after her decline.[182] The northwest and west of France was attracted to the new European world-economy and its Atlantic and Baltic trades.[183] The south of France was developing the system of *métayage* we previously discussed, part of the general movement of the Christian Mediterranean toward primary production, toward export-oriented, capitalist agriculture.[184]

For Henri Hauser this motley assortment of activities and orientations adds up to a "happy condition in which [France] could dispense with her neighbours while they could not do without her."[185] He even wishes to call this "autarchy." To me, it seems quite the opposite, a situation in which France is the sum of centrifugal economic forces. It is in order to counter this fractionation that the controllers of the state machinery move so strikingly to reinforce it, to create Europe's strongest state, what will become under Louis XIV the very model, for contemporaries and for history, of the absolute monarchy.

One of the critical sources of the economic dilemma of France arises out of a change in the technological substratum of the European world-economy. To appreciate its importance, we must first dissect some conflicting evidence on the relative costs of sea and land transport in pre-industrial Europe. On the one hand, there are the frequent and seemingly obvious statements that in pre-industrial Europe, "land transport was still extremely expensive and the nations which had the best command of sea-borne trade secured the fastest economic growth."[186] Furthermore, as Kristof Glamann suggests, the theory of widening circles as a result of economic intercourse particularly applies to maritime trade. Indeed, he says, "international trade [via water routes] is in many cases cheaper and easier to establish than domestic trade."[187] On the other hand, Wilfrid Brulez points out:

> In the 16th century, . . . land transport retained a primordial role. This fact is indisputable for the trade between the Low Countries and Italy: although they had Antwerp, a first-rate maritime outlet and what's more a world center, the Low Countries undertook the overwhelming majority of their commercial relations with Italy by land route. [Shipments by sea] occurred between the two countries, but their importance remained minimal.[188]

The situation seemed to be different by the seventeenth century. What had happened? Very simple. It seems that, although there was technological advance in both land and sea transport at this time, the rate of improvement was different, such that it came to be the case that "for very heavy and bulky goods water transport was the most economical under all circumstances [with the exception of live cattle]."[189] The development of the Dutch *fluyt* referred to previously was probably of central importance in this regard.Conversely, in the sixteenth century, land remained a cheaper, more efficient, and safer means of transport for men, for light and expensive manufactures, and for precious metals.[190]

What is the significance of this for France? We presented the politics of the "first" sixteenth century as revolving around the attempts by Spain and France to transform the European world-economy into a world-empire. Despite the Atlantic explorations, these attempts were primarily oriented to land routes. Indeed, this may be a supplementary reason for their failure. The politics of the "second" sixteenth century was oriented to the creation of coherent nation-states obtaining politico–commercial advantages within the framework of a nonimperial world-economy. These attempts were primarily oriented to the maximum utilization of sea routes (external and internal). The natural geographic advantages of the northern Netherlands and England served them well here. The politics of France was a tension, often inexplicit, between those who were land-oriented and those who were sea-oriented.[191] The critical difference between France, on the one hand, and England and the United Provinces, on the other, was that in the latter cases, to be sea-oriented and to wish to construct a strong polity and national economy were compatible options, whereas for France, because of its geography, these options were somewhat contradictory.

The first strong hint we have of this comes in the religious controversies and civil wars that racked France from the death of Francis II in 1560 to the truce enshrined in the Edict of Nantes in 1598.

Let us just look briefly at some of the class and geographic coordinates of the religious struggle. As long as France was primarily oriented to a struggle with the Hapsburg empire and counted on Lyon as their contestant for chief international trading center, religious toleration was possible.[192] After Cateau-Cambrésis the international financial need for religious toleration disappeared. At the same time, the prosperity of Lyon declined, both because of its lessened importance as a financial center and because it was a major battleground of the Wars of Religion.[193] The wars had brought together many disparate forces whose politics often became detached from their original motivations, as usually happens in the heat of extended political turmoil. Nonetheless, it should be possible for us to disentangle some of the strands. Hurstfield's account of the origins of the civil wars in the *New Cambridge Modern History* runs as follows:

> In France during this period the tension between monarchy and nobility flared up into a long and bloody struggle. It is, of course, well known that the French civil wars derived from powerful secular no less than religious causes. . . . The Calvinist movement in France had first, in the mid-sixteenth century, taken hold upon the merchant and the artisan; and its early martyrs—as in Marian England—came from the humblest stock. But by the time the civil wars began in 1562

the nobility, both high and provincial, had joined in and indeed taken over control. Contemporaries in France recognized the importance of distinguishing between the wings of the movement describing the one group as "Huguenots of religion," and the other group as "Huguenots of state." These latter stood for much more than religious dissent. They represented the long-standing hostility of the ruling families of provincial France to the power of Paris; to the crown and its ally, the Catholic church; and above all, to the Guises, the family most closely identified with that church and most bitterly opposed to the aims and interests of those provincial and often decaying noble houses. (The traditional use of the expression "provincial nobility" in part confuses the issue: most of its members would be regarded in England as belonging not to the nobility but to knightly and gentry families.)[194]

Hurstfield thus draws a picture of France close to that Trevor-Roper draws of England, of the Country versus the Court. And such a picture evokes all the unclarity that the English analogy does—were nobility (or gentry) "rising" or "declining?" In whose interests did the state in practice operate?

Let us put next to Hurstfield the picture as drawn by Koenigsberger in the same volume of the *Cambridge History:*

> After the bankruptcy of 1557, Henry II squeezed another seven million livres in extraordinary taxes out of his unfortunate subjects. Nevertheless, the limit had been reached. There were *peasant* revolts in *Normandy* and *Languedoc*. The nobles, though exempt from taxation, had spent their incomes and mortgaged or sold their estates in the king's service on the heavy ransoms demanded of noble prisoners after the disaster of St. Quentin (1557). . . .
>
> In the towns, the *small artisans* and *shopkeepers* had been hit by heavy taxation and by the periodic collapse of rural purchasing power that followed bad harvests such as that of 1557. The *journeymen* saw food prices rising faster than wages and found that the growing influence and rigidity of the *guilds* blocked the advance of the majority to mastership. . . .
>
> After 1559 the *nobility joined the movement in large numbers, especially in the south.* . . .
>
> It was only [in 1573] that Huguenot organization reached its full development, in a broad arc stretching from *Dauphiné* through *Provence* and *Languedoc* to *Béarn* and *Guienne*. As in the Netherlands, the successful revolution tended to become *localised*, both by an alliance with provincial feeling against an interfering central government and by the hopes of the military situation.[195]

In reaction to this, Catholic local unions arose, also emphasizing their regional identity and claims to (traditional) provincial autonomy. Paris local-ists sided with the Catholic League.[196] Furthermore, both camps were linked to outside forces, the Huguenots to England and the Protestant princes of Germany, the Catholics to Rome and the rulers of Spain and Savoy. "Thus, all revolutionary movements of the period were linked to powers and interests outside their national boundaries."[197]

King Henry III, attempting to arbitrate the struggle, in the end dealt blows to and alienated both camps. In a sense, it was a brilliant tactical coup to seek to de-escalate the conflict by recognizing the Protestant pre-tender, Henry of Navarre (Henry IV), as his successor, provided he became a Catholic. It was then that Henry IV issued his famous: "Paris vaut une messe." Note that it was Paris, not France, and it was Navarre who said it.

Henry IV switched camps which was easy enough since his motivation was different from that of his mass base. The nobility then by and large withdrew from the conflict and became Catholicized. This defused the religious content of the conflict and hence weakened the strength of the political opposition.[198] It also frustrated the lower classes who turned to angry but relatively ineffectual *jacqueries*.[199] In the end, the Huguenots were more strongly regionally based than ever. They had lost their congregations in the north and east and remained strong in the south.[200]

One of the underlying tensions clearly was regional. On the one hand, Normandy and Brittany were pulling away; on the other hand, so was the whole of the south whose separatism had remained latent since its defeat in the thirteenth century. The reasons for the pulls were in both cases that the creation of a strong national economy served to limit rather than expand profit opportunities for the local notables: the bourgeoisie of the maritime west who sought to use their money to break into the Atlantic–Baltic trade rather than construct a state bureaucracy and army; the landed capitalists of the south who sought a free international market. The partisans of the center were not anticapitalist in orientation. They had essentially a middle-range orientation: first strengthen the state and commercial possibilities will follow.

As in England, the monarchy was caught in the contradiction of wishing to create a national economy based on new forces that could compete successfully in the new world-economy and being the apex of a system of status and privilege based on socially conservative forces. Wishing not to choose rashly, the king—in France as in England—felt more comfortable in his aristocratic penchant than in a role as the harbinger of the new. What was different however was that in England the nascent capitalist elements, both rural and urban, felt they stood to gain from a stronger national economy. France however had merchant elements who felt they were being sacrificed to a remote Paris, and capitalist agriculture in the south whose structure and hence needs were nearer to those of landowners in peripheral countries like Poland (who needed an open economy before all else) than to landowners in England within whose domains the new cottage industries were growing up. In England, there was a sense in which the king could count on his opponents to restrain themselves since his "national" stance was in their "short-run" interests. The king in France could not, and had to use sterner means to hold the country together: hence civil war in the second half of the sixteenth century, and bureaucratic centralism, which was to come in the first half of the seventeenth century.

The price however was heavy. The Wars of Religion would facilitate the rise of absolutism, to be sure. But as Mousnier adds: "Unlike in England, the development of trade, of industry and of the bourgeoisie was retarded (*freiné*)."[201] Nor had the price been yet fully paid. The era of Louis XIII and Richelieu was to see a further cost exacted. In order, however, to assess this price, we must now shift back to the general situation of the world-economy.

The "long" sixteenth century was now drawing to an end. And, so say most historians, the evidence is that there was a crisis. Crisis or crises? For there was an economic recession in the 1590s, an even bigger one in the 1620s, and what some see as a coup de grâce around 1650. We shall not dwell too long on the debate of dates—whether the ideal cutting point for the story is 1622 or 1640 or 1650. Spooner indeed argues that one of the key phenomena to notice about this "culminating point and watershed" of the long sixteenth century was that the turning point "was spread over a fairly wide period of time."[202] We have chosen 1640 as the terminal date for a variety of reasons, and do not pledge even so not to transgress this boundary. The main point is nonetheless that, virtually without exception, historians accept the idea that there was some kind of critical turning-point somewhere around this time.[203]

Of what did it consist? First, a price reversal, the end of the price inflation which had sustained the economic expansion of the European world-economy. The price trend did not reverse itself all at once. It is crucial to the understanding of this period and to the subsequent development of the world-economy to see that, in general, the reversal occurred earlier in the south than in the north, earlier in the west than in the east, and earlier in areas on the sea than inland in the continent.[204] There was a gap, and of not a few years.

Trouble began in Spain shortly after the defeat of the Spanish Armada. Trade still had however its ups and downs. Chaunu's data show 1608 as the highpoint of the Spanish Atlantic trade. Then a sort of plateau until 1622, which Chaunu attributes to the economically relieving qualities of temporary peace,[205] followed by the definitive downturn. The military–political defeat of the Armada merely however punctured a balloon, stretched thin by the exhaustion of the resource base of Spanish prosperity. Spanish exploitation of the Americas had been of a particularly destructive variety, a sort of primitive hunting and gathering carried out by advanced technology.[206] In the process, Spain exhausted the land and its men. Furthermore, Spain not only used up Indian labor; she used up, in other ways, as we have seen, her own labor.[207]

One very important consequence was the fall in bullion import. For example, bullion annually imported on the average into Seville from the Americas in the period 1641–1650 was 39% of that imported in the period 1591–1600 in the case of silver and only 8% in the case of gold. The output of bullion had fallen "victim to the relentless law of diminishing marginal returns and declining profits."[208] Since however trade did not suddenly diminish—indeed it was still expanding—devaluation was inevitable.

Here for the first time the existence of a single world-economy of uneven national development made a crucial difference. The countries of northwest Europe devalued far less than those of southern, central, and eastern Europe.[209] These are of course bullion prices. René Baehrel has a very brilliant excursus in which he demonstrates that shifts in bullion prices bear no necessary relationship to shifts in prices and that men make their real economic decisions primarily in terms of the latter.[210] It is significant, however, that he does this in a book devoted to discussing the economy of the seventeenth and eighteenth centuries. A. D. Lublinskaya makes the point that what distinguishes the seventeenth from the sixteenth century is precisely the fact that, after 1615 for the first time, there is "an *independent* movement of prices, *not* dependent on the influx of gold and silver."[211] She asserts that this fact defines the end of the "price revolution." Ruggiero Romano insists that there occurs a sudden aggravation of devaluation in the years 1619–1622: "What matters is the intensity of the phenomenon. . . ."[212] There was such an abundance of money in 1619 that the interest fell to 1.2%, "the absolute minimum interest rate for the whole period 1522–1625."[213]

From the general depression, only Holland and to some extent (to what extent we shall soon see) England escape.[214] Indeed Romano argues that Holland not only escapes, but that plus or minus 1590–*1670* are a period of Dutch agricultural *expansion.*[215]

Why should northwest Europe have been relatively so insulated against the winds of ill fortune? Chaunu has an explanation which is rather complex. In the sixteenth century, prices in northwest Europe rose less sharply than those in Spain because of the time lag in the arrival of bullion. Northwest Europe however always obtained part of its bullion in contraband. The proportion of contraband bullion rose as time went on. Hence the inflationary impact of the contraband bullion was rising in percentage of total impact just as Spanish prices were beginning to drop. "The prices of northern Europe, by a lesser receptivity to depressive factors, tend thus to come closer to the Spanish price-levels."[216] This seems a bit farfetched, since it depends for its plausibility on assuming that there was no significant decline in the absolute as opposed to relative supply of contraband bullion, which, it can be inferred from Spooner's figures, was probably not the case.

Pierre Jeannin seems nearer the mark in analyzing the resistance of northwest Europe to depressive forces as deriving from advantages this region had within the world-economy.[217] He cites geographic location (on the Atlantic at a crossroads between the breadbaskets and forests of the northeast and the countries in need of their exports); industrial aptitudes (rooted in the past, as Dutch and English textiles; or in economic potential released by the extension of the international economy, as Swedish iron). Furthermore, the very expansion of productive forces in the north meant a continued rise in population at the very moment of demographic decline in the Mediterranean region. Pierre Chaunu estimates that between 1620 and 1650 the population of the Empire went from 20 to 7 million, Italy declining by 2 million between 1600 and 1650. *Relatively* sheltered from the demographic decline were England and, this time, France.[218]

As a geopolitical phenomenon, this meant the end of the Spanish Atlantic and the establishment of a European Atlantic.[219] The war whose resumption in 1624 marks in fact a crushing blow to the Spanish economy began with the Dutch attack on the Portuguese colony of Brazil, Portugal at the time belonging to the Spanish crown.[220] In terms of the Asian trade, and especially pepper, between 1590 and 1600, the Dutch and English invaded what was hitherto a Portuguese–Spanish monopoly, which accounts for a collapse in spice prices.[221] One can well understand how it was that the men of that era developed a mercantilist perspective that led them to feel that "the sum of prosperity in the world was constant, and the aim of commercial policy . . . was to secure for each individual nation the largest possible slice of the cake."[222]

But it was not in fact constant. On the one hand, one could argue that the end of the sixteenth century meant for all of Europe "collapse of profit, the flight of rent, economic stagnation."[223] But one must be specific. Romano insists that the sixteenth century was "just like the 12th and 13th centuries, a century of large *agricultural* profits."[224] It is the decline of the *easy* agricultural profits that is going to explain the increased role of large-scale capitalist agriculture based on ever more coerced and lowly-paid agricultural labor in the late seventeenth and eighteenth century. Romano's comments are apt:

> These vast phenomena, which Fernand Braudel has called on the one hand "faillite," "trahison de la bourgeoisie," and on the other hand "réaction seigneuriale," do not seem to be, on closer inspection, two separate and distinct types, but only one: almost the very same people, or at least, the descendants of one family who *betrayed* their bourgeois origins (and above all their bourgeois functions), and entered the system of the *réaction seigneuriale*, a phenomenon which when dealing with the Italian case I have called "refeudalization."[225]

But once again, as Romano observes, Holland and to a lesser extent England are exceptions.

We must not however get ahead of our story. It is crucial to understanding the subsequent era to look closely at how England and France coped with the closing convulsions of the "long" sixteenth century. The consolidation of the European world-economy which was to occur in the seventeenth and eighteenth centuries would center around the competition of England and France for primacy. But in a sense the crucial cards were dealt in the period 1600–1640.

When G. N. Clark seeks to explain the "remarkable" advance of industry in England in the "second" sixteenth century, he suggests that the root lay in international commerce. And when he analyzes England's international commerce in this period, he finds three main contrasts between the end of the period and the beginning: (1) although England's international trade expanded absolutely, it declined in relation to internal industry in providing for consumption needs; (2) although Amsterdam succeeded Antwerp as the pivot of the European world-economy, England's relationship to the Netherlands shifted from one of dependence and complementarity to one of rivalry; (3) England's external trade became far more diversified within Europe, and England began systematic trade with Russia, the Levant, the Indian Ocean area, and the Americas.[226]

Before the end of Elizabeth's reign, however, these changes had not yet occurred to a noticeable degree. Nor did they develop in so smooth a fashion as Clark implies. For these changes upset the delicate social and political equilibrium that the Tudors had attempted with so much skill to create and laid bare the conflicting interests that were to tear the English political system apart. Let us take each of these changes in turn.

It is no doubt true that international trade declined as a proportion of the gross national product, and that this might be interpreted as a sign of England's long-term economic health. But this misses the point that the very process of internal industrialization made England's social structure more, not less, dependent on the vagaries of the world market. Barry Supple points out that, unlike in the period after the Industrial Revolution, fixed capital played a small role in the industrial economy and hence fluctuations in the national economy were not caused by excess capacity nor were they intensified by fluctuations of a capital goods industry. Fluctuations in credit also were a lesser factor than later. Hence the prosperity of the home market was largely a function of harvest fluctuations (induced by climate variations) and "overseas demand which was frequently the strategic determinant of alterations in internal activity."[227] And such alterations were politically critical precisely because of England's industrial development:

> Cloth production was sufficiently far advanced to have ceased, in the main, to be a by-employment for a predominantly agrarian population. Hence for the government and for the community at large the existence of the textile industry meant the perennial threat of an outbreak of distress and disorder among a landless, and even propertyless, class. The situation had helped produce the Elizabethan Poor Law and made generations of statesmen wary of encouraging industrial growth.[228]

What might England then do to assure economic, hence political, stability? One solution Supple indicates: It was to draw back still further. F. J. Fisher observes that "Bacon looked back on the reign of Elizabeth as a critical period during which England had been dangerously dependent on foreign grain. . . ."[229] Over time, this is the path of deindustrialization which northern Italy took. Another solution might be to push outward and overcome the supply squeeze by obtaining additional sources of supply and the demand squeeze by securing new markets.[230] This is the path on which the northern Netherlands was embarking. To try one or the other solution meant making critical options in terms of England's internal social structure. These were precisely the decisions that the Tudors spent all their energy avoiding. The result was a halfway house. Lawrence Stone's examination of the volume of Elizabethan overseas trade leads him to conclude that the "famous expansion of trade in the reign of Elizabeth appears to be a pious myth."[231]

If then we turn to degree to which England had liberated itself from Dutch economic tutelage by 1600, we find to be sure that the process of growing control by the English commercial bourgeoisie over English internal trade had been more or less completed by such acts as abolishing Hanseatic privileges first in 1552 and definitively in 1598.[232] This was to the advantage of closed monopolies like the Merchant Adventurers.[233] The interest of such groups lay largely in the uneasy equilibrium of the halfway house.

When, under the Stuarts, other merchants obtained the legal rights to make a more forthright challenge of the Dutch role in industrial finishing of textiles—the so-called Alderman Cockayne's Project[234]—they failed. For Supple this failure demonstrated that

> the international division of labour by which the Dutch dyed and dressed England's semi-manufactured textiles was not an arbitrary phenomenon sustained by artificial survivals of company regulation. On the contrary, by the early seventeenth century it reflected economic realities against which England might tilt only at her peril.[235]

Hence, Elizabethan constraint in hesitating to expand outwardly may not have been so unwise.[236] The Tudors had been thereby postponing internal social conflict until they had strengthened the political autonomy of the state machinery from outsiders, so that England would have the strength to tolerate the explosive but inevitable readjustment of political and social forces.

Finally, to what extent was the Elizabethan era one of diversification overseas? To be sure, it was at this time that the English ships returned to the Baltic and began to make voyages to the Mediterranean, to Russia, to Africa. And this was the time of the constitution of the first chartered companies. But we must be careful not to exaggerate. On the one hand, eastern Europe was still more closely linked with the economies of France and Spain (via Amsterdam) than with England[237] and, on the other hand, it is the trade with France and the rebel Dutch provinces that is still fundamental to England in the period of Elizabeth.[238]

The realities of the English commercial scene are both cause and consequence of the policies of the Tudor monarchs. They were straddling a fence.[239] The international economic crisis of the period 1590–1640 made this fence-straddling increasingly impossible, and hence the political stability of the monarchy and the monopolies it sheltered increasingly tenuous. Stability is not always everyone's *summum bonum*. To some it was "irksome."[240] By 1604, the chafing of those merchants who sought to pursue the possibilities of commercial expansion found expression in various free trade bills pushed in Parliament. The immediate impetus was probably the peace with Spain which had opened changed trade perspectives as peace is wont to do, both by eliminating certain obstructions to trade, and by dint of the unemployment, so to speak, of the previously flourishing band of privateers.[241]

For the next decade, things looked bright for the English cloth industry which reached an export peak in 1614. But it was to be, in Supple's phrase, "a transitory Indian summer."[242] It was followed by an "unrivalled" economic depression, which "ensured a permanent restriction of the overseas market for old draperies."[243] What caused this sudden downfall? Actually it was not so sudden, but rather as R. W. K. Hinton says, "a sudden worsening of a situation that had been deteriorating for some time."[244] What happened was that the devaluation of continental currencies by reference to England created highly unfavorable terms of trade which "priced the English cloth out of their north and central European markets."[245] This led to an outflow of bullion which was made worse by the need for foreign grain as a result of bad harvests in 1621 and 1622.[246] The dramatic loss of bullion "was of great significance in an unsophisticated economy dependent on steady supplies of a secure metallic coinage."[247]

J. D. Gould argues that England now paid the price of having "wasted" her international price advantage of 1550–1600 "in a scramble for privileges." Consequently, now that the price advantage had been reversed, "England was left saddled with a rigid, ologopolistic, high-cost economy, ill-fitted to cope with a competitor [the Dutch] who throve on low costs, adaptability, and up-to-dateness."[248] The Dutch were now able to break into England's own import trade,[249] and textile exports to Germany and eastern Europe were hit by both Dutch and local competition.[250]

Both the merchants and the government were alarmed. The merchants reacted by demanding more protection, such as limiting the rights of non-English to import the goods into England, increased mandatory use of English shipping, the freedom to re-export Baltic grain which both enlarge the cloth trade and bring in bullion for the grain.[251] The government had quite a different perspective. First, the agricultural interests well represented in parliament were pushing for a ban on the *import* of corn, because of their need for protection against low prices.[252] Second, the government concentrated on how to reconcile its needs "to alleviate local destitution, in order to prevent riots and tumults, and to revive commerce, in order to maintain economic stability and power."[253] To do the first, the government was tempted by the solution of governments of twentieth-century underdeveloped countries, the creation of employment. But, like today, such a solution is not easy.[254] Rather than provide new protection, the government moved in the direction of loosening monopolies, to see if that would revive commerce and industry.[255] But they could not go very far in this direction because the arrangement of privileged companies had too many advantages for the government. It secured the loyalty of a quasi-public bureaucracy which performed consular and customs functions, was a source of income via loans and taxation, and even substituted for the navy as a protective device in international commerce.[256] "The patents and monopolies, the cloaking of selfish aims beneath verbose platitudes, were an integral part of the fabric of Stuart government."[257] If the government moved at all in the direction of antimonopolism, it was in fact only under the pressure of parliament, "vociferously representative of the outports and the lesser gentry."[258]

Nor was England in luck as far as the gods were involved. The trade revival of 1623–1624 was set back by the plague of 1625 as well as by a poor harvest. The resumption of war with Spain, so harmful to Spain as we have seen, was no aid to England. The renewed need for grain led to another balance of payments crisis.[259] Thus the traditional heart of English industry came to find itself "in the middle of an extended history of decline, painful adaptation, and widespread redundancy."[260] Crown interference did not solve the problem; it only aggravated the situation by creating a "crisis of mercantile confidence."[261]

It was apparently not so easy for the English textile industry to cut costs. It was partly that the merchants were too closely imbricated in the state-machinery for the Crown to be able to force the industrialists to run a leaner shop.[262] Also it must have been that the workers were relatively strong enough to withstand the introduction of significant wage cuts.[263] The only solution, therefore, other than de-industrialization, was to circumvent the vested interests by the development of new industries. It was here in fact that England found its commercial salvation, in the so-called "new draperies,"[264] which saw a remarkable rise as an export item precisely as the "old draperies" fell.[265]

There was a second solution to the dilemma of high prices: England developed a re-export trade. And it was this aspect of England's commercial policy that stimulated the two most striking new features of the seventeenth century: the interest in colonial expansion, and the Anglo–Dutch rivalry. Both trends would crystallize after the Civil War but both were in evidence before it.[266]

New products required new markets. And it was Spain and the Mediterranean area in general that provided the most important new arena of English export,[267] an area relatively free from the constrictions of the old English monopolies.[268] The Spanish market in particular was attractive because of "internal inflation and colonial purchases."[269] England was beginning to eat off the carrion of the Spanish Empire. And as Italian industry declined, English exports partially filled the gap.[270]

As for colonization, we must remember that for a long time it was not necessary for England (France, or Holland) to engage in direct colonial enterprises. The Treaty of Cateau-Cambrésis, no doubt as a sign in part of weariness with imperial expansion, included the extraordinary clause which read: "West of the prime meridian and south of the Tropic of Cancer . . . violence done by either party to the other side shall not be regarded as in contravention of the treaties."[271] This concept, popularly known as "No peace beyond the line," was reaffirmed at Vervins in 1598. It allowed, to be sure, the freedom to create new settlements, but also the freedom to plunder. And for fifty-odd years plunder was far more profitable than settlement would have been.[272] Colonization, by contrast, seemed a dubious venture. It was assumed that the Spaniards had already gotten the good spots and "even the mercurial Elizabethans—and most certainly the queen herself—were aware of the hopelessness of prospecting at random over a vast continent."[273] Besides, England had Ireland as an outlet for homestead emigrants.[274]

These attitudes changed in the period after 1600. England consolidated her links with Scotland by the union of the two thrones in the person of James I. The colonization of Ireland took on a new seriousness, both for England and for Scotland.[275] Ireland became integrated into the British division of labor. Her woods were used up to supply England with timber.[276] She would become in the course of the next 100 years the site of a major iron industry controlled by Englishmen.[277] And England would begin to create settlements in North America. Parry ascribes the change to the decline of Spanish prestige, and to the search for raw materials—cheap food, especially fish,[278] and strategic supplies (timber, hemp and pitch) whose Baltic sources might be cut off in wartime. In addition, they would be a new market for manufactures and a place to export paupers.[279] All true no doubt but, except for the consideration of Spain's military strength, all would have been largely true a century earlier. Is not the new scramble for colonies by the three powers of northwest Europe merely a sign of their competitiveness? Was it not largely a pre-emptive colonization, especially in the wake of Spain's decline?

The impact of these international economic convulsions forced a political crisis in England. I think Perez Zagorin has caught quite accurately the nature of the conflict:

> [T]he genesis of the English revolution is not to be found in a class struggle—for the leading sections of both sides in the Civil War included many who were drawn from the same economic class, whose development had been steadily proceeding during the preceding century. It is to be found, rather, in a conflict within this class among England's governing groups.[280]

And this internecine warfare within the governing class was not merely forced by the exigencies of international economic arena but made possible by prior elimination of two great dangers to the English political system, as Stone asserts: "The ring [had been] cleared of interference by the poor or by the Spaniard. . . ."[281]

There are two somewhat silly arguments relating to the onset of the Civil War. One is whether it was or was not inevitable. To Tawney's assertion that "the fall of the monarchy was hastened by the measures taken by the Tudors to preserve it,"[282] Trevor-Roper asserts that the main problem was a wasteful administration, which could have been reformed by Parliament. "For, of course, monarchy itself was no obstacle. It is absurd to say that such a policy was impossible without revolution."[283]

We shall see shortly the consequences for France of the administrative reforms Trevor-Roper retrospectively recommends to the Long Parliament. But "inevitability" is a pointless game to play. If one element had been different, of course the results would have been different. But if one, why not two, three? The reality is that the Civil War did in fact occur and the task of the student is to explain it.

The other silly question is whether or not the "real" issues dividing England were not beliefs about liberty and religion. Mr. Hexter insists that these were the issues and affects some surprise that so many of his partners and antagonists in the controversy agree (Hinton, Stone, Pocock, Hill, Trevor-Roper speaking for himself and Tawney.) He welcomes them to his "Whiggish" company.[284] J. G. A. Pocock at least takes umbrage, insisting he is a "post-Marxist" rather than a "neo-Whig."[285] But it is a silly argument because of course the protagonists of the Civil War expressed many of their divisions in ideological terms revolving around political freedom and religious perspectives. And of course they meant it. And of course the outcome of the Civil War was to have consequences for the normative system governing English political life.

To dissect the ideological coordinates of a political and social conflict is however never meaningful unless one can root that analysis in the social relations prevailing at the time and thereby comprehend the implication of ideological demands for these relationships. The debate is *really* about the totality of these relationships, about whether they should remain as they are or change in some specific direction.

The English Civil War was a complex conflict, as all major social upheavals are. *One* major thrust of it was that between those who emphasized the role of the monarchy, who hoped thereby to hold on to a slipping system of privilege and deference,[286] whose fears of social revolution outweighed other considerations, who were somewhat paralyzed before the forced choices of the world-economy, and those, on the other hand, who gave primacy to the continued commercialization of agriculture, who welcomed some change in social patterns, who saw little virtue in the extravagance of the Court, who were oriented to maximizing England's advantage in the world-economy.

Let us turn to France, where things were the same, but most importantly were not the same. Davis Bitton says of the years 1560–1640 that they were "a crucial phase of the transition from the French nobility of the late Middle Ages to the French nobility of the Old Regime."[287] So were they in England. But what a different transition was made in France. In the great debate between Boris Porchnev and Roland Mousnier—which we shall get to in a moment—Porchnev argues in essence that what happened in France in this era was that "the venality of offices brought about not the 'embourgeoisement' of power, but the 'feudalization' of the bourgeoisie."[288] To which Mousnier replies: "There was no such thing as a 'feudal-absolutist' order. To the extent that there was a tendency toward absolutism, it was involved in a struggle against the feudal order. What remained of the feudal order tended to paralyze absolutism."[289] Although I think the debate is partially semantic, and that for the rest Porchnev had the better of the argument, what might be said is that Mousnier is closer to the truth if one applies his reasoning to explain England and that of Porchnev to explain France. That is to say, schematically and in an oversimplified fashion, one might assert that in England the aristocracy lost in the short run and gained in the long by transforming itself into bourgeois capitalists, while in France the aristocracy gained in the short run and lost in the long run by forcing the bourgeoisie to abandon its proper function and thus to some extent contribute to economic stagnation. Why this should have been so, we are arguing, is essentially a function of their differing relationship to the world-economy.

But first let us review once again to what extent this is a fair description of the French social system. For reasons we have already outlined, the French state in 1600 was stronger than the English state. This meant that the bureaucracy was "for the bourgeoisie the main means of rising in the social hierarchy,"[290] much more so than in England. In turn this venality led to a greater direct interest of the bourgeoisie in the French monarchy.[291] This leads Mousnier to argue that there was a relatively open class situation in France at this time.[292] But Mousnier himself shows how difficult was the ascent. He points out that for a *roturier* to make it up to the status of *maître des requêtes* required normally four generations.[293] I think in fact Porchnev catches the class situation with more subtlety. It is less that there is very much interclass mobility than that there exist strata of people for whom the sentiments of class attachment vary according to the concrete situation. The most significant such stratum is the bureaucracy of bourgeois origin, the *noblesse de robe:*

> At the moment that a worker, who has retained his links to his village, loses his job in the factory, he becomes once again a peasant. In the same fashion, when one sought

to take back from the *officiers* their property rights and privileges, that is to say deprive them of their status as privileged nobility, they automatically fell back virtually
into their original status as bourgeois. . . . [The] *officiers* negatively affected by [the
decisions of] Mazarin felt themselves to be bourgeois and, at the beginning of the
Fronde, their attitude was the same as that of the whole of the bourgeois class.[294]

It is precisely because of the relative ease of acquiring formal aristocratic
status in France (true in England under the Stuarts, too, but less so) that
there arose in the sixteenth century that "ambiguity of noble status" of
which the French aristocracy complained and which led to their "intense,
obsessive concern with honorific privileges,"[295] and also to the very great
emphasis on strict rules of behavior and the theory of *dérogeance*.[296]

The traditional description of the absolute monarchy as being in alliance
with the bourgeoisie against the nobility always ran up against the fact
that the so-called classic regime of the absolute monarchy of Louis XIV
was also the prime example of the reassertion of the seigniorial privilege.
Marc Bloch solved this dilemma by arguing that the seigniorial reassertion
was the more fundamental of the two antipathetic phenomena, and that
without the absolute monarchy, this tendency would have had full force.
In other words, one could say that "the victory of the absolute monarchy
limited the extent of the 'feudal reaction.' "[297]

A. D. Lublinskaya essentially agrees,[298] drawing this picture of France
in the "second" sixteenth century. After 1559, the role of foreign bankers
declined in France, both because of the decline of Italy and Germany
and the religious wars. These wars however prevented the French commercial bourgeoisie from filling the gap. In order to obtain funds, therefore,
the French government created a system of tax farming. Eventually the
tax farmers became fused into the state's financial machinery. "Tax farming
was a profitable business. It was on this fact that the government founded
its system of forced loans from the chief tax-farmers, turning the latter
into its creditors."[299] Hence the intimate links between "financiers" and
the state, so much so that their own survival depended on the strength
of the state, provided that the "strong government which they wanted
. . . remained strongly in need of credit from them."[300] Although it was
perhaps not true that the monarchy imposed no taxes on the nobility,[301]
it was the very dependence of the venal *officiers* that made this most difficult
since, Lublinskaya asserts, tax reform necessarily would have involved the
cash outlay of repurchasing the offices, which was far too expensive.[302]
Anything which increased state indebtedness reinforced the position of
these *officiers*. In particular, "war was very profitable to the financiers."[303]

That some of the reasoning here is very ad hoc can be seen by quick
reference to England where "fiscal feudalism" or revenue farming by
syndicates of businessmen became common practices under Elizabeth and
the early Stuarts,[304] with no religious wars to explain it and no large-scale
growth of a venal bureaucracy subsequent upon it. Furthermore, to the

extent that tax profiteering was constrained, this was the result of administrative reform whose immediate motivation was the exigencies of war finance and the need to reduce significantly the cut of the fiscal intermediaries between state and taxpayer.[305]

No matter, however. There was a more fundamental attack on this line of reasoning launched by Boris Porchnev. Porchnev unleashes a full-scale assault on the argument that "venality was a form of the political supremacy of the bourgeois,"[306] a theory he attributes to Pagès and then Mousnier. Porchnev wishes to argue that seventeenth century France was "in its main features, still a feudal society characterized by the predominance of feudal relations of production and feudal forms of economy."[307]

Porchnev argues that capitalist forms exist but that the bourgeoisie "participated in the political power of the feudal state only to the degree that it did not act as a class of capitalist society."[308] The bourgeoisie sought titles for reasons of vanity and cupidity and also adopted an aristocratic life style. In addition, they were induced to abandon true bourgeois economic activities because of the fiscal advantages of using money as credit capital rather than as industrial or agricultural capital.[309]

Hence when peasant uprisings occurred in the period 1623–1648 (to which we shall come in a moment), the bourgeoisie vacillated. On the one hand, they too were unhappy about high taxes. On the other hand, they identified with the interests of the aristocracy and feared the plebeians. Some revolted; some fled the country; and others came to terms with the state by purchasing offices and putting their money into credit operations.[310]

If one asks how come that England and Holland produced a nobility that was *"embourgeoisée"* but France did not, the answer is that "in France, feudalism had a perfection and a classical vitality which prevent any *embourgeoisement* of the nobility."[311] It was not that France was more backward, but that "the qualitative particularities of the French economy made impossible a grouping of classes that would have permitted a bourgeois semi-revolution on the English model."[312] The lucidity of Porchnev's arguments flounders at this crucial comparison where he has to fall back on unexplained perfections, undefined particularities, and the conceptual vagueness of "semi-revolution."

It is just at this point in the argument that Corrado Vivanti offers a helping hand to Porchnev. Agreeing completely with Porchnev's rejection of Mousnier's arguments that the Fronde was an isolated element in French history, he suggests that Porchnev has not followed the logic of his own argument to the end, but instead gets bogged down in denouncing the bourgeoisie for betraying the revolution. They could do no other, for they "did not yet form a social group sufficiently strong and autonomous" to do otherwise.[313] Vivanti poses this hypothesis in the form of a question:

To what extent can the "feudal reaction" or "restoration" and the very "betrayal

of the bourgeoisie" in the 17th century be said to lay the base—in a different
fashion from what one may find elsewhere, in analogous conditions of crisis—for
that capital accumulation which the [French] economy of the 16th century had
not succeeded in creating?[314]

That is to say, given "those objective obstacles which finally precluded the
Third Estate from engaging in autonomous action in the political and
social arenas,"[315] was this path not second best? If it did not permit France
the degree of development which England would come to have, it nonetheless prevented France from descending to the role of a semiperipheral
state like Spain and Italy. Even southern France, which went down the
road of sharecropping, did not regress economically to the extent of
neighboring Mediterranean areas. Le Roy Ladurie insists that one can
say of southern France (and Catalonia), unlike northern Italy and Castile,
that the state of the economy "is becalmed and restrained, is modified
and grows heavy, but it does not yet turn around. . . . The drama of
Languedoc is not the fall, but the inelasticity, the rigidity of agricultural
production; not regression [*décroissance*] but absence of marked growth."[316]
It would happen to southern France eventually, but 50 years later than
to other areas.

Lucien Goldmann makes a parallel critique of the theory of the alliance
of the absolute monarchy and the bourgeoisie. He argues that, on the
contrary, the basic alliance was between the monarchy and the nobility,
with, however, the monarchy safeguarding its flank by creating a new
bourgeoisie. Then, however, Goldmann argues, precisely to keep this
bourgeoisie bourgeois and not pseudo-aristocratic, the monarchy introduced the reform of the *paulette* in the early seventeenth century.[317]
The *paulette* by instituting in effect a tax on offices kept the bureaucracy
venal and hence kept the bourgeoisie bourgeois,[318] and thus also dependent on the monarchy.[319]

Goldmann's explanation centers on distinguishing between two varieties
of state officials: an older one made up of *notables* and the *noblesse de
robe,* the *officiers* and members of the *Cours souverains* and *parlements,* and
a newer one, who were the *commissaires* and *Conseillers d'Etat,* and who
served as *intendants* and *maîtres de requêtes.* Goldmann sees the latter as
displacing the former "in the first half of the seventeenth century, and especially from 1620 to 1650."[320] Goldmann analyzes the impetus behind this
new system as an attempt of the monarchy "to regain ground after the
coming to power of Henry IV in 1598,"[321] ground that had been lost
during the religious wars.

Since the *officiers* had been a great aid to the monarchy during the religious
wars and hence expected that their power and importance would grow
not fall, they were upset both by the *paulette*[322] and the rise of the *commissaires.*
The tension between *officiers* and *commissaires* grew, reaching a high point

around 1637–1638. This Goldmann links up with the rise of Jansenism among the *officiers*, an ideology that "insisted upon the essential vanity of the world and upon the fact that salvation could be found only in solitude and withdrawal."[323]

While Goldmann's portrait of the monarchy is close to that of Porchnev, his portrait of the bourgeoisie is closer to that of Mousnier, who avows "feeling an extreme repugnance to considering the 17th century as a 'feudal' epoch, since it was rather one in which 'commercial capitalism' has profoundly penetrated the country"[324]—the whole of the country and not just the towns. The monopolies were not a break in the rise of capitalism but "a condition of its development at this stage."[325] But Mousnier is most outraged at the assimilation of the *officiers* to nobility. He reacts with the flair of a true aristocrat.

> An *officier* of some importance is judicially a noble. A noble, but not a gentleman nor a seignior *(un féodal)*. Porchnev never makes the distinction. Would we call the Venetian nobility, those great merchants, a feudal corps? In France, the public insisted on the distinctions. An *officier*, ennobled by his office, remained a bourgeois. People deplored the fact that the true nobility, that of gentlemen, was without employ by the state and public office was the prerogative of those who were called ironically the "gentlemen of pen and ink." Bourgeois, that is what one still was, whether *officier* or *commissaire*, even seated on the *fleur de lys* and wearing the purple of office, even rigged out in a title of knight, even baron, even president of Parliament or member of the Royal Council.[326]

Mousnier concludes by denying that either he or Pagès had ever suggested that the bourgeoisie controlled the monarchy. "It is the monarchy which subjected all the classes in reconstructing the state. But in this work it was aided by the bourgeoisie. . . ."[327]

It is important to notice that in this debate a number of issues have gotten scrambled together. One is the nature of the system. Another is the nature of the relations between the classes. A third is the role of the monarchy. We have already explained in a previous chapter why we believe the term "feudalism" with respect to agricultural production at this time (market-oriented cash crops, even if based on coerced or semicoerced labor) is confusing and unhelpful to analysis. To insist that France is primarily involved in a capitalist world-economy at this time does not necessarily entail arguing, however, that the bourgeoise wielded substantial political power. Obviously it did not. In eastern Europe, the aristocrats were capitalist farmers and the indigenous commercial bourgeoisie was on its way to extinction. Nor does it speak necessarily to the particular role the monarchy played in France as opposed to other states in this world-economy. J. H. M. Salmon observes that "like the debate over the gentry and aristocracy in England, the controversy [concerning early seventeenth-century France] is concerned with the character of early modern society and government."[328] Precisely!

Mousnier is probably more right than Porchnev in seeing the monarchy as an institution which, far from clearly dominating the situation, was struggling to assert its political preeminence, even in France. But Porchnev is more right than Mousnier in seeing that one of the developments that most clearly distinguishes France from England is the comparative political success in France of the old aristocracy whose short-run interests were not conducive to the long-run ability of France maximally to profit from the division of labor in the world-economy.

Let us now turn to the closing "crisis" of the "long" sixteenth century and see exactly what impact this had on the French political arena. We start with the fact that the fall of prices in France in the period 1600–1610 was in fact economically favorable to France and its bourgeoisie.[329] Even Porchnev admits that it would be too much to argue that industrial capitalists were of no significance in France. He accepts the fact that "the evolution of capitalism continued on its path, but at a slower pace."[330]

The problem was in large part in foreign trade, the importance of which to national economies we argued previously when discussing England's reaction to the commercial crisis. Although France between 1600–1610 had somewhat recouped the losses occasioned by the disruptions of the religious wars, another great decline set in after 1610, this time largely the consequence of Dutch and to some extent English competition. And what made the Dutch and even the English able to outprice the French in this period was that, at a moment of a contracting world market, the accumulated edge of industrial capital and technology of the prior 50–60 years was critical:

> France lagged behind her competitors in respect of all the important indices. The division of labour in French manufactories was at a lower level; the shortage of skilled workers did not allow the entrepreneurs to establish an adequate hierarchy of wage-levels. State subsidies, which were absolutely necessary at that time, were casual and sporadic, and small in amount, while accumulation of money was not on a large enough scale; France was excluded from that direct plundering of colonies which nourished primitive accumulation ·in Holland and Spain, and industry in England as well.
>
> The consequences of this was that French industrial products were comparatively expensive. As a result, the French commercial and industrial bourgeoisie was unable to compete successfully with the Dutch and the English in its own home market, and to some extent also in foreign markets. It was obliged to use its capital in other ways. . . . French shipbuilding and navigation, and therefore also French trans-oceanic trade, was behind English and Dutch, technically and economically. . . .
>
> For all these reasons, the French bourgeoisie was very interested indeed in increased protection, and the government of France endeavored to meet its needs in this respect.[331]

This then fitted France into the world-economy at a middle layer. While the French were able to exploit to some extent Spain and Germany, the

English and Dutch could exploit the French market as well as that of Spain.[332]

The relative strength of the French state machinery compared to England and the United Provinces did not necessarily serve it well in regard to this dilemma. Had the French monarchs of the time been unreservedly committed to the development of industry and the interests of the bourgeoisie, no doubt France might have overtaken the after all not so great lead that the other two countries had. But the French monarchs were ambivalent. Their intrusion was not always conducive to maximizing national commercial interest in the world-economy. Indeed, Nef attributes one of England's secrets of success not to a difference of royal intent but to the fact that the French were more efficient in their interference with bourgeois enterprise.[333] Similarly, Nef argues, England's comparative isolation from European wars in this period meant less emphasis on the "habits of obedience of the royal authority"[334] than in France. The ability of the French monarch to tax combined with the ability of the nobility to be exempted from taxation meant a heavier burden not only on the populace, but on the bourgeoisie as well.

Finally, we must not miss the link between achieved position in the world-economy as of say 1610 and future position. The French difficulties in competing with the Dutch and the English in their home markets encouraged them to concentrate in the production of those goods in which they had some historical edge and a relatively larger home market than other European countries—luxury products, especially silks.[335] But the cheaper goods for the wider markets would in the long run provide a surer industrial base.

The Thirty Years' War placed great pressures on the French. As the military expenses rose and the armies expanded, so did the size of the state bureaucracy and, as cause and consequence, the degree of taxation, both directly by the state and de facto in addition by means of the depredations of the troops in the countryside.[336] The impact of war on the price of Baltic grain and hence on food prices in general we have already mentioned. This was all considerably aggravated by the great epidemics that raged between 1628 and 1633, and especially in 1630–1631. Whether poor harvests led to the spread of disease, or disease led to a grain shortage, the two occurred together and hit France badly.[337]

Given this analysis, it is easy to see why peasant uprisings should have been so extensive in France at this time. Not only were state exactions of the peasantry rising but the nobility was having difficulty getting its rents and dues from the peasants because of their economic squeeze.[338] No doubt this meant in many instances that the nobles and the peasants of an area were simultaneously upset with the monarchy, and that to some extent "the sense of loyalty and mutual obligation [between seignior and peasant] did persist"[339] in early seventeenth-century France, but it would be an error to push this idea too far, as some are inclined to do. For surely it is not only present-day analysts but peasants of the time who could perceive that, after the Wars of Religion, the seignior, as Salmon puts it, "whether of the old *noblesse* or the new, was less a companion in peasant misery than its partial cause."[340] It was after all precisely the political doing of the nobility that accounts for the slow progress of economic development.[341] At the same time, the partial industrialization of France ensured that such discontent spread from rural to urban areas, the two being linked by the growing numbers of persons, a sort of lumpenproletariat without fixed employment, who moved back and forth and whose margin of existence was too small to endure much aggravation of crisis.[342]

Robert Mandrou contributes to this debate by asking us to consider the popular uprisings of 1623–1648 in the context of the ongoing history of France which saw such uprisings both earlier and later. He reminds us that the various taxes "must be seen as the signs of a greatly deteriorated economic situation and not simply as the only or most immediate cause of the revolts."[343] Mandrou then urges us back to a most fruitful route. He asks us to be:

> attentive to localizations, to cartography: the West, Normandy, Guyenne, the Center (Marché, Berry, Bourbonnais), this is the area most often affected, the most stimulated by these chain-reactions of troubles. May we see in this a consequence of the greater participation of these provinces that face the break in the rise of the "long 16th-century": the ebb of the years 1620-1680 leading to a more evident depression here than in the areas that are more continental, more undeveloped (*fruste*)? But are not these zones of rural and urban agitation of the 17th century also the provinces in which the religious wars were the most ardent in the preceding century?[344]

This is indeed a precious clue and one that fits very well into our overall hypothesis, furthermore one on which both Mousnier and Porchnev agree. Mousnier says:

> The study of each uprising cannot be separated from research on the local economies and social structures. Why did the rural uprisings occur principally in the West, the Center, and the Southwest? Would it not be possible to classify towns according to the degree of development of capitalism therein and to examine whether it does not correlate with some constants in the revolts?[345]

Porchnev notes that the uprisings of 1623–1648 were preceded by three series in the sixteenth century. The first two were those of 1520–1550, linked to the Reformation, and those of 1570–1590, during which the popular movements "placed their hopes in the Catholic League of which they declared themselves to be partisans." Then, from 1590–1600, there was a last wave which had now become non-religious in format.[346] Indeed,

Porchnev argues further that the popular disgust with the religious wars led to the desanctification of authority, which in turn accounts for the great need felt to reassert state authority in the early seventeenth century.[347]

This argument of Porchnev raises once again some questions about the meaning of religious movements and affiliations in early modern Europe, their links to the assertion of national entities and conversely to religious centrifugal forces. We have earlier spoken of Koenigsberger's treatment of the Huguenots as a French national revolutionary movement.[348] It is certainly within the realm of reasonable speculation that the Huguenots might have consolidated in the south and west of France in a manner parallel to the consolidation of the Calvinists in the north of the Netherlands, which could have resulted in a partition as in the Netherlands. This was certainly a fear at the time.[349] Within the framework of such a perspective, it is not surprising that the Huguenots at one point called upon Catholic Spain for aid. The liquidation of the Huguenots was then part and parcel of the drive to maintain the integrity of France as a state,[350] and Mousnier points out the role that the venality of office played after 1620 in buying off the Calvinist cadres.[351]

That the regionalism was more fundamental than the religious schism is clearly indicated in the way in which southern France, the Occitania of old, switched from being a Huguenot stronghold. Henri Espieux speaks of the Reformation finding its strongholds "both in Occitania and in the fringes of the ancient Roman Gaul of the 6th century, while Catholicism is essentially northern. . . ."[352] But, he notes, when Henry of Navarre becomes king "to the detriment of the Occitan cause," then "by a singular turnabout, Occitania became sympathetic to the League *(ligeuse)*—the only way remaining to it to pursue its difference. . . ."[353] Finally, Espieux argues, the Occitans embraced Jansenism in the same "non-conformist spirit," a cause that "contributed to the maintenance of their rebellious attitude *(humeur frondeuse)*."[354] Espieux sees this rebelliousness as Occitania's method of resisting the integration into France imposed upon it in the sixteenth century, achieved and reinforced by the fiscal burdens it was made to bear, and made more unpalatable still by the economic decline of Marseilles and Bordeaux in the "second" sixteenth century, not only with regard to Paris, but even in relation to Barcelona and Genoa—once again layers within layers.[355]

Porchnev's description of the uprising in Normandy in 1639 records similar themes. As he traces the story, peasants in Normandy had a heavier seigniorial burden in the fourteenth and fifteenth centuries than elsewhere in France. Because of this fact as well as the destructions of the Hundred Years' War, peasants fled, thus creating an acute labor shortage, which led to the relatively rapid decline of perpetual leases in favor of term leases more favorable to the peasantry. The price revolution, and France's emerging role in the world-economy, led to a setback for the peasant pro-

prietors—higher rents, smaller plots, the partial return to a natural economy, in short, a brake on capitalist development.[356] At a time when the
English yeoman farmer was benefiting from the enclosures of arable land,
his Norman equivalent was losing out. As for the bourgeoisie, Porchnev
points to the division between its two segments: the magistrates, tied to
local interests, and hence playing with rebellion; and the financiers, firmly
tied to the state and hence bent on sustaining the local aristocracy.[357] The
rebellion can be seen as discontent with the politics of the center which
was depriving the Norman peasant proprietor (and local bourgeois) of the
benefits of fuller participation in the new world-economy.

In the west as in Occitania, the monarchy was being viewed as pursuing
a French "national" perspective that was economically regressive. In the
name of the traditional, the outer provinces were demanding more not
less economic progress.[358] It was no accident then that the Normandy uprising of 1639 was followed by uprisings in Provence, Bretagne, Languedoc,
and Poitou.[359] Nor was it an accident that the immediate background of
the Normandy uprising was the monarch's unwillingness to relieve the
tax burden of Normandy in the wake of the economic difficulties following
upon the epidemic of 1632–1633 because: "His Majesty being burdened
by too heavy expenses cannot relieve his people as he would wish."[360] This
he could not do, because the money was being spent on creating the French
national entity.

Suppose—great historical game—that France had been a differently
shaped geographical entity, covering only the north and west of France
with Rouen as the capital. Suppose Occitania had been a separate state
from the thirteenth century on. Might not such a truncated France have
found that the national interests of the central state machinery and the
commercial interests of the bourgeoisie were somewhat more in harmony
one with the other? Might not such a France, seemingly weaker, have
been able to do what England did—respond to the emerging world-economy
by creating an industrial base? Perhaps.

But such a France did not exist. The France that did exist was, as we
said, neither fish nor fowl, and rent by religio-regional strife. The pressure
toward a one-religion state was as powerful in sixteenth-century Europe
as the pressure toward a one-party state in twentieth-century Africa, and
for the same reason, the need to combat centrifugal forces. But the price
was heavy. For France the price was coming to terms with the aristocracy
largely on its terms—the *"réaction seigneuriale,"* the *"féodalisation"* of
the bourgeoisie. There was to be no civil war in the seventeenth century, only
the *Fronde.* The bourgeois revolution would come in 1789, at another epoch,
for another purpose, and in some ways too late. In the seventeenth century,
the French administrative bourgeoisie, the *noblesse de robe,* was constrained
to remember that it could not afford the luxury of pursuing its narrow
interests too far since, if it did, the integrity of the state and hence the

economic foundation of this administrative bourgeoisie was threatened.

The differing roles (roles, not intents) of the monarchies in England and France was in the end a critical factor. One way to look at this is to define the political struggle as one in which the monarchies of the era were trying to erode the privileges of all non-state groups and to observe, as Cooper does, that by and large they succeeded better against the towns (and hence segments of the bourgeoisie) than against the landed classes.[361] Braudel speaks of the towns being "held in check" or "disciplined" by the monarchies.[362] In this view, the landed classes were seeking to use the state to aid them to stay out in front in the swift currents of economic expansion. In this perspective, the Frondeurs, though they lost, won, whereas the English aristocracy, though there was a Restoration, lost. In the end, Braudel argues, English primacy in the world would be that of London, "which constructed England to its requirements (*à sa guise*) after the peaceful revolution of 1688."[363]

In the vacillation between the demands of the bourgeoisie and the aristocracy, the monarchies of both England and France moved ever closer to the demands of the aristocracy. The difference was that in England the interests of the commercial bourgeoisie were linked with a strong center, whereas in France to some extent they were linked to the national periphery. This difference was a consequence of geographical considerations within the framework of the European world-economy.

One consequence was that, in order to hold an intrinsically more rambunctious bourgeoisie in check, the French monarchy had both to strengthen itself and to buy them off by the venality of office, which in turn diverted them from industrial investment. In England, the aristocracy to survive had to learn the ways of and partially fuse with the bourgeoisie. In France, the pressure was on the bourgeoisie to survive. In France and England, the center won out against the periphery. But in England, this meant furthering the cause of the national bourgeoisie, whereas in France it was a setback for the bourgeoisie.

The English Civil War occurred at the last possible moment. The resurgence of the landed classes in the next 150 years was to be great everywhere, even in England. But there at least the bourgeoisie had won *droit de cité*. And the landed classes meant less the aristocracy and more the gentry who were in the end *bons bourgeois*. In France, the bourgeoisie was far too weak in the seventeenth century to produce a Cromwell. It would not be until 1789 that they would find their interests consonant with those of the state as state. By then, the world-economy had evolved and it would be too late for France to achieve primacy within it.

6

THE EUROPEAN WORLD-ECONOMY: PERIPHERY VERSUS EXTERNAL ARENA

Figure 7: "The (Dutch) fleet off Mozambique, and the capture of a (Portuguese) carrack near Goa," an illustration from the "Journal of Observations of an East Indian Voyage by Cornelis Claeszoon of Purmerent, steersman of the ship Bantam, which sailed in the service of the mighty Lords of the United Company," published in 1651.

The boundaries of an entity defined in political terms are relatively easy to ascertain. If we want to know the territory covered by the Chinese empire in the year 1600, we need to consult some archives which tell us of the juridical claims as of that date. To be sure, there will always be marginal regions, where sovereignty is contested by two rival state structures, or one in which the imperial authority can scarcely be perceived as existing de facto which may lead us to consider the claim to be juridical fiction. But the criteria are fairly straightforward: The combination of asserted authority with some measure (however gross) of effective authority (however thin) will generally give us what we need.

But what shall we say of the boundaries of a social system not defined in political terms, of a "world-economy" such as we have been dealing with here. By saying that in the sixteenth century there was a *European* world-economy, we indicate that the boundaries are less than the earth as a whole. But how much less? We cannot simply include in it any part of the world with which "Europe" traded. In 1600 Portugal traded with the central African kingdom of Monomotapa as well as with Japan. Yet it would be prima facie hard to argue that either Monomotapa or Japan were part of the European world-economy at that time. And yet we argue that Brazil (or at least areas of the coast of Brazil) and the Azores were part of the European world-economy. There was a transit trade across Russia between western Europe and Persia.[1] Yet we argue that Persia was certainly outside this world-economy and so even was Russia. Russia outside, but Poland inside. Hungary inside, but the Ottoman Empire outside. On what basis are these distinctions determined?

It is not a question of the simple volume of trade or its composition. Celso Furtado says:

> Apart from gold and silver, little that could be produced in the Americas during the first century of colonization was marketable in Europe. Unlike the East Indies, which produced articles of great value per unit of weight, such as spices, silks and muslins, the Americas produced nothing that could become the basis of a lucrative trade.[2]

Nonetheless, the Americas inside, and the East Indies outside, or at least so we contend.

We shall denote this distinction as one between the periphery of a world-economy and its external arena. The periphery of a world-economy is that geographical sector of it wherein production is primarily of lower-ranking goods (that is, goods whose labor is less well rewarded) but which is an integral part of the overall system of the division of labor, because

199

the commodities involved are essential for daily use. The external arena of a world-economy consists of those other world-systems with which a given world-economy has some kind of trade relationship, based primarily on the exchange of preciosities, what was sometimes called the "rich trades." We shall try to demonstrate this distinction primarily by analyzing the differences between Russia and various parts of eastern Europe and those between the Indian Ocean area and Hispanic America *in the sixteenth century.*

At first glance, both Russia and eastern Europe seem to have great similarities. They both seem to experience the rise of large domains engaged in cash-crop production and based on coerced labor. Indeed, as Braudel points out, this occurs also in the Ottoman Empire at this time.[3] In both areas, the coercion of the peasants is primarily the result of actions by the state authorities. In both areas, the landlord class seems to emerge from this era greatly strengthened and the bourgeoisie weakened. Furthermore, both areas seem to be affected by the Price Revolution and to conform to its general parameters with reasonable faithfulness. Yet a closer look will reveal some differences.[4]

We shall treat the differences between Russia's relations with western Europe and eastern Europe's relations with western Europe as coming under three principal headings: (a) a difference in the nature of the trade, (b) a difference in the strength and role of the state machinery, and (c) as a consequence of the two prior points, a difference in the strength and role of the indigenous urban bourgeoisie.

The great prerevolutionary Russian historian, V. O. Kluchevsky, constructed his history of Russia on the assumption that "the principal fundamental factor in Russian history has been migration or colonisation, and . . . all other factors have been more or less inseparably connected therewith."[5] To the extent that this is true, it is a phenomenon of the sixteenth century when, just as the rest of Europe, Russia "entered upon a new era of economic growth. . . ."[6] It is commonly asserted that the conquest of the Volga khanate of Kazan in 1552 followed by that of Astrakhan in 1556 was a turning point.[7] In the following century Russia colonized the forest-steppe zone to the south, along the Don to the Azov Sea and along the Volga to the Caspian. It also pushed a large part of the way across Siberia. At that same time, the Ukrainians (then under Polish rule) advanced along the Dnieper, all of which would become part of Russia in 1654. The expansion southward and eastward by Russia was an important event in modern world history and it is important to note that the direction of the expansion is a function of the strength of the regimes in the regions surrounding Russia. As George Vernadsky reminds us, it was at "the very time when the Russians were checked and thrown back in the west [that] they started advancing in the east toward Siberia."[8]

Hence, in the case of Russia, Western traders were faced with a country far more immense than Poland or Bohemia or Mecklenburg, and one that was itself clearly an imperial structure. Whereas the external trade of Poland was almost exclusively with western Europe, Russia traded *both* westward and eastward and, as Jerome Blum says, the "Eastern trade was probably of more importance to Russia than her commerce with the West."[9]

It is not only that the trade eastward was larger in volume but that it was of such a nature and volume that it tended to create a world-economy, or as some writers put it, working in a slightly different theoretical framework, a national market. A. G. Mankov points to the crucial role of grain production, a concept with which we are already familiar: "One cannot speak of the effective development of commercial relations within feudal society before the time when cereals become merchandise—which testifies to a certain level of differentiation between agriculture and crafts *(métiers)*."[10] Let us therefore examine the phenomenon of expanding wheat production, known both in Poland and in Russia in the 15th and 16th centuries. Poland, as we have already argued, is by the sixteenth century integrated into the European world-economy, on whose markets wheat is sold, and for whose markets wheat is grown. As Braudel and Spooner put it: "The dominating feature of the end of the [sixteenth] century is clearly the fact that Polish wheat is now absorbed into the general pool of European prices."[11] This was crucial both for Poland and for the rest of Europe, for which Poland had become at that time "the greatest exporter of cereals."[12]

The rise of a Polish wheat-exporting economy meant, as we have seen, the rise of large domains with coerced cash-crop labor. It meant also the rise of the political strength of the *nobility,* whose economic interest in removing obstacles to trade matched that of western European merchants. Their combined efforts maintained Poland as an open economy.[13] How dependent the prosperity of the Polish nobility was on this open trade was clearly illustrated by the economic difficulties provoked by the blockade of the Vistula by Gustavus Adolphus of Sweden between 1626–1629, who sought thereby to "cut the nerve" of Poland.[14] The fact that "cereal export via the Baltic ports had rapidly taken on [in Poland] proportions such that it dominated the entire economic structure of the country"[15] is used by Jerzy Topolski then to explain the devastating effects of seventeenth-century regression in Poland, effects that varied in different parts of Poland according to the degree to which the local economy was export-oriented.[16]

It may be objected that the value of the wheat involved is rather small as a proportion of the total product of the European world-economy, but Boris Porchnev replies that "it is not the quantities of merchandise exported (not too great in point of fact) which ought to be the object of the attention of scholars, but rather the rate of profit which was shared between the merchant middlemen and the landed proprietors exploiting the labor of the serfs."[17] And Stanislaw Hoszowski points out that in the overall inflation of the sixteenth century, not only did Polish prices start to rise even before those of western and central Europe, before the impact of American treasure on prices,[18] but also, within Poland, it was the "landed proprietors who obtain(ed) the maximum benefit of [the rise in prices] while peasants and the townsmen only los(t) by it."[19] The counterpart of this economic squeeze of the peasants was the frequency of peasant revolts.[20]

Let us now compare the role of wheat production in Russia at this time. Let us start with Mankov's assertion about sixteenth-century Russia: "one can speak at this time only of an internal cereals market."[21] That is, although almost no wheat is exported, "there existed already, in the sixteenth-century, a link between local markets, sometimes very far apart from each other."[22] Thus capitalist agriculture emerged at this time, and in similar forms, both in Poland (and other countries of eastern Europe) on the one hand, and Russia on the other. But whereas the former produced for an expanding west European market, in Russia, "seigniors produced for the expanding domestic market."[23] Indeed, in the sixteenth century, "special permission was required of the tsar to ship [grain] out of the country."[24] The specialization of the sixteenth-century European world-economy was being replicated in smaller form within the Russian world-economy. The core of the Russian world-economy was exporting manufactured goods (metal wares, textile products, leather goods, weapons, and armor) in return for luxury goods, cotton cloth, horses, and sheep.[25] In addition, they *re*exported Western manufactured goods eastward, "though this activity was apparently not of much significance in the sixteenth century."[26] Russia was feeling the happy effects of being the focal point of an economic community: "Furs, salts, hides, and other wares streamed into the older regions from the colonies, creating new wealth and stimulating commercial and industrial activity."[27]

But what about Russian trade with the West? Did it not parallel Polish trade? We must be careful not to read back into the sixteenth century phenomena of the eighteenth and nineteenth centuries, by which time a separate Russian world-economy had indeed disappeared and Russia had become one more peripheral area of the European world-economy.[28]

It is true, on first glance, that what was happening in the sixteenth century was that "in her trade with the West, Russia exchanged raw materials and semi-finished goods for manufactured wares."[29] Russia exported various raw materials used for naval stores (flax, hemp, grease, wax) plus furs and imported luxury articles and metal goods (including munitions). But in neither direction does it seem the trade was critical. For western Europe, not until the seventeenth century could it be said that Russia was important as a "reservoir of grain and forest products."[30] T. S. Willan sees Russia's chief value for England, the western country with which Russia traded most in the sixteenth century, "as a source of essential materials for the navy." But he adds:

> It is a little difficult to say whether the trade was equally valuable for the Russians.

Their equivalent for the naval stores exported to England was perhaps the arms and munitions which the company was alleged to be sending to Russia, especially in the "fifties" and the "sixties."[31]

"Especially in the 'fifties' and the 'sixties' "—we shall return to that observation. A. Attman suggests that the crucial import was not the metal goods but rather silver in form of bullion and of art objects. He offers as verification of this hypothesis the extraordinary accumulation of silver in the churches, monasteries and palaces as well as important finds of metal bars.[32] If one remembers that a major export was that of furs, "then the livery of dignity and wealth,"[33] one of the so-called "rich trades," we can consider the major portion of Russian–Western trade in the sixteenth century to be an exchange of preciosities, a method of consuming surplus rather than producing it, hence dispensable at moments of contraction, and consequently not central to the functioning of the economic system. This is not to say it was unimportant. Middlemen profited by it. No doubt the state obtained some customs revenue from it. No doubt also it reinforced the system of social prestige accumulation. The point however is that if a blockade had occured equivalent to that of Gustavus Adolphus of the Vistula in 1626, the impact on Russia's internal economy would have been far less than on Poland's.

We have been using Poland as our example of a country in the periphery of the European world-economy (as opposed to being in the external arena). But Poland was in many ways an extreme case. Would there be any difference if we looked at other countries in the periphery? The answer is there would be some but it does not seem crucial.

For example, in both Bohemia and Hungary, the "forced labor" of the "serfs" was not always exclusively in the form of the *corveé* but sometimes in the form of "forced wage labor."[34] Josef Válka notes that this intermediate form of labor service in Bohemia is linked with the fact that agricultural production is diversified and directed to an internal market.[35] Josef Petráň similarly points out in various of the smaller territories of central Europe (Bohemia, Silesia, Saxony, Austria), there was less of a tendency for the growth of large estates and he suggests that we are witnessing the birth of specialization not only between agriculture and industry but within agriculture itself, where however "naturally the specialization could not be complete."[36] Malowist points out that agricultural specialization in Denmark parallels that of eastern Europe, for, during the sixteenth century, the Danish and Holstein nobility "developed an economy based on the labour of serfs, as well as on the trade of agricultural and dairy products, and also on the product of their serfs, whose chances of engaging in commerce were limited to a minimum."[37] But he says that this social process of aristocratic appropriation "which can be seen most clearly in Poland, Brandenburg, Pomerania, Mecklenburg and Livonia, showed itself *more feebly* in Denmark."[38]

What we can say about these examples is that they show the texture of the European division of labor to be getting more complex already in the sixteenth century. However, the meaning of a low export ratio for Bohemia, a small country surrounded by the rest of the European world-economy and a similar low ratio for Russia, a large empire on the edge of the European world-economy, must have been quite different. Bohemia's freedom of political action was ultimately far smaller and hence her economic dependence ultimately far greater. This is a case where the analyst must look at absolutes for minima and proportions for maxima.[39] Bohemia had less give in case of a trade cutoff than Russia. Therefore its economic activities had to be developed more consciously within the framework of the needs of the European world-economy.

Let us now return to the remark of Willan about the 1550s and 1560s. It should be obvious from our exposition thus far that the line between periphery and external arena is fluid, both in the sense that it is hard for an analyst to fix it and in the sense that it shifts easily. One way to look at the history of Russia in this period is to see it as reacting to a tentative attempt of Europe to include it within the world-economy. This attempt failed then because Europe's technology and economy was not yet sufficiently strong. Eventually, in a later era, it would succeed. Robert Reynolds states this process somewhat ethnocentrically:

> As far as we can tell, it was the English who opened a gateway and detonated
> Russian expansion. . . . England's opening of the [northern] route [in 1553] gave
> Russia a tremendous market for furs, which stimulated the Cossacks on the frontier
> and the Stroganovs with their capital and managerial talent to push as fast as pos-
> sible to the eastward and the northward. Each year they took up new sections for
> the fur trade, exactly as the French and English furtraders, and then the Americans,
> pushed farther and farther to the west in North America. With the great market
> for fur, the possibility was opened to buy fine textiles, metal goods, and other
> things from western Europe.[40]

How did this English thrust into the Russian world fit in with the latter's internal political developments? It is to this picture we must now turn, to see how Russia reacted to "bringing it into Europe" and how this reaction further differentiated Russia from eastern Europe. Malowist notes that the grain grown in central Russia was sold in the north and northeast of European Russia and in Siberia.[41] Thus the development of Russian wheat production "had facilitated the colonization and conquest" of its own very rich territories of the north and east which in turn "furnished immense riches, first of all for the treasure of the Czars, and later, for the merchants."[42]

To appreciate the role of the Russian state, we should recapitulate what we argued in the previous chapter about the role of the state in the core states of western Europe, proceed to look at the role of the state in the peripheral states of eastern Europe, and then compare both with the role of the state in Russia. We presented the absolute monarchy as a structure in which the king and his entourage aspired to political primacy with the direct assistance of a patrimonial and venal bureaucracy and mercenary standing armies. On the one hand, the king sought the assistance of favored segments of the urban commercial bourgeoisie who supplied him with money and some political counterweight to the centrifugal tendencies of the old nobility. On the other hand, the king was the pinnacle of the system of traditional social status and was ultimately the protector of the nobility against the corrosive effects of the developing capitalist system.[43]

In terms therefore of the two social strata, the old nobility and the commercial urban bourgeoisie, the absolute monarchy was for each a lesser evil, and its strength grew on the basis of their lack of alternatives. For it served them both well by creating the possibility of enabling the country as an entity to get a disproportionate share of the surplus product of the entire European world-economy. In the sixteenth century, we can speak at most of state "fiscalism" or "precocious mercantilism." From about 1650 on, the Western states engaged in a full-scale mercantilist policy designed to strengthen their relative position in the world-economy even further.

While the sixteenth century was a period of the rise of state power in western Europe, it was an era of decline for state power in eastern Europe, both cause and consequence of the latter's economic position. This is a further instance of the cumulative impact of social changes. As the landed aristocracy of Poland grew stronger through its profitable role in international trade and the indigenous bourgeoisie grew weak, the tax base of the state frittered away which meant that the king could not afford to maintain an adequate army.[44] The magnates then needed to assure their own protection, but this in turn made for the possibility of private wars.[45] Some of these private armies equalled in size that of the Crown.[46] The king became an elected king, and the central legislature, the *Seym,* began to turn over much of its authority to local diets.

From this point on, disintegration of the state machinery proceeded apace. Janusz Tazbir shows how one step led to the next:

> From 1613 decisions concerning taxation were, as a rule, transferred to the local diets. This decentralization of the fiscal system led to a situation in which some districts had to pay bigger taxes than others. The chaos was further deepened when the local diets were entrusted with the voting of taxes even for the defense of the State (1640). All this was bound to result in a decline of the revenues of the treasury which, in turn, rendered payments to the army virtually impossible.
> The soldiers, who [were] owed arrears of pay, organized military leagues or

confederations which ravaged the country constituting dangerous centres of political ferment.[47]

In western Europe, royal property grew at the expense of church property, even in Catholic Spain, but not in Poland. During the first impact of the Reformation some parochial Church lands were confiscated by Protestant gentry, but even then the bulk of major Church property was untouched. Then the Counter-Reformation triumphed for reasons we have already elucidated. However because of the very weakness of the State, royal property declined.[48]

Similar processes were occurring elsewhere in eastern Europe. Most people today associate the state of Prussia with two phenomena: the strong state and a strong Junker class. The sixteenth century precisely saw the rise of a strong Junker class in the areas that would later constitute Prussia. But it was also a century in which the state grew weaker, not stronger.

For one thing, the system of estates based on tiny cottage holdings and *corvée*[49] which grew up in east Elbia at this time and was called *Gutsherrschaft,* replacing the older feudal form called *Gutswirtschaft,* differed from the older form most markedly, as the very name would indicate, in the internal system of authority. In the new system, as Friedrich Lütge puts it, "the estate [was] something like a small political unit within the State: its inhabitants [were] only indirectly subjects of the territorial prince."[50] Second, as in Poland, the Hohenzollerns were using their crown estates and even the former church lands[51] as security for loans, a process which steadily undermined their strength. These measures, taken *in extremis* by the Crown, were extremely beneficial to the Junker class.[52]

This process of decline of princely power in Germany continued throughout the sixteenth century and reached a low point in 1648 with the Peace of Westphalia, which concluded the Thirty Years' War, a peace which A. J. P. Taylor argues was "not the cause of German decline and weakness, but rather the result. . . ." Although peace was "imposed" by foreign powers, without their intervention matters would have been still worse. "The only alternative in 1648 was not less foreign interference but more—the continuance of the war until most of Germany was actually partitioned between Sweden, France, and the Habsburgs."[53]

The position of Sweden is worth brief attention, as the evolution of Sweden's state machinery approached the model of western Europe rather than that of the periphery, although it was economically very underdeveloped at this time. It was strong, not because its commerce and industry was strong, although iron production grew steadily beginning in 1540;[54] it was paradoxically rather that its agriculture was weak, and its aristocrats wished to take hold of the profits of other lands for want of being able to create them on their own. Or, so at least, Malowist argues:

[I]t would be worth our while to go over certain aspects of Swedish domination of the Baltic. In fact, the beginnings of Swedish expansion, modest at first, are also to be found in the 15th century. Furthermore, Sweden in the 15th and 16th centuries was economically a very backward country, not only by comparison with western Europe, but even by comparison with east Germany or Poland. . . . Thus it should be noted that there was nothing in the situation of the Swedish merchants which can explain Sweden's aggression against its neighbors, since these merchants made infinitesimal profit out of Sweden's conquests and even, on occasion, sought to oppose the policy of conquest, considering it to be rather a source of ever-increasing taxation.

On the contrary, the group which strongly supported expansion was the aristocracy, the nobility, unable to increase its income, rather small at that time, at the expense of a peasantry that was strong and well-organized. And it was precisely to the great lords and the nobility that the conquests and the administration of conquered territories brought important sources of new revenue.[55]

And if we ask why the peasantry was so strong, may it not be precisely the fact that Sweden at that time was endowed with "an agriculture which could barely supply its own needs," and hence its only real source of immediate wealth was to be "something of a parasite living on the weakness of her neighbours, a consequence of the enormous growth in the power of the nobility."[56]

Sweden as a mild deviant case thus illustrates the process well. As a peripheral state with a weak bourgeoisie, it was an arena in which the political power of the aristocracy grew with the economic expansion of the sixteenth century. But the growth of wheat was hindered by the climatic downturn of the time which affected negatively in particular the Scandinavian countries.[57] The nobility hence needed conquest and for that they needed a strong, not a weak, state. Once they had the strong state, they would be able in the seventeenth and eighteenth centuries to use mercantilism as a lever of industrial advance, and hence be spared the fate of Poland.

We are now ready to look at Russia. One key piece of evidence for the hypothesis that Russia was *not* part of the European world-economy is precisely the growth of the absolute monarchy in Russia in a manner that bears substantial parallels to developments in western Europe and is strikingly different from eastern Europe.

What are the facts? The rise of coerced cash-crop labor in sixteenth-century Russia was the product of state intervention in the economy, directly linked to the creation of military benefices called *pomestia*, used to reward supporters of the tsar. In a sense, there is some parallel here to the *encomiendas* in Hispanic America. Unlike in Hispanic America, however, the system of coerced labor could not be as suddenly introduced because land first had to be expropriated from the old nobility (the *boyars*) and the monasteries. Nor was there any equivalent to the *cacique* as an intermediary, except insofar as the Russian Orthodox priest might be considered to play an analogous role in some areas. Rather, legislative enforcement of "serf-dom" came at the end of a process in which the "refeudalization" had been set in motion by a process of growing peasant debt. V. O. Kluchevsky describes how this worked:

> [T]he landlord's loan gave rise to relations wherein the seigniorial peasant had to choose between a definite term of insolvent peasanthood and an indefinite term of slavery [that is, working off the debt in the form of personal labor]. Yet this restriction was not [a] police attachment to the place of domicile . . . but a mere industrial dependence, through debt, upon an individual (i.e. upon the landowner) under the general civil law of the country. Thus the close of the sixteenth century saw the peasant's right of removal expire of itself, and without any abrogation by law. . . .
> [The] peasant, when bargaining with the landowner for a plot and a loan, of himself, and in perpetuity, renounced (through his tenancy-contract) the right of ever, or by any means whatsoever, terminating the obligations which by that contract he assumed.[58]

Voluntary enserfment, however, became insufficient in Russia when the military successes of Ivan the Terrible in the middle of the sixteenth century led to the incorporation of large vacant lands in the southeast of what is today European Russia. To keep the peasant population from running away to these new lands, which meant for the holders of *pomestia* losing their manpower and thereby for the government its taxpayers, "restrictions on peasant liberty to move were introduced."[59] As Alexander Gerschenkron remarks, "the process of enserfment is almost inconceivable without the power of the state. How else could it be achieved in a country so open towards the vast empty space in the south and the east as was the great Russian plain?"[60] The active role of the state machinery was hence very closely linked with the fact that Russia was involved in a conquest operation.

So of course was Spain. But Spain, because of the bullion, the Italian creditors, and the Hapsburg links, was and remained intimately linked with the European world-economy. Russia sought to create its own world-economy. Nonetheless the original process of Russian state creation had some parallels to that of Spain. Spain was created as the result of a *reconquista* of its territory by a Christian crusade against Moslem conquerers from North Africa. Russia was created as a process of overthrowing the "Tartar yoke," of reconquering its territory by a Christian crusade against Moslem (or Islamized) invaders from Central Asia. Muscovy's role paralleled that of Castile and the élan of a common struggle greatly aided Muscovy's triumph.[61]

As part of the price of getting the assistance of the traditional warrior class, the *boyars*, in this reconquest, the Muscovy tsars had to concede to them a claim to perpetual primacy according to a rank order early in historical time.[62] This system, known as *mestnichestvo*, was one of those important traditions created by the process of change. In order to balance off this new strength of the aristocracy, Ivan III in the late fifteenth century created a new system of nonallodial fiefs called *pomestia* which were granted as a prebend in return for military service. The *pomestia* were created out of conquered frontier lands, from land confiscated from monasteries and errant *boyars*, and also from free peasant land.[63]

For lack of a Reformation, however, the Church was able to fight back and the existence of two kinds of land tenure, *pomestia* and the old manorial form known as *votchina*, gave the monasteries a great opening, as owners of *votchini* began to sell or donate their lands to the Church, especially after 1550, in return for life tenancies. There were religious justifications to be sure, but the key factor seems to be socio–political.[64]

It was the creation of new forms of tenure, the *pomestia*, not based on traditional reciprocal feudal obligations and often in frontier areas, combined with the fact of territorial expansion and hence the ready availability of land, that led the government down the path of making peasant work and residence obligations increasingly compulsory throughout the sixteenth century, beginning with the Code of 1497 and culminating in the Assembly Code of 1649.[65] Without such restrictions, the peasants would have refused service. The political strength of the Church meant that the state was unable to stem this drain of land out of the taxation system. The only alternative was to increase the taxes on the remaining land, further squeezing the peasants.[66] Since, in addition, peasants were offered more favorable terms on monastic lands, increased taxation served as a further impetus to peasant emigration.

This is the background to the question of "the fifties and the sixties." The reign of Ivan IV (the Terrible) from 1547–1584 was a critical period in Russian history, for Ivan by a single-minded concentration on the objective of increasing state authority crystallized the form of internal social structure that Russia was to know for several centuries to come, while trying to establish the autonomy of the Russian state from the European world-economy. As we shall see, he was successful in the latter goal in the short run. Or to put it another way, he held off the wolves at the door long enough to make it certain that when Russia would later be absorbed into the world-economy, it came in as a semiperipheral state (like seventeenth and eighteenth century Spain) rather than as a peripheral state (like Poland).

Within Russia, the main weapon of the tsar in increasing state power was by the creation of a patrimonial state machinery (as in western Europe), linked in the case of Russia even more than in the case of France and England to the redistribution of land rights. One key reform was the abolition of the *kormlenie* system of regional administration, a system of tax-farming prebends, and replacing it with a bureaucracy paid partly in cash and partly by the grant of land.[67] This reform not only created a central bureaucracy; it created at the same time its tax base.[68] This was combined with the creation of local government institutions firmly in the hands of local gentry whose rise was favored by and part of the expansion of the tsar's authority.[69] It was at this time (1556) that military service was firmly linked to the holding of *pomestia,* thus giving the tsar an assurance of a relatively loyal standing army.[70] The growing of *pomestia* and hence the growing complexity of supervising the operations of the system led to the creation of a central land office in Moscow for the *pomestia.*[71]

Meanwhile, externally Ivan IV was pursuing a policy of expansion not only toward the frontier lands in the south (at the time, the Crimea) but in the west toward the Baltic, the so-called Livonian war which dragged on for twenty-five years (1558–1583). Its object was to establish Russia as a Baltic power. It was a long and essentially inconclusive war.[72] Had it been more conclusive, Russia might have been definitively drawn into the European world-system at that time.

One can understand why expansion westward tempted the tsar in his capacity as entrepreneur. Unlike the rulers of the various countries of eastern Europe, the tsar was in a position to profit directly from the expansion of trade because of the already stronger state machinery. In Poland it was the aristocracy which managed to gain a monopolistic control on the export trade; in Russia it was the tsar. He reserved these rights for himself and those he favored.[73] Thus foreign trade was of interest to the tsar not only as a source of customs revenue but as an outlet for the very large amount of goods delivered to him in kind by his peasants. As the city served the medieval feudal lord, so Ivan IV sought to use all of Europe. Since the enterprise was vast, he found it convenient and profitable to enlist the cooperation of a commercial bourgeoisie (both foreign and indigenous) to handle the merchandise. When Polish aristocrats eliminated Polish commercial middlemen, they thereby escaped paying certain taxes on their goods. Thus the state lost revenue and the Polish bourgeoisie declined. When the landlord is the sovereign, any taxes dispensed or saved are simply bookkeeping transactions. Ergo, in Russia, there were no great financial advantages in making the individuals who supervised the transfer of goods members of the firm's staff as opposed to independent entrepreneurs. Since they were the latter to start with, it was easier to let them remain that.

Hence, in Russia as in western Europe, the indigenous commercial bourgeoisie survived, and the state machinery was strengthened at the same time.[74] Had Tsar Ivan IV succeeded, it is not certain that the Russian merchants would have fared quite as well as they anticipated. We shall never know, since when the Livonian war ended in stalemate externally, all that had really been accomplished was to bring to a head an internal social and economic crisis within Russia.

In the intrinsically unstable political arenas of the time, lack of continuous success by a state in the international area led to open clashes of interest at home which always bore the risk of disintegration of the state. To counteract this inner turbulence, Ivan IV resorted to strong police measures—the notorious *Oprichnina* for which he earned the title of "the Terrible." It essentially involved the creation of a special palace guard, with the aid of which the tsar drastically purged his enemies, especially among the aristocracy. The weapons were two: death and confiscation of property, the latter enabling the tsar to redistribute land to those whose loyalty he hoped to keep.

It was politically successful in that it ended the fear of *coup d'état*. But, in the opinion of many, it backfired. Blum for example says:

> The shock of the *Oprichnina,* together with the steady drain of the long and unsuccessful Livonian War . . . upon the country's resources, deranged the social and economic structure of the realm. . . . The confiscation of the great landed complexes and their subdivisions into pomestia did violence to the agricultural system upon which the nation's economy was based, setting back techniques, cutting down on production, and creating new tensions between seigniors and peasants.[75]

Blum also blames the heavy taxation combined with plagues, crop failure, and invasions for mass flights of peasants.[76] A sharp and sudden inflation between 1575 and 1590 reflected these happenings and accentuated them. A. G. Mankov, on the basis of his study of Russian price movements in the sixteenth century, is willing to go so far as "to see in the crisis of the years 1580–1590 a generalized crisis of the national economy,"[77] a view he asserts he shares with Soviet historical writing generally.[78]

Vernadsky argues in a similar vein that the Livonian War was a dreadful error, because Russia had no choice but to continue fighting on the Crimean front and hence by opting to fight in Livonia, Russia was opting for a two-front war, a policy with disastrous results.[79] This seems to me to miss the crucial point that Russia may equally well have had no choice in Livonia. Vernadsky views the Livonian War as a failure, one in which the Russians were "lucky to be able to conclude an armistice with Sweden on August 5, 1583, even though the terms of it were highly unfavorable."[80] Perhaps, alternatively, we could think of it as a gigantic success. Russia was *not* pulled into the European world-economy. Her bourgeoisie and her monarch were spared, at least for the moment, the fate of their Polish counterparts.

This is not entirely fanciful. Boris Porchnev analyzes the grand pattern of international relations in Europe in the sixteenth century as one in which the opponents of the Hapsburg–Catholic objective of creating a single imperial system sought to encourage the creation of an eastern barrier of states—Sweden, Poland (later Poland-Lithuania), and the Ottoman

Empire, "directed primarily against central Europe" but which also became "a barrier isolating, from the rest of Europe, Russia which was becoming ever stronger."[81]

As Catholicism regained ground in Poland, however, the state of Poland-Lithuania became an ally of Spain. When, in the years following Ivan IV, the Russian state was rent by internal quarrels culminating in the so-called "Time of Troubles" (1610–1613), Poland, secretly supported by the Hapsburgs and, for separate motives, Sweden, engaged in an "attempt to dismember and subjugate Russia,"[82] an attempt which failed. Furthermore, Vernadsky asserts there was also English interest at this time in establishing "a protectorship over all or part of Russia."[83] No doubt a major contributing factor to the failure was the existence of the sharp divisions of the Thirty Years' War which constantly diverted Russia's immediate enemies into more pressing tasks.

But Russia was coming ever nearer to absorption by Europe. Ivan IV's "disastrous" policies delayed this. See Kluchevsky's description of what was happening at the end of the "long" sixteenth century:

> We see England and Holland helping [Tsar] Michael [1613-45] to become reconciled to his enemies, Poland and Sweden, for the reason that Muscovy was a valuable market for the former, and also a convenient road to the East—to Persia, and even to India. Again, we see the French King proposing to conclude an alliance with Michael, in order to meet the commercial interests of France in the East, where she was the rival both of England and of the Dutch. . . . The Empire of Tsar Michael was *weaker* than the Empire of Tsar Ivan [IV] and Theodor [1584-98], *but* far *less isolated* in Europe.[84]

Should not the "but" read "and therefore?" What Ivan had been seeking was the creation of a Russian Empire, not a piece of the European pie. That was to be the objective at a later time of Peter the Great.

The third great difference between Russia and eastern Europe was, as we have indicated, the direct consequence of the different structure and direction of commerce and the differing strengths of the state machinery. In Russia the cities and the indigenous bourgeoisie survived the "long" sixteenth century whereas in eastern Europe they very largely did not. And the land, although for the most part in the same large estate form as developed in eastern Europe, was in Russia in the hands of "new men," sometimes called "gentry," sometimes "lesser nobility" (we have already seen how little relevant this distinction is). These were men descended not from the old *boyar* class, but drawn from two groups, the *dvoriane* (a sort of court nobility) and the so-called "sons of boyars" who were in earlier epochs minor and outlying aristocrats. Those boyars who survived were largely "non-royal kinsmen of the tsar."[85] Thus, especially after the Time of Troubles, when Tsar Michael was able to carry through to their logical conclusion the policies of Ivan IV, a new class of magnates emerged.[86]

Eventually the new aristocracy took over all the formal appurtenances of the old. *Mestnichestvo* was abolished in 1682. The *pomestia* became de facto transferable by sale and inheritance, thus vitiating the distinction from the *votchini*.[87] The Code of Laws of 1649 lessened considerably the distinction between the two forms of property[88] and in 1731 the two forms would be legally merged.[89]

The rise of "new men" of course occurred everywhere—certainly in western Europe as we have seen, in many ways in eastern Europe as well. But Blum catches the essential point:

> The Russian experience . . . differed in one important respect from the rest of Eastern Europe (and resembled that in the West). In the other Eastern lands the ascent of the lesser nobility was made possible by the decline in the powers of the sovereigns. In Russia the gentry owed its rise to the increase in the tsar's power. It was the tail of the kite of the new absolutism.[90]

Finally, the contrast between eastern Europe and Russia is clear in the urban areas. Towns declined more in eastern Europe, the indigenous urban bourgeoisie declined more and native industry declined more. It was to be sure a relative matter. Russia in comparison to *western* Europe may be considered to have declined, relatively if not absolutely. And the decline was not total in eastern Europe. Yet the evidence seems to indicate a qualitative gap between eastern Europe and Russia.

The difference may have been less in the "first" sixteenth century.[91] But as the landed proprietors engaged more and more in direct trade, they pursued openly "antiurban" activities in eastern Europe.[92] With the rise of "kinglets" in Poland and *Gutsherrschaft* in east Elbia, the prince as landowner found little in his own immediate needs to make him sympathetic to townsmen.[93] And as the towns declined the nobility grew still stronger.[94] In Russia, Kluchevsky might speak of the "extraordinarily slow and painful growth of Russian towns and town industries during the sixteenth and seventeenth centuries,"[95] but at least it was growth not decline. Blum is more positive. He says:

> The new importance of exchange in economic life [in the 16th century] was signalized by the reemergence of the city as a center of industry and commerce and as a market for farm goods and other wares produced in Russia and in foreign lands. Old towns were revivified, new ones established, and some rural settlements (as Novgorod land registers show) began to abandon agriculture for trade and industry.[96]

Along with the strength of the towns went the strength of the indigenous commercial bourgeoisie. The local aristocracies not only took over the export trade from the local merchants, "depress[ing] them into the role of agents"[97] but shared the import trade with a *foreign* bourgeoisie.[98] The indigenous bourgeoisie of one country was the foreign bourgeoisie of another. German merchants who could find no place in the economies of east Elbia were more than welcome in Poland, and were appropriately grateful politically.[99] Indeed one might speculate as to whether the later recuperative power of the German bourgeoisie is not due to the fact that they survived in places like Poland and Slovenia. In Russia, on the contrary, though indigenous merchants ran into competition from large landholders, including the monasteries, and most especially the tsar himself, they nonetheless survived.[100] One factor that helped was that the leading merchants, known as *gosti*, were allowed to play the double role of agents of the tsar, both commercial and fiscal, and merchants on their own account.[101] Eventually then they could break away from their connections with the tsar, even became effective rivals to him. And in the end, "private enterprise did carry, in point of fact, a large share of the Russian expansion to the Pacific, though rarely supported by the state, but rather competitive with it."[102]

As for the handicrafts industries, these seemed to decline everywhere, largely because the absence of tariff barriers allowed the ever more economical products of western European industry to outsell the local products.[103] To the extent that local industries survived, as for example lace in Czechia, it was by serving as rural cottage industries for merchant houses outside their area.[104] Still and all, this made some difference as it encouraged a diversification of agriculture and prepared the way for the later industrial development of Bohemia.[105] In Russia, however, because it was its own world-economy, some of the accumulated capital went into industrial development.[106] Even in the case of the most important export industry of the European world-economy, textiles, where one would have thought the Russian industry would have collapsed before the competition, the local industry retained most of the mass market and even a part of the quality market.[107]

We could make a similar analysis of why the Ottoman Empire was not part of the European world-economy.[108] It is perhaps more to the point to turn our attention to the issue of the Portuguese Indian Ocean trade and how that differed from the Spanish Atlantic trade.

We must begin by dispensing with the myth of the role of the Turks in the rise of the Portuguese Indian Ocean trade. Far from the rise of the Ottoman Empire having led to a closure of the eastern Mediterranean to western Europe and hence having motivated Portugal's search for the Cape route to Asia, it is now generally recognized both that Portugal's overseas explorations predated the rise of the Ottomans and that the decline of the eastern Mediterranean spice trade predated Portugal's entry into it. Indeed, A. H. Lybyer precisely attributes the Levant's "decline" not to cultural resistances to modern technology, but to the structural diversion of trade and hence its noninclusion in the expanding European world-economy.

> [The Turks] were not active agents in deliberately obstructing the routes. They did not by their notorious indifference and conservatism greatly, if at all on the whole, increase the difficulties of the oriental traffic. Nor did they make the discovery of new routes imperative. On the contrary, they lost by the discovery of a new and superior route. Had there been no way around Africa the whole story of the Levant since 1500 might have been very different. In the first place, the Mameluke sultans might have found in their uninterrupted trade sufficient financial support to enable them to resist successfully the attack of the Turks in 1516. But if the Turks had conquered Egypt while the full steam of oriental trade still ran through it, they must either have been deprived far sooner than was actually the case of the control of these routes, or they would have had to accomodate themselves to the great and increasing trade through their dominions. In the latter case they might have been forced into adopting modern ways, and into adding to their wonderful capacity for territorial unification a parallel scheme of organizing their trade. . . . The shifting of the trade-routes was done, not by the Turks, but in their despite and to their disadvantage.[109]

We have, in an earlier chapter, sought to explain the complex of forces within Portugal (and Spain) which led to the explorations of the fifteenth century and the overseas trade and empires of the sixteenth. It is striking when one reflects upon how the economic motivations of the Iberian expansion pointed heavily to Atlantic areas (the Western Hemisphere, though they did not know it, and West Africa) but not to Asia, even though the ideology of the explorations set great stock on the search for a route to the Indies. For example, when Vitorino Magalhães-Godinho makes a long list of the factors which dominated the early phase of Portuguese expansion (from the lack of gold, to the grain shortage, to land and slaves for sugar production, to the need for fishing areas), there is no mention of pepper or spices or drugs, of silks or porcelain or precious stones, in short, of all that the Portuguese would in fact import from Asia in the sixteenth century.[110] But in the last quarter of the fifteenth century Portuguese interest in the spice trade awakened,[111] and the search for Prester John became linked to this interest in the mind of King John II, "for [the] kingdom [of Prester John] would serve him as a way-station on the route to India, from whence Portuguese captains would bring back those riches heretofore distributed by Venice."[112] And the gold of West Africa plus the pepper and spices of Asia would in fact make up more than half the revenue of the Portuguese state by 1506 with the portion of the Asian trade growing thereafter, constituting thus the "underpinning of the imperial economy."[113]

Vasco de Gama came, saw, and conquered far more and far faster than Julius Caesar. It is indeed extraordinary that, in a very few years, Portuguese ships comletely dominated the extensive trade of the Indian Ocean. What was the structure of this enterprise and how did it come to be so quickly established?

The answer to the latter is relatively easy: the technological superiority of the gunned ship that had been developed in Atlantic Europe in the two prior centuries, and to which a crucial technological innovation—the cutting of ports for guns in the actual hulls of the ships as opposed to the superstructure—had been achieved in 1501.[114] Was this technological advantage enough to explain Portuguese success, or must we add thereto the belief that Portugal "went to Asia in a spirit of determination to succeed, which was stronger than the will of the Asiatic peoples to resist," as George B. Sansom insists?[115] Perhaps, although I tend to feel that cultural qualities, such as a spirit of collective psychology, are the product of very specific social structural conjunctures and do not long outlive their base.

In any case from about 1509 when the Portuguese defeated the Egyptian fleet at Diú, the Portuguese navy held "uncontested hegemony"[116] in the Indian Ocean. In addition, during the sixteenth century (but only until 1570 for the Straits of Malacca) Portuguese traders were to be found not only there but in the China Sea, on the coasts of Africa east and west, in the south Atlantic, in Newfoundland, and of course in Europe. "Thus, present everywhere, a Portuguese economy."[117]

The Portuguese system of control in Asia was basically very simple: a fleet of two squadrons (one to block the Red Sea and one to patrol the western coast of India), a Governor-General at Goa and seven fortresses on the periphery.[118] For commercial purposes they maintained a series of trading posts *(feitoria)* and established three great intermediate markets: Malacca, Calicut, and Ormuz, and a subsidiary stop at Aden.[119] The greatest of them was Malacca which became a giant store house and entrepôt, located there almost obligatorily because the monsoons forced the sailing ships coming from points east to unload there.[120] This structure was evolved by Portugal's leading figure on the scene, Affonso Albuquerque, who worked it out as a solution to the military dilemmas of the enterprise.[121]

By and large the trade was in the hands of the state,[122] and when Portugal's role began to wane in the latter part of the sixteenth century, the private sector pulled out of the reduced trade entirely because of the increased risk.[123]

In a few small areas, the Portuguese exercised direct sovereignty. In several areas, such as Cochin or Ceylon, the local ruler was under Portuguese "protection." But in most places, the Portuguese made no pretense at political rule, instead "circulating and trading in conformity with the laws, usages, and customs of the states in which they found themselves."[124] As Donald F. Lach puts it, the Europeans at that time were "mainly interested in those countries where effective unity and central authority help(ed) to provide stable conditions for trade and a favorable climate for evangelizing."[125]

To appreciate why we do not consider the Indian Ocean trading area to be part of the European world-economy despite the fact that it was so completely dominated by a European power, we must look successively at the meaning of this dominance for the Asian countries affected, its meaning for Europe, and how it compares with those parts of the Americas under Iberian rule.

There seems little doubt that a major element in Portugal's lightning ascendancy first in the Indian Ocean then in the China Sea, was the "vacuum in sea-borne trade," as Trevor-Roper calls it, that existed at this time in both areas: "The vast trade of Asia—of which the long-distance trade with Europe was but a fragment—lay open to the first comers. The Portuguese came and took it; and while the vacuum lasted—until Europe overtook them or Asia resisted them—it was their monopoly."[126] The vacuum was not economic but political, for it is central to the understanding of the situation that the Portuguese did not create the trade. They took over a pre-existing trade network, in the hands at that point of time of Moslem merchants (Arabs and Gujeratis) in the Indian Ocean and *Wako* pirates in the China Sea.[127] The ouster of the Moslem traders, which comes first in time, was "by brute force and not by peaceful competition."[128] It was primarily due to politico–naval superiority.[129]

The great import from Asia to Lisbon was pepper, or pepper and spices. Already at the end of the fifteenth century before Portugal was in the picture, Europe probably consumed a quarter of Asia's production;[130] and, to meet the increased demand of Europe, Asian production doubled over the course of the century.[131] In return, what Asia principally got from Europe was bullion, silver and gold.[132] The silver came largely from the Americas and Japan.[133] The gold seems largely to have come at first from West Africa,[134] then from southeast Africa, Sumatra and China.[135]

Given Europe's passionate hoarding of bullion, it is strange indeed that this kind of formal imbalance of payments should persist for so long. But if Europe wanted Asia's offerings, it seems that this was the price they had to pay. This points to one fundamental sense in which Asia was not part of the European world-economy at this time, since from 1500 to 1800 Europe's relations with Asian states "were ordinarily conducted within a framework and on terms established by the Asian nations. Except for those who lived in a few colonial footholds, the Europeans were all there on sufferance."[136] And this despite Europe's military superiority. For we must remember that this military superiority was only a *naval* superiority.[137]

From an Asian point of view, the Portuguese traders differed in one fundamental respect from those that had preceded them historically. The buyers were "not merchants—private entrepreneurs—but a formidable naval power, acting, in the name of a foreign state, on behalf of its merchants and itself."[138] This meant that trade relations—indeed prices—were fixed by treaties recognized under international law. But states had to deal with states. And it took the Portuguese a while to accustom themselves to the high level of state dignity they encountered.[139] Initially, the Portuguese were willing to make the enormous profits that seizures would bring, but after 10 short years, they realized this was a very shortsighted policy.[140] They turned instead to becoming the arbiters of and intermediaries for *intra*-Asian trade, the profits from which they used to capitalize the Cape route trade, bringing both spices *and* bullion to Portugal. It was, as Godinho says, a "grandiose dream," an "enterprise beyond her possibilities *(démesurée)*."[141] They sacrificed the bullion (and more) for the spices, but they did achieve a "centralized intra-Asian trade," and that was "something quite new in Asia."[142] Translated into terms of the European world-economy, the Portuguese role as middlemen meant that "a good deal of European imports derived from invisible exports of shipping and commercial services."[143] The degree to which intra-Asian trade was central to the economics of Portuguese involvement in Asia is highlighted by the fact that it was only after 75 years, in 1578, that the first nonstop express ship *(une 'carrière' de droiture)* went from Lisbon to Malacca.[144]

Thus, for Asia, Portuguese traders meant two things: Asian traders had to deal with a state as the agent for traders, and *intra*-Asian trade was rationalized. Yet J. C. van Leur does not think this adds up to enough to warrant the designation of social change:

> The Portuguese colonial regime . . . did not introduce a single new economic element into the commerce of Southern Asia.⁻ . . . The Portuguese regime only introduced a non-intensive drain on the existing structure of shipping and trade. The next period [that of the Dutch] would in its time organize a new system of foreign trade and foreign shipping, it would call into life trenchant colonial relationships, and it would create new economic forms in Europe—not perhaps as a direct result but rather as a parallel development bolstered by the system. . . .
>
> The international Asian character of trade was maintained, while the political independence of the Oriental states remained practically uninfringed upon by European influence. The great intra-Asian trade route retained its full significance.[145]

The literature tends to support van Leur's assessment.[146] The Portuguese arrived and found a flourishing world-economy. They organized it a little better and took some goods home as a reward for their efforts. The social organization of the economy as well as the political superstructures remained largely untouched. The major change occurs in the production of pepper, the only spice which "gave rise to mass production."[147] But the technology of pepper is so simple that it required very little labor to expand production by more extensive production, for pepper has an important quality: "Once planted, it does not need to be cared for."[148] Hence, a century of Portuguese dominance meant for most of Asia principally that Portuguese rather than Arabs made the profit. The Indian historian K. M. Pannikkar sums up this perspective by saying:

It made no difference to Indian rulers whether their merchants sold their goods to the Portuguese or to the Arabs. In fact, the Portuguese had an advantage in that they were able to sell to Indian rulers arms and equipment that they required. So far as the Indian merchants were concerned, very soon they worked out a system of permits by which they were able to carry on their trade without the competition of Arab merchants, and in that sense the Portuguese monopoly may be said to have helped them.[149]

This is why despite the fact that "the enterprises of the Portuguese kings . . . combined monopolies of protection, of transportation, and of products transported,"[150] Charles Boxer can call Portuguese maritime dominance an "inherently brittle superstructure."[151] Asia, or even Indian Ocean border regions, did not become part of the European world-economy in the sixteenth century. Asia was an external arena with which Europe traded, on somewhat unequal terms to be sure. That is to say, elements of monopoly imposed by force intruded on the market operations. There was, in Chaunu's phrase, a "thalassocratic *Conquista*"[152] by Portugal. But Asia's inner life remained basically unchanged by the contact. Surely it would be hard to argue that Asian primary production was an integral part of this time of the European division of labor.

Further evidence can be found if we look at the impact of Portuguese Asian trade on Europe. Europe did not conquer Asia in the sixteenth century because she could not. Her military advantage was only at sea.[153] On land she was still retreating in the face of Ottoman attack,[154] and this military balance would only change with the Industrial Revolution.[155]

What Asia provided for Europe at this time was luxuries. Now luxuries are important and not to be sneered at, but they take second place to food (grain, cattle, fish, sugar) and the manpower needed to raise them. They took second place also to bullion, not hoarded bullion but bullion as money (although it was only magic that bullion could be used as money, the magic lying in the possibility of its eventual use as a commodity, if need be). Compared to food and even to bullion, a world-economy can adjust relatively easily to the shifts in luxury supply.

Pepper, it may be argued, was not quite a luxury, nor even spices, for they were essential to the preservation of food and as medicine.[156] Once again, it was a matter of degree. The food that was preserved was largely meat, not quite a luxury but not quite destined either for those on subsistence diets. Likewise the medicines.[157] Of course, as Chaunu argues, with a rising standard of living in Europe and a changing balance of power in the world, pepper was becoming less of a luxury. The question, I suppose, is how much less:

When does [pepper] first appear in West? Traditionally one points to several turning-points [*jalons*]. The first of them are the contacts between East and West in the 12th and 13th centuries in the Mediterranean, at the time of the Crusades.

> To tell the truth, two factors must be taken into account. The rise of the consumption
> of pepper must certainly be tied to the increase in the 14th and 15th centuries
> of meat consumption, a phenomenon that has been clearly established. Much more
> lasting however the development of consumption-patterns involving far-off and
> costly products seems to me inseparable from the shift in the power-situation from
> the 12th and 13th centuries. The spices procured *in the conditions of the 13th* [*century*]
> constituted a luxury. To get them required developing that power which would
> permit Western Christianity to develop slowly its potential [*le lent décollement de
> ses moyens*]. This power allowed the West to come to have one after the other
> those various stimulants to the taste-buds and the nervous system that Latin Christian-
> ity had been less clever in producing than Oriental civilizations.[158]

In any case, to the extent that pepper was not a luxury but a seminecessity,
it was precisely the *malaguette* of West Africa, not Asian products, which
was the most important in *quantity*, if not in price.[159]

There is of course no question that the Asian trade was *profitable* to
Portugal. That after all was the point of it. Godinho spends 25 pages
evaluating this. One example, perhaps spectacular, will suffice. The
merchandise which returned was evaluated in 1512 by Albuquerque as
eight times the worth in Portuguese currency of that sent out.[160] It is easy
to see therefore why pepper was "the most notable speculative commodity
of the [sixteenth and seventeenth centuries], attracting the attention of
the greatest merchants and capitalists of the age."[161] The divisibility and
durability of pepper, as well as its profit margin, "rendered it an excellent
object for speculation."[162]

This speculation was not simply that of the capitalists as individual entrepreneurs. It was preeminently that of the Portuguese state which sought
"to increase national wealth by the use of military power," in the formulation
of Frederic Lane.[163] We shall consider below the costs of this policy. It
is pertinent however at this point to insert Lane's evaluation of this collective "speculation":

> In the long run of fifty or a hundred years, a more peaceful policy, fostering
> a greater development of the Eastern trade, might have made the nation richer.
> Although the conquest of India increased Portuguese national income for a time,
> it was followed by a decrease later in the productivity of the nation's labor. It
> does not therefore supply a clear case of success in using armed force to increase
> the nation's prosperity.[164]

But could Portugal have pursued a "more peaceful policy?" This is doubtful,
partly as Lane himself suggests, because of the kind of capital and labor
that existed in Portugal in 1500.[165]

Nonetheless, the discussion on profitability makes clear the limitations
to profit by trade in an external arena. The profits, when all is said and
done, are those of plunder. And plunder is over time self-defeating, whereas
exploitation within the framework of a single world-economy is self-
reinforcing.

Perhaps this will be clearer if we now seek to compare systematically Iberia in Asia and Iberia in the Americas. A word should be said first about the relations of Portugal and Spain. The papal bull, *Inter Coetera,* in its second version of June 1493 drew a famous line, supposedly allocating various parts of the non-European world to the care of Portugal and Spain for the purposes of evangelization.[166] For the Atlantic regions, this came to mean that Portugal's sovereignty was recognized over Brazil and the Atlantic non-Caribbean islands but that of Spain over the bulk of the continent. Presumably Asia was "allotted" to Portugal. But Magellan convinced Charles V to reinterpret the map, it being difficult in the sixteenth century to estimate longitudes, and he laid claim on behalf of the Spanish Crown to the Philippines in 1520,[167] which however was not in fact occupied until 1564. Indeed it is only when Portugal begins to falter as a source of pepper supply because of the revival of Venice's role that Spain sends her expedition to the Philippines in search of pepper, there and in China.[168]

Thus we have a largely Hispanic role in the Americas with a Portuguese corner, and a largely Portuguese role in Asia with a Spanish corner. It is striking how *Iberian* policy was roughly similar in both areas. For in the sixteenth century, Iberia establishes *colonies* in the Americas, but *trading-posts* in Asia.[169]

We have already written of Spanish policy in the Americas and Portuguese policy in Asia. It is noteworthy that each sought to generalize from its dominant experience to the other area but, realizing its error, each came to adapt itself to the requirements of the area. The Portuguese sought to limit their involvement in Brazil to an entrepôt arrangement, but were forced to colonize it as a preemptive measure as of 1530.[170] Similarly the Spaniards sought to utilize an *encomienda* system in the Philippines, but the international commerce was insufficient to sustain the costs and they reverted to the Portuguese pattern. "The trade of Manila thus settled down to a straight exchange of silver from New Spain against Chinese wares."[171]

The reasons for the two different policies seem to be, as we have already hinted, twofold. On the one hand, the rewards of American colonization were in some sense greater. On the other hand, the difficulties of colonizing Asia were much greater. The combination of the two meant that the Americas became the *periphery* of the European world-economy in the sixteenth century while Asia remained an *external arena.*

By rewards we do not mean short-run profit, although even here the Americas seem to do better than Asia by about 50%,[172] but long-run profits in terms of opportunity costs. The Asian trade was an *import trade,* especially that part of it which bypassed the Levant.[173] Indeed one of the reasons Spain eventually gave up the Manila Galleon was precisely opposition at home to the bullion drain it represented.[174] To be sure, this is not, as we have indicated, without some exceptions. It seems for example that Indian teak forests were to some extent incorporated into the European world-economy as suppliers of timber for ships built in dockyards at Goa.[175]

But this is minor compared to the harvest of bullion, wood, leather and sugar from the New World, which evolved during the century from a gathering technique to a stable form of production using cheap labor and European supervision,[176] and thus *transformed* the social structure of the areas involved, incorporating them into the European world-economy.[177]

It is only when Europe had no choice, could not get a product within the framework of its own world-economy that it went to the outside arena to get it at higher cost. Take for example silk. Woodrow Borah has described the reasons for the collapse of Mexican raw silk production in the late sixteenth century.[178] It is just then, as Chaunu points out, that we have "the apogee of the Galleon trade, the massive, brusque and ephemeral arrival of Chinese silk on the Indies market."[179] Of course, when the Spaniards have no more American silver to offer the Chinese, they cannot buy the silk and the Manila Galleon trade collapses about 1640.[180]

As a general rule, the geographical bounds of a world-economy are a matter of equilibrium. The dynamics of forces at the core may lead to an expansionist pressure (as we saw happened in Europe in the fifteenth century). The system expands outward until it reaches the point where the loss is greater than the gain. One factor is of course distance, a function of the state of the technology. Early on, we mentioned the concept of a sixty-day world. There are many ways of estimating time. Compare Chaunu's description of time from Iberia to the Americas, and time from Iberia to Asia. Of the first he says: "Outward passage one month, return six weeks, round trip including loadings and unloadings, in an annual cycle including everything between the winter dead periods."[181] Of the other he says:

> At the point of maximum distance—let us say the Seville-Manila axis as of 1565—the universe born of the long transformation of the 15th and 16th centuries is a five-year universe. That is, five years is the average time necessary for a round trip from Spain to the Philippines.[182]

Clearly the difference was considerable.

But the resistance of distance was compounded by the resistance of estabished authority. The Americas were easily conquered. Even the structured states, like the Aztecs and the Incas, were no match for European arms. Asia was another matter altogether. Neither Portugal, nor even its seventeenth-century successors, were able to summon the firepower to make significant land conquests. For lack of this, they could not establish a system, as in the Americas or eastern Europe, where a little force permits a large expropriation of surplus. On the contrary, it required a lot of force (the Portuguese against their maritime rivals) to achieve the acquisition of a lesser amount of surplus (because the local rulers could insist on a far larger percentage). One way to look at this is to estimate the profitability of alternative uses of force. Frederic Lane conceptualizes it thus:

> I venture to propose as a hypothesis that the [colonial] enterprises which used force to plunder and to prevent the trade of rivals [for example, the Portuguese in Asia] were in general subject to diminishing returns, but that many enterprises using force to create protection [against the destruction or seizure of its capital and the disruption of its labor force], including many that imposed forced labor [for example, the Portuguese in Brazil], enjoyed the advantage of increasing returns.[183]

Handling oneself in the periphery and in the external arena are different skills. It is only in the periphery that the economically more powerful group is able to reinforce its position by cultural domination as well. The Portuguese understood this far better than the Spanish. The latter took Christian evangelization as a greater priority than did the Portuguese, who were more sensitive to the limits of their power in this great Christian–Moslem encounter in sixteenth-century Asia. Chaunu points out that the Spanish put great effort into stopping Moslem penetration of the Philippines. They succeeded to some extent, but they paid an economic price: "This deep-seated hostility to Islam, this inability to make deals with the Moslem princelets of the Moluccas, is this not the true explanation, far more than Portuguese hostility, why the Spaniards in the Philippines could not make a success of the spice trade?"[184] Compare this with the Portuguese decision in the Kongo where first they played with evangelization, colonization, even cash-crop agriculture, then later realized the costs were too high and retreated to an entrepôt relationship in which they sought primarily slaves and ivory.[185]

In Asia, the Portuguese dominance of the Indian Ocean and the Straits of Malacca faced increasing challenge as the "long" sixteenth century went on—from the Arabs *cum* Venice (the old Levant route), from the rising stars of northwest Europe (England and Holland), and from resurgent indigenous forces in Asia.

In an earlier chapter, we already treated the revival of the Eastern Mediterranean in the "second" sixteenth century. Thus, let us merely briefly review the matter here. To cut off the Levant required a costly blockade. The core of the matter was that the "Portugal was not rich enough to maintain this vast network, its fortresses, its costly squadrons, its functionaries.[186] By the 1530s, the Turks were once again able to land in the Persian Gulf, and from that point on the Portuguese share of the trade declines.[187] By 1560, Alexandria was exporting as much spices to Europe as in the late fifteenth century,[188] though, to be sure, it was proportionately less. The Portuguese furthermore were unwilling or unable to lower their prices to meet Venetian competition.[189] And of course we are only referring to the pepper trade, since the trade in drugs seems at no point to have become a Portuguese monopoly.[190] Indeed Portuguese decline is to be measured by the fact that eventually, after 1580, they sought for a cut in the Venetian trade itself.[191] The decline of Portugal was therefore very real. Godinho warns us not to go to the other extreme and see a rosy picture for Venice in its upswing,[192] a view we have already had occasion to expound. For Venice could not pick up all that Portugal dropped.

An even more effective rival was northwest Europe. We should not forget that when the Crowns of Spain and France both declared bankruptcy in 1557, the Portuguese Crown followed suit in 1560. We shall not review the reasons for the rise of Holland and England. But we should take note of one crucial factor in the spice trade, which is that there were in fact *two* spice trades, often called "the Asian contract," and "the European contract." That is to say, there were profits on the spices brought from Asia to Lisbon (or Venice or later Amsterdam) and there were profits on these same spices as they were resold to their ultimate European consumers, who were principally to be found in northern Europe.[193]

The Portuguese did not have the network to sell the pepper in Europe, especially after the decline of Antwerp, with whom they had had close relations. Chaunu says of Portugal in 1585:

> Cut off from the North, the king of Spain, who rules in Lisbon since 1580, offers in vain the contract of Europe. Italy is not strong enough [*n'est pas du taille*]. No one in Spain can dream of it. He must substitute for Antwerp all the strength of German capitalism, that of the Welsers and the Fuggers.
> How can it be said more clearly? The contract of Europe in the end takes priority over the contract of Asia.[194]

But the Welsers and the Fuggers, in turn, are not strong enough to stand up to the English and the Dutch.[195] And the rise of the Dutch is in fact the final blow to Venice because Amsterdam, "more efficient than [Lisbon], breaks the neck of the old Mediterranean commerce."[196]

The Dutch (and English) not only had advantages in Europe. Their naval superiority in the Indian Ocean had an extra financial advantage. They could make profits not only from the trade but from plundering Portuguese ships as well.[197] Even so, the Dutch (and English) did not yet intrude a new element on the Asian scene. They continued the Portuguese role of middlemen.[198]

This brings us then to what is happening in Asia. As the Portuguese collapse, some control is recovered by Asian rulers. For example, from 1570 on in the Straits of Malacca, the Javanese take over the spice trade, at least until the intrusion of the Dutch in 1596.[199] For a while the Portuguese compensated for this by their new monopoly of carrying trade between China and Japan.[200] But as the Japanese came to overcome internal anarchy, they no longer needed the Portuguese. Originally the Ming Emperors had forbidden the Japanese to trade because of anger at the *Wako* pirates.

Once the *Wako* were under control, direct trading was once again possible. Furthermore, now the Dutch and English came on the scene with no kind words for Spain(–Portugal). The Japanese grew uncomfortable with the Jesuits, and it was possible now for Japan to withdraw from the world, especially since indigenous manufacturers were eliminating the need for Chinese silk.[201]

It is perhaps the case that Japan's withdrawal was occasioned by the evangelistic overaggressiveness of the Christian Church, as C. R. Boxer asserts.[202] One has to take seriously an hypothesis which comes from Boxer, whose breadth of knowledge and historical judgment command respect. However, there is little concrete empirical evidence presented by him to back up this judgment. Might they not have withdrawn in any case, given their growing internal strength and the thinness of the links they had to any world-economy?

Portuguese citizens themselves drew the lesson of the decline of the entrepôt boom. They began to cut themselves off from the home country, and adjust to survival in Asia. They became, in economic terms, largely Asians of European extraction, though less so in political terms and doubtless not at all in cultural terms. J. B. Harrison describes the ever-increasing military and political autonomy of the *Estado da India* in the course of the sixteenth century, a process that went along with the growing importance for the Portuguese of the intra-Asian trade.[203] With the growing conflict of interests between the Portuguese at home and in India,

> the Portuguese encrust themselves into the worlds of the Orient, installing themselves everywhere as *casados* [literally, those who maintain a household], fit themselves into local or regional interests, give themselves over to local or inter-regional operations.[204]

When Spain absorbs Portugal in 1580, this accentuates the process further. The local Portuguese do not wish to cut the Castilians into their market, and the King of Spain has not got the strength to force them.[205] But this means that instead of edging into the status of a peripheral area, a century of Iberian involvement pushed Asia further away. It would not be until a century or so later that Europe would be strong enough to begin to incorporate these regions.

7

THEORETICAL REPRISE

Figure 8: "Richmond Palace," or "The Thames at Richmond," an oil painting of the first quarter of the seventeenth century, done by David Vinckenboons (1578–1629), a Flemish artist who migrated to England and painted on Royal Commissions in the time of both James I and Charles I.

Theorizing is not an activity separate from the analysis of empirical data. Analyses can only be made in terms of theoretical schema and propositions. On the other hand, analyses of events or processes must include as a starting point a whole series of specific values of certain of the variables, on the basis of which one can explain how the final outcomes were arrived at. In order to convey the historical explanation with clarity, it is often the case that one has to assume or glide over the exposition of the formal interrelations between variables.

Consequently, it often makes sense to review the material a second time more briefly and abstractly at the conclusion. No doubt this should be useful to the reader. But it is even more important for the author, in forcing a degree of rigor in the analysis whose absence might readily pass unnoticed amidst the complexity of detail. The empirical material treated thus far has surely been complex—indeed, far more complex than it was possible to portray. Hence, I propose to review what I have been arguing in this book.

In order to describe the origins and initial workings of a world system, I have had to argue a certain conception of a world-system. A world-system is a social system, one that has boundaries, structures, member groups, rules of legitimation, and coherence. Its life is made up of the conflicting forces which hold it together by tension, and tear it apart as each group seeks eternally to remold it to its advantage. It has the characteristics of an organism, in that it has a life-span over which its characteristics change in some respects and remain stable in others. One can define its structures as being at different times strong or weak in terms of the internal logic of its functioning.

What characterizes a social system in my view is the fact that life within it is largely self-contained, and that the dynamics of its development are largely internal. The reader may feel that the use of the term "largely" is a case of academic weaseling. I admit I cannot quantify it. Probably no one ever will be able to do so, as the definition is based on a counterfactual hypothesis: If the system, for any reason, were to be cut off from all external forces (which virtually never happens), the definition implies that the system would continue to function substantially in the same manner. Again, of course, substantially is difficult to convert into hard operational criteria. Nonetheless the point is an important one and key to many parts of the empirical analyses of this book. Perhaps we should think of self-containment as a theoretical absolute, a sort of social vacuum, rarely visible and even more implausible to create artificially, but still and all a socially-real asymptote, the distance from which is somehow measurable.

Using such a criterion, it is contended here that most entities usually described as social systems—"tribes," communities, nation-states—are not in fact total systems. Indeed, on the contrary, we are arguing that the only real social systems are, on the one hand, those relatively small, highly autonomous subsistence economies not part of some regular tribute-demanding system and, on the other hand, world-systems. These latter are to be sure distinguished from the former because they are relatively large; that is, they are in common parlance "worlds." More precisely, however, they are defined by the fact that their self-containment as an economic-material entity is based on extensive division of labor and that they contain within them a multiplicity of cultures.

It is further argued that thus far there have only existed two varieties of such world-systems: world-empires, in which there is a single political system over most of the area, however attenuated the degree of its effective control; and those systems in which such a single political system does not exist over all, or virtually all, of the space. For convenience and for want of a better term, we are using the term "world-economy" to describe the latter.

Finally, we have argued that prior to the modern era, world-economies were highly unstable structures which tended either to be converted into empires or to disintegrate. It is the peculiarity of the modern world-system that a world-economy has survived for 500 years and yet has not come to be transformed into a world-empire—a peculiarity that is the secret of its strength.

This peculiarity is the political side of the form of economic organization called capitalism. Capitalism has been able to flourish precisely because the world-economy has had within its bounds not one but a multiplicity of political systems.

I am not here arguing the classic case of capitalist ideology that capitalism is a system based on the noninterference of the state in economic affairs. Quite the contrary! Capitalism is based on the constant absorption of economic loss by political entities, while economic gain is distributed to "private" hands. What I am arguing rather is that capitalism as an economic mode is based on the fact that the economic factors operate within an arena larger than that which any political entity can totally control. This gives capitalists a freedom of maneuver that is structurally based. It has made possible the constant economic expansion of the world-system, albeit a very skewed distribution of its rewards. The only alternative world-system that could maintain a high level of productivity and change the system of distribution would involve the reintegration of the levels of political and economic decision-making. This would constitute a third possible form of world-system, a socialist world government. This is not a form that presently exists, and it was not even remotely conceivable in the sixteenth century.

The historical reasons why the European world-economy came into existence in the sixteenth century and resisted attempts to transform it into an empire have been expounded at length. We shall not review them here. It should however be noted that the size of a world-economy is a function of the state of technology, and in particular of the possibilities of transport and communication within its bounds. Since this is a constantly changing phenomenon, not always for the better, the boundaries of a world-economy are ever fluid.

We have defined a world-system as one in which there is extensive division of labor. This division is not merely functional—that is, occupational—but geographical. That is to say, the range of economic tasks is not evenly distributed throughout the world-system. In part this is the consequence of ecological considerations, to be sure. But for the most part, it is a function of the social organization of work, one which magnifies and legitimizes the ability of some groups within the system to exploit the labor of others, that is, to receive a larger share of the surplus.

While, in an empire, the political structure tends to link culture with occupation, in a world-economy the political structure tends to link culture with spatial location. The reason is that in a world-economy the first point of political pressure available to groups is the local (national) state structure. Cultural homogenization tends to serve the interests of key groups and the pressures build up to create cultural-national identities.

This is particularly the case in the advantaged areas of the world-economy—what we have called the core-states. In such states, the creation of a strong state machinery coupled with a national culture, a phenomenon often referred to as integration, serves both as a mechanism to protect disparities that have arisen within the world-system, and as an ideological mask and justification for the maintenance of these disparities.

World-economies then are divided into core-states and peripheral areas. I do not say peripheral *states* because one characteristic of a peripheral area is that the indigenous state is weak, ranging from its nonexistence (that is, a colonial situation) to one with a low degree of autonomy (that is, a neo-colonial situation).

There are also semiperipheral areas which are in between the core and the periphery on a series of dimensions, such as the complexity of economic activities, strength of the state machinery, cultural integrity, etc. Some of these areas had been core-areas of earlier versions of a given world-economy. Some had been peripheral areas that were later promoted, so to speak, as a result of the changing geopolitics of an expanding world-economy.

The semiperiphery, however, is not an artifice of statistical cutting points, nor is it a residual category. The semiperiphery is a necessary structural element in a world-economy. These areas play a role parallel to that played, *mutatis mutandis,* by middle trading groups in an empire. They are collection points of vital skills that are often politically unpopular. These middle areas (like middle groups in an empire) partially deflect the political pressures which groups primarily located in peripheral areas might otherwise direct against core-states and the groups which operate within and through their state machineries. On the other hand, the interests primarily located in the semiperiphery are located outside the political arena of the core-states, and find it difficult to pursue the ends in political coalitions that might be open to them were they in the same political arena.

The division of a world-economy involves a hierarchy of occupational tasks, in which tasks requiring higher levels of skill and greater capitalization are reserved for higher-ranking areas. Since a capitalist world-economy essentially rewards accumulated capital, including human capital, at a higher rate than "raw" labor power, the geographical maldistribution of these occupational skills involves a strong trend toward self-maintenance. The forces of the marketplace reinforce them rather than undermine them. And the absence of a central political mechanism for the world-economy makes it very difficult to intrude counteracting forces to the maldistribution of rewards.

Hence, the ongoing process of a world-economy tends to expand the economic and social gaps among its varying areas in the very process of its development. One factor that tends to mask this fact is that the process of development of a world-economy brings about technological advances which make it possible to expand the boundaries of a world-economy. In this case, particular regions of the world may change their structural role in the world-economy, to their advantage, even though the disparity of reward between different sectors of the world-economy as a whole may be simultaneously widening. It is in order to observe this crucial phenomenon clearly that we have insisted on the distinction between a peripheral area of a given world-economy and the external arena of the world-economy. The external arena of one century often becomes the periphery of the next—or its semiperiphery. But then too core-states can become semiperipheral and semiperipheral ones peripheral.

While the advantages of the core-states have not ceased to expand throughout the history of the modern world-system, the ability of a particular state to remain in the core sector is not beyond challenge. The hounds are ever to the hares for the position of top dog. Indeed, it may well be that in this kind of system it is not structurally possible to avoid, over a long period of historical time, a circulation of the elites in the sense that the particular country that is dominant at a given time tends to be replaced in this role sooner or later by another country.

We have insisted that the modern world-economy is, and only can be, a capitalist world-economy. It is for this reason that we have rejected the appellation of "feudalism" for the various forms of capitalist agriculture based on coerced labor which grow up in a world-economy. Furthermore, although this has not been discussed in this volume, it is for this same reason that we will, in future volumes, regard with great circumspection and prudence the claim that there exist in the twentieth century socialist national economies within the framework of the world-economy (as opposed to socialist movements controlling certain state-machineries within the world-economy).

If world-systems are the only real social systems (other than truly isolated subsistence economies), then it must follow that the emergence, consolidation, and political roles of classes and status groups must be appreciated as elements of this *world*-system. And in turn it follows that one of the key elements in analyzing a class or a status-group is not only the state of its self-consciousness but the geographical scope of its self-definition.

Classes always exist potentially *(an sich)*. The issue is under what conditions they become class-conscious *(für sich)*, that is, operate as a group in the politico-economic arenas and even to some extent as a cultural entity. Such self-consciousness is a function of conflict situations. But for upper strata open conflict, and hence overt consciousness, is always *faute de mieux*. To the extent that class boundaries are not made explicit, to that extent it is more likely that privileges be maintained.

Since in conflict situations, multiple factions tend to reduce to two by virtue of the forging of alliances, it is by definition not possible to have three or more (conscious) classes. There obviously can be a multitude of occupational interest groups which may organize themselves to operate within the social structure. But such groups are really one variety of status-groups, and indeed often overlap heavily with other kinds of status-groups such as those defined by ethnic, linguistic, or religious criteria.

To say that there cannot be three or more classes is not however to say that there are always two. There may be none, though this is rare and transitional. There may be one, and this is most common. There may be two, and this is most explosive.

We say there may be only one class, although we have also said that classes only actually exist in conflict situations, and conflicts presume two sides. There is no contradiction here. For a conflict may be defined as being between one class, which conceives of itself as the universal class, and all the other strata. This has in fact been the usual situation in the modern world-system. The capitalist class (the *bourgeoisie*) has claimed to be the universal class and sought to organize political life to pursue its objectives against two opponents. On the one hand, there were those who spoke for the maintenance of traditional rank distinctions despite the fact that these ranks might have lost their original correlation with economic function. Such elements preferred to define the social structure as a non-class structure. It was to counter this ideology that the bourgeoisie came to operate as a class conscious of itself.

But the bourgeoisie had another opponent, the workers. Whenever the workers became conscious of themselves as a class, which was not too frequently in the sixteenth century, they defined the situation as a polarized two-class situation. In such circumstances, the bourgeoisie found itself in a deep tactical dilemma. To the extent that they maintained their own *class*-consciousness, they abetted by this fact workers' class-consciousness, and thereby risked undermining their own political position. To the extent that, in order to deal with this problem, they muted their class-consciousness, they risked weakening their position vis-à-vis the tenants of traditional high rank.

The process of the crystallization of class-consciousness of a bourgeoisie, thinking of itself as a universal class, drawing its members from all social ranks, has been illustrated in our discussions of the emergence of the gentry as a social category in Tudor England or the rise of the burghers in the northern Netherlands. One of the ways they supported their claim to be a universal class was by the development of national sentiment, which gave a cultural veneer to their claim.

The deep dilemma of a bourgeoisie trapped by insurrection on the left, so to speak, and fearing an alliance between its two sets of opponents taking the form of regionalist claims, has been illustrated in our discussions of France in the "second" sixteenth century. The bourgeoisie there opted for temporary retreat. They perhaps had no viable alternative. But this retreat was to have its long term consequences in the later social radicalism of the French revolution (however momentary), and in the long-run lag in economic development of France behind England.

Our examples here are of bourgeoisies that became conscious, but conscious within the bounds of a nation-state. This was clearly not the only choice. They could have become conscious of themselves as a world class. And many groups pushed for such a definition. On the one hand, there were the various communities of international merchant–bankers. On the other hand, there were the many sets of capitalist farmers in the peripheral areas.

In the heyday of Charles V, there were many in the Low Countries, in southern Germany, in northern Italy and elsewhere who tied their hopes to the imperial aspirations of the Hapsburgs (some prudentially keeping a foot in the door of the Valois as well). If these groups remained a social stratum and did not yet form a conscious class, they were moving in that direction, and it seemed only a matter of time. But with the failure of empire, the bourgeoisies of Europe realized that their economic and social future was tied to the core-states. And those who, by virtue of their ethnic–religious affiliations, could turn to the national state as their arena of political operation did so.

As for the capitalist farmers of the periphery, they would gladly have thought of themselves as part of an international gentry class. They willingly sacrificed local cultural roots for participation in "world" cultures. But to constitute an international class, they needed the cooperation of the capitalist strata of the core-states, and this was not to be forthcoming. So increasingly these peripheral capitalist farmers became the antiquated and snobbish Spanish-American *hacenderos* or east European nobility of later centuries, retreating from potential international class-consciousness into local status solidarities—which served well the interests of Western European bourgeoisies.

Geographic concentration of particular economic activities serves as a continuing pressure to status-group formation. When the local dominant strata are threatened by any incipient class-consciousness of lower strata, emphasis on local culture serves well to deflect local internal conflict, creating instead local solidarity against the outside. If, in addition, these local dominant strata feel themselves oppressed by higher strata of the world-system, they are doubly motivated to pursue the creation of a local identity.

Obviously, one does not construct an identity out of thin air. One builds on what one finds—in terms of language, religion, and distinctive life-styles. Nonetheless it is quite clear that both linguistic and religious homogeneity and passion (*a fortiori* devotion to separate life-styles) are social creations which cannot be accounted for as simple continuities of tradition eternal. They are social creations molded with difficulty in times of travail.

The sixteenth century was such a time of travail in much of Europe. It was of course the era of the Reformation and the Counter–Reformation. It was the era of great religious civil wars. It was the era of international religious "parties." But in the end, as the dust settled, all the religious upheaval resulted in a pattern of relative religious homogeneity of the various political entities within the framework of international laissez-faire—*cuius regio eius religio*.

We have tried to indicate in our discussion of various specific developments why various forms of Protestantism ended up as the religion of the core-states (except France, and again why) and Catholicism as the religion of the periphery and semiperiphery. We have been skeptical that the tenets of the various theologies had too much to do with it, although they may have facilitated the task. Rather the tenets of the theologies, as they evolved in practice as opposed to their original conception, reflected and served to sustain the roles of the various areas in the world-system.

It is often said that Charles V missed a great opportunity of creating a united German Protestant state by attempting to remain an arbiter of the religious split instead of a protagonist. But such a critique neglects the fact that Charles V sought to create a world-empire, not a core-state within a world-economy. Empires thrive on multiple religions reflecting multiple roles, few of which are concentrated within specific political boundaries. National homogeneity within international heterogeneity is the formula of a world-economy.

At least this is the formula at the simple beginnings. Core-states because of their complex internal division of labor begin to reflect the pattern of the system as a whole. In the sixteenth century, England was already moving in the direction of becoming Britain, which would have regional homogeneity within a relative heterogeneity for the nation as a whole.

Religion does not have to be the defining cultural trait of the major status-groups; one can use language. Language indeed began to play such a role in the sixteenth century, and its importance was to increase as the centuries passed. Religious reinforcement of role specialization in a world-economy has, however, advantages over linguistic reinforcement. It interferes less with the ongoing communications process within the world-economy. And it lends itself less (only less) to isolationist closures, because of the underlying universalist themes of world religions.

The European world-economy of the sixteenth century tended overall to be a one-class system. It was the dynamic forces profiting from economic expansion and the capitalist system, especially those in the core-areas, who tended to be class-conscious, that is to operate within the political arena as a group defined primarily by their common role in the economy. This common role was in fact defined somewhat broadly from a twentieth-century perspective. It included persons who were farmers, merchants, and industrialists. Individual entrepreneurs often moved back and forth between these activities in any case, or combined them. The crucial distinction was between these men, whatever their occupation, principally oriented to obtaining profit in the world market, and the others not so oriented.

The "others" fought back in terms of their status privileges—those of the traditional aristocracy, those which small farmers had derived from the feudal system, those resulting from guild monopolies that were outmoded. Under the cover of cultural similarities, one can often weld strange alliances. Those strange alliances can take a very activist form and force the political centers to take account of them. We pointed to such instances in our discussion of France. Or they can take a politically passive form that serves well the needs of the dominant forces in the world-system. The triumph of Polish Catholicism as a cultural force was a case in point.

The details of the canvas are filled in with the panoply of multiple forms of status-groups, their particular strengths and accents. But the grand sweep is in terms of the process of class formation. And in this regard, the sixteenth century was indecisive. The capitalist strata formed a class that survived and gained *droit de cité*, but did not yet triumph in the political arena.

The evolution of the state machineries reflected precisely this uncertainty. Strong states serve the interests of some groups and hurt those of others. From however the standpoint of the world-system as a whole, if there is to be a multitude of political entities (that is, if the system is not a world-empire), then it cannot be the case that all these entities be equally strong. For if they were, they would be in the position of blocking the effective operation of transnational economic entities whose locus were in another state. It would then follow that the world division of labor would be impeded, the world-economy decline, and eventually the world-system fall apart.

It also cannot be that *no* state machinery is strong. For in such a case, the capitalist strata would have no mechanisms to protect their interests, guaranteeing their property rights, assuring various monopolies, spreading losses among the larger population, etc.

It follows then that the world-economy develops a pattern where state structures are relatively strong in the core areas and relatively weak in the periphery. Which areas play which roles is in many ways accidental. What is necessary is that in some areas the state machinery be far stronger than in others.

What do we mean by a strong state-machinery? We mean strength vis-à-vis other states within the world-economy including other core-states, and strong vis-à-vis local political units within the boundaries of the state. In effect, we mean a sovereignty that is *de facto* as well as *de jure*. We also mean a state that is strong vis-à-vis any particular social group within the state. Obviously, such groups vary in the amount of pressure they can bring to bear upon the state. And obviously certain combinations of these groups control the state. It is not that the state is a neutral arbiter. But the state is more than a simple vector of given forces, if only because many of these forces are situated in more than one state or are defined in terms that have little correlation with state boundaries.

A strong state then is a partially autonomous entity in the sense that it has a margin of action available to it wherein it reflects the compromises of multiple interests, even if the bounds of these margins are set by the existence of some groups of primordial strength. To be a partially autonomous entity, there must be a group of people whose direct interests are served by such an entity: state managers and a state bureaucracy.

Such groups emerge within the framework of a capitalist world-economy because a strong state is the best choice between difficult alternatives for the two groups that are strongest in political, economic, and military terms: the emergent capitalist strata, and the old aristocratic hierarchies.

For the former, the strong state in the form of the "absolute monarchies" was a prime customer, a guardian against local and international brigandage, a mode of social legitimation, a preemptive protection against the creation of strong state barriers elsewhere. For the latter, the strong state represented a brake on these same capitalist strata, an upholder of status conventions, a maintainer of order, a promoter of luxury.

No doubt both nobles and bourgeois found the state machineries to be a burdensome drain of funds, and a meddlesome unproductive bureaucracy. But what options did they have? Nonetheless they were always restive and the immediate politics of the world-system was made up of the pushes and pulls resulting from the efforts of both groups to insulate themselves from what seemed to them the negative effects of the state machinery.

A state machinery involves a tipping mechanism. There is a point where strength creates more strength. The tax revenue enables the state to have a larger and more efficient civil bureaucracy and army which in turn leads to greater tax revenue—a process that continues in spiral form. The tipping mechanism works in other direction too—weakness leading to greater weakness. In between these two tipping points lies the politics of state-creation. It is in this arena that the skills of particular managerial groups make a difference. And it is because of the two tipping mechanisms that at certain points a small gap in the world-system can very rapidly become a large one.

In those states in which the state machinery is weak, the state managers do not play the role of coordinating a complex industrial–commercial–agricultural mechanism. Rather they simply become one set of landlords amidst others, with little claim to legitimate authority over the whole.

These tend to be called traditional rulers. The political struggle is often phrased in terms of tradition versus change. This is of course a grossly misleading and ideological terminology. It may in fact be taken as a general sociological principle that, at any given point of time, what is thought to be traditional is of more recent origin than people generally imagine it to be, and represents primarily the conservative instincts of some group threatened with declining social status. Indeed, there seems to be nothing which emerges and evolves as quickly as a "tradition" when the need presents itself.

In a one-class system, the "traditional" is that in the name of which the "others" fight the class-conscious group. If they can encrust their values by legitimating them widely, even better by enacting them into legislative barriers, they thereby change the system in a way favorable to them.

The traditionalists may win in some states, but if a world-economy is to survive, they must lose more or less in the others. Furthermore, the gain in one region is the counterpart of the loss in another.

This is not quite a zero-sum game, but it is also inconceivable that all elements in a capitalist world-economy shift their values in a given direction simultaneously. The social system is built on having a multiplicity of value systems within it, reflecting the specific functions groups and areas play in the world division of labor.

We have not exhausted here the theoretical problems relevant to the functioning of a world-economy. We have tried only to speak to those illustrated by the early period of the world-economy in creation, to wit, sixteenth-century Europe. Many other problems emerged at later stages and will be treated, both empirically and theoretically, in later volumes.

In the sixteenth century, Europe was like a bucking bronco. The attempt of some groups to establish a world-economy based on a particular division of labor, to create national states in the core areas as politico–economic guarantors of this system, and to get the workers to pay not only the profits but the costs of maintaining the system was not easy. It was to Europe's credit that it was done, since without the thrust of the sixteenth century the modern world would not have been born and, for all its cruelties, it is better that it was born than that it had not been.

It is also to Europe's credit that it was not easy, and particularly that it was not easy because the people who paid the short-run costs screamed lustily at the unfairness of it all. The peasants and workers in Poland and England and Brazil and Mexico were all rambunctious in their various ways. As R. H. Tawney says of the agrarian disturbances of sixteenth-century England: "Such movements are a proof of blood and sinew and of a high and gallant spirit. . . . Happy the nation whose people has not forgotten how to rebel."[1]

The mark of the modern world is the imagination of its profiteers and the counter-assertiveness of the oppressed. Exploitation and the refusal to accept exploitation as either inevitable or just constitute the continuing antinomy of the modern era, joined together in a dialectic which has far from reached its climax in the twentieth century.

BIBLIOGRAPHIC ESSAY

There are three journals I found essential: *Annales E.S.C.*, *Economic History Review*, and *Past & Present*. *Annales E.S.C.* publishes in French but there has recently been a translation into English of material from *Annales* particularly relevant to this period, edited by Peter Burke, *Economy and Society in Early Modern Europe* (New York: Harper and Row, 1972). The *Economic History Review* has extracted some of its most important articles into a three-volume collection edited by E.M. Carus-Wilson and entitled *Essays in Economic History* (New York: St. Martin's Press, 1965). Volumes I and II are particularly relevant, and include among other things Tawney's essay on the gentry, and the articles by Phelps-Brown and Stokes on wage-levels. The articles in *Past & Present* about the nature of the seventeenth-century "crisis" by Hobsbawm, Trever-Roper, and others have been republished, edited by Trevor Aston, as *Crisis in Europe, 1560-1660* (New York: Doubleday, 1965).

Reading Fernand Braudel's *The Mediterranean* (New York: Harper and Row, 1973) is the most rewarding further reading that can be done. A much briefer but far less accessible essay is his "European Expansion and Capitalism: 1450-1650" in *Chapters in Western Civilization* (New York: Columbia Univ. Press, 1966, 3rd. ed., Vol. I).

For the medieval prelude, Marc Bloch's work *Feudal Society* (Chicago: Univ. of Chicago Press, 1961) is the classic. See also *French Rural History* (Berkeley: Univ. of California Press, 1966), which covers a wider time span. George Duby's *Rural Economy and Country Life in the Medieval West* (Columbia: Univ. of South Carolina Press, 1968) is also extremely helpful. The Dobb–Sweezy debate, in which many others joined, has recently been made readily available in a collection edited by Rodney Hilton entitled *The Transition from Feudalism to Capitalism* (London: New Left Books, 1976).

The basic data on agriculture are to be found in B.H. Slicher van

Bath, *The Agrarian History of Western Europe, A.D. 500–1850* (New York: St. Martin's Press, 1963). On the expansion of Europe and its socioeconomic consequences, reading Pierre Chaunu is very important. Unfortunately, his very extensive corpus exists only in French. The most useful single item that is of reasonable length is *Conquête et exploitation des nouveaux mondes (XVIe siècle)*, No. 26bis in the Collection Nouvelle Clio (Paris: Presses Universitaires de France, 1969). Also useful is Carlo M. Cipolla, *Guns, Sails, and Empires* New York: Pantheon, 1966).

Price history is crucial, and the progenitor of the debate on the impact of price inflation was Earl Hamilton, whose work regrettably is scattered in many journals, not always easy to obtain. He résuméd his views in "The History of Prices Before 1750," which he wrote for the XIth Congress of Historical Sciences at Stockholm in 1960 and which was published in Vol. I of their *Rapports* (Göteborg: Almqvist and Wiksell, 1960). The reader will also find an essay by Hamilton in the *Journal of Economic History* (1952).

On the general patterns of economic development in early modern Europe, see Maurice Dobb, *Studies in the Development of Capitalism*, rev. ed., (New York: International Publ., 1964); Vol. IV of the *Cambridge Economic History of Europe* (London and New York: Cambridge Univ. Press, 1967), edited by E.E. Rich and C.H. Wilson (which contains the magisterial essay by Fernand Braudel and Frank C. Spooner on "Prices in Europe from 1450 to 1750"); and Vol. II (*The Sixteenth and Seventeenth Centuries*) of the *Fontana Economic History of Europe* (New York: Watts, 1973), edited by Carlo M. Cipolla. See also various essays by Ruggiero Romano, but all in French and Italian. The most important is in *Rivista Storica Italiana* (Vol. LXXIV, 1962). Finally, on climate and its social consequences, the one serious overview is Emmanuel Le Roy Ladurie, *Times of Feast, Times of Famine* (New York: Doubleday, 1971).

On the absolute monarchy and statism, much has been written and yet it is hard to recommend a few basic readings. Joseph Strayer has a small and worthwhile book, *On the Medieval Origins of the Modern State* (Princeton, New Jersey: Princeton Univ. Press, 1970). Charles Tilly has recently edited a collection of papers on *The Formation of National States in Western Europe* (Princeton, New Jersey: Princeton Univ. Press, 1975). On the important subject of banditry, a very interesting book, available only in Italian, is Rosario Villari, *La revolta antispagnola a Napoli: le origini (1581–1647)* (Bari: Laterza, 1967).

The history of Spain and the Hapsburg Empire is well served. The Spanish historian, Jaime Vicens Vives is found in English translation: for example, *An Economic History of Spain* (Berkeley: Univ. of California Press, 1970, 2nd ed.). This can be complemented by J.H. Elliott,

Imperial Spain, 1469–1716 (New York: Mentor, 1966) and the essay on "The Age of Don Quixote" by Pierre Vilar translated in *New Left Review* (No. 68, July–August 1971).

On the Habsburg empire in relation to Europe, there is H.G. Koenigsberger, *The Hapsburgs and Europe, 1516–1660* (Ithaca: Cornell University Press, 1971). On social upheaval in Germany, see F. Engels, *The Peasant War in Germany* (Chicago: Univ. of Chicago Press, 1967). On the Italian city-states, particularly Venice, see the collection edited by Brian Pullan, *Crisis and Change in the Venetian Economy in the Sixteenth and Seventeenth Centuries* (New York: Barnes and Noble, 1968), and Frederic Lane's collection, *Venice and History* (Baltimore: Johns Hopkins Press, 1966), which also includes his essays on "protection rent."

On the Netherlands Revolution, the modern classic is Pieter Geyl, *The Revolt of the Netherlands (1599–1609)* (London: Benn, 1968). A recent, stimulating contribution is J.W. Smit, "The Netherlands Revolution" in a volume edited by R. Forster and J.P. Greene, *Preconditions of Revolution in Early Modern Europe* (Baltimore: Johns Hopkins Press, 1970). The rise of Amsterdam is recounted by Violet Barbour, *Capitalism in Amsterdam in the Seventeenth Century* (Ann Arbor, Michigan: Ann Arbor Paperbacks, 1963).

The literature on the crucial English-French comparison is voluminous. For the debate about England, a minimum is to read the following works by major participants: R.H. Tawney, *The Agrarian Problem in the Sixteenth Century* (New York: Harper Torchbooks, 1968), H.R. Trevor-Roper; *The European Witch-Craze of the 16th and 17th Centuries and Other Essays* (New York: Harper, 1969); Lawrence Stone, *The Crisis of the Aristocracy, 1558–1641* (London: Oxford Univ. Press, 1967); J.H. Hexter, *Reappraisals in History* (New York: Harper, 1963); Christopher Hill, *Puritanism and Revolution* (New York: Schocken Books, 1958).

The debate about France tends to be in French. There is however a good summary of the views of Porchnev, Mousnier, and others in the article by J.H.M. Salmon in *Past & Present* (No. 37, 1967). In addition, two major works have been translated into English: Lucien Goldmann, *The Hidden God* (New York: Humanities Press, 1964), and A.D. Lublinskaya, *French Absolutism: The Crucial Phase, 1620–1629* (London and New York: Cambridge Univ. Press, 1968).

Economic comparisons of England and France are to be found in the collection of essays by J.U. Nef, *The Conquest of the Material World* (Chicago: Univ. of Chicago Press, 1964), and a major effort of analysis of England's process of transformation has been collected by Joan Thirsk as Vol. IV, *1500–1640* of *The Agrarian History of England and Wales* (London and New York: Cambridge Univ. Press, 1967).

Material on the periphery and on Europe's "external arena" is harder to find in English. On eastern Europe and the Baltic, the best single source is Marian Malowist. His essays have been collected in a French edition, *Croissance et régression en Europe, XVIe et XVIIe siècles* (Paris: A. Colin, 1972). An English version of three of these can be found in the *Economic History Review* (1959, Vol. XII and 1966, Vol. XIX), and in *Past & Present* (No. 13, 1958). On Hispanic America, a good, short introduction is Stanley J. and Barbara H. Stein, *The Colonial Heritage of Latin America* (London: Oxford Univ. Press, 1970). On Russia, see Jerome Blum, *Lord and Peasant in Russia from the Ninth to the Nineteenth Century* (Princeton, New Jersey: Princeton Univ. Press, 1961). Finally, on the Indian Ocean area, the story is told in C.R. Boxer, *The Portuguese Seaborne Empire, 1415–1825* (Oxford: Clarendon Press, 1963), which also is useful for what happened in Portugal.

Finally, whenever the reader's knowledge of political history falters for a particular zone or moment of time, a compact and clear exposition will usually be found in Volumes II and III of *The New Cambridge Modern History* (London and New York: Cambridge Univ. Press, 1958 and 1968). And many, many excellent articles are to be found (however, in many different languages) in the papers of the five successive International Congresses of Economic History beginning in 1960.

C 8
D 9
E 0
F 1
G 2
H 3
I 4
J 5

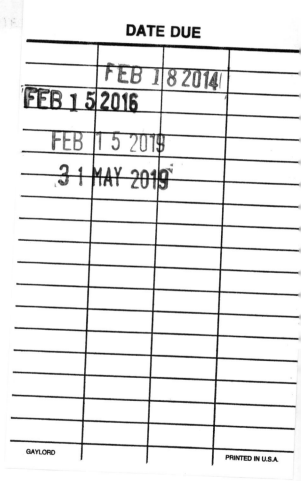